D0910306

LEONARD G. RATNER
Professor of Music
Stanford University

MUSIC
THE LISTENER'S ART
THIRD EDITION

McGRAW-HILL BOOK COMPANY

New York St. Louis San Francisco Auckland Bogotá Düsseldorf
Johannesburg London Madrid Mexico Montreal New Delhi Panama
Paris São Paulo Singapore Sydney Tokyo Toronto

Library of Congress Cataloging in Publication Data

Ratner, Leonard G
    Music, the listener's art.

    Bibliography: p.
    Includes index.
    1. Music—Analysis, appreciation.   I. Title.
MT6.R24 1977   780′.15   76-23395
ISBN 0-07-051221-3

MUSIC: THE LISTENER'S ART

1 2 3 4 5 6 7 8 9 0   DODO   7 8 3 2 1 0 9 8 7

This book was set in Plantin by York Graphic Services, Inc.
The editors were Robert P. Rainier and David Dunham;
the designer was Anne Canevari Green;
the production supervisor was Angela Kardovich.
R.R. Donnelley & Sons Co., was printer and binder.

Cover illustration, *Appollo and Pan,* c. 1530, engraving, Benedetto Montagna.
Stanford University Museum of Art.
Gift of Mrs. Robert M. Loeser.

CONTENTS

PREFACE

This third edition of *Music: The Listener's Art* retains the basic framework of the second edition. It aims to provide listeners with the tools by which they can better analyze, evaluate, and appreciate the music they hear.

This third edition is considerably shorter than the previous edition, thus making it more suitable for a one-semester course. Descriptions are more concise, most speculative or corollary material has been eliminated, and the number of musical examples has been reduced. Explanations have been condensed and simplified, especially in Chapter Two, "Musical Elements and Their Relationships."

Chapter Eight, on twentieth-century music, has been expanded to include sections on chance music, electronic music, exotic music (Japanese, African, Indonesian, and Indian music), and popular music (jazz, rock, and country music).

As in previous editions, we start with the listener's reaction to music. First, we listen. What are the immediate impressions? Sound itself, its strength, its color, then the movement of sound, how it is set in motion, its pace, its regularity, how it reaches a point of arrival. These effects carry expressive values; they become our first criteria. Thus, at the very outset, listeners can interpret their impressions in nontechnical terms.

Afterwards, we discover how specific musical elements and processes—melody, rhythm, texture, harmony, phrase structure—help to create musical impressions. In this way we begin to see the relationship between musical techniques and expressive values in music. In order to show how fundamental musical procedures underlie various types of expression, we have drawn the material for the first section (Chapters One and Two) from a wide range of sources, from medieval to modern music, from folksong to symphony. This will enable the listener to make his or her way more confidently and quickly within the various areas of musical style and expression. The criteria established in the first chapters are used throughout the entire book to guide us in our listening.

The approach described above invites comparison for fuller understanding and greater satisfaction. For this reason, the historical framework is used. It enables us to illustrate systematically different kinds of music; it helps us to visualize the growth which, during history, has given rise to many and various musical styles. A perspective is developed and a sympathy awakened for perhaps unfamiliar modes of musical expression. At no time, however, does historical data take precedence over the actual experience of listening to the music itself. Throughout the second section of this book (Chapters Three to Eight) there is constant reference to the ideas explained in the first section—sound, movement, departure, arrival.

When lay people come to a music-appreciation class or take up a book on music, they want to retain their musical experience, to have it illuminated; they want the instruction to be organized around what they can hear, what they can grasp by listening. This need of the listener has been the guiding principle in organizing the entire presentation of this book. It has resulted in establishing the nontechnical criteria of the first chapter and, throughout the book, in offering the music first, and then discussing it. It is an approach that is sympathetic with the listener's already strong motivations for wanting to know music better.

The greatest organized demand for a book of this kind is in the courses offered in colleges and universities for the general student, courses which usually have such titles as "Music Appreciation," "Survey of Music," and "Introduction to Music." It is hoped that this book will help serve the needs of such instruction. But the musical needs and curiosities of students in such courses are no different from those of lay people who listen to music at home or at a concert. From the public at large there is perhaps an even greater demand for help in musical understanding. The approach adopted in this book—from impression to evaluation, and then to some insight into the qualities and structures of music—will, we hope, appeal to all listeners.

Leonard G. Ratner

MUSIC
THE LISTENER'S ART

CHAPTER ONE

THE MUSICAL EXPERIENCE

Why do you listen to music? If this question were asked of a number of people, they might answer: "I like the beat," "I like music for dancing," "I like a good tune," "I am moved by the sound of choral singing," "I like music for many reasons, but I could not begin to describe them." For most of us music evokes a response.

Many listeners want to go beyond an immediate response. They want to understand how music creates its many effects, how it can stir the feelings. This book is intended for such listeners. It takes up various aspects of the art to show how they can communicate and thereby contribute to the musical experience.

We start with *sound.* All music stirs the feelings of the listener by means of sound, whether it be the twang of Oriental theater music, the pulsation of tribal drums, or the rich tapestry of sound in a Brahms symphony. Such sounds are worlds apart in quality, yet each says something of importance to some listeners. Our experience today with new sound sources demonstrates that any sound can become musically evocative.

Yet sound alone is not music. Sound must *move* forward in time to suggest some kind of action, as in a series of drum beats or in the successive tones of a melody. As we listen to music we sense the *movement* from one instant to the next.

As music moves, we expect it to have some direction, to reach some goal, some *point of arrival.* In a series of drum beats, the beats themselves are points of arrival. On a larger scale, the opening of "Jingle Bells" has a rather strong point of arrival on the word "way":

Jingle bells / jingle bells / jingle all the way /

On the largest scale, the final note of a symphony or opera is the ultimate point of arrival for all the musical action that has preceded it.

Thus, *music is made up of sound moving in time to points of arrival.* By observing how sound, movement, and arrival work together, we can learn a great deal about a composition. These three will be our first criteria to make contact with music, to get some idea of how it is shaped and what it may express.

THE FIRST CRITERIA OF ANALYSIS

SOUND

The first sound in a piece sets a mood for the listener. It may be high, low, soft, loud, heavy, light, the sound of a single voice, a drum beat, the blare of a trumpet, or a totally novel effect. As we direct our attention first to sound and its various qualities, especially at the beginning of a composition, we are on the way to an appreciation of what it may be expressing.

QUALITIES OF SOUND

Musical sound has the following basic attributes: (1) level or pitch, (2) strength or degree of loudness, (3) color.

Pitch: low, middle, high

We tend to associate levels of pitch with degrees of lightness or heaviness. The Scherzo from Mendelssohn's *A Midsummer Night's Dream* fixes our attention upon a high pitch to suggest the lightness and agility of the magical wood creatures of Shakespeare's play; Liszt's *Les Préludes* opens on a low pitch to set the mood of introspection that prepares the listener for the episodes to follow—romantic, pastoral, agitated, triumphant. The opening of Brahms's Symphony No. 1, Op. 68, covers a wide range of pitch to create a massive, deliberate effect, proper for a piece in a heroic vein.

Strength: loud, soft

Strength of sound—the degree of loudness—has an immediate expressive effect. Loud music has strong, direct, commanding impact; soft music can be subtly persuasive, gently gratifying. The loud beginning of Brahms's Symphony No. 1 is one of the most arresting opening gestures in all music; the soft notes at the beginning of the Mendelssohn Scherzo draw us gently into the playful mood. When a piece begins with a moderate degree of strength, we look for other values than loudness or softness to set the expressive mood.

Color of Sound: bright, dark; rich, thin

The *kinds* of sound used for musical purposes are limitless. Color of sound—*tone color* or *timbre*—is one of the principal concerns of the composer. It may be bright, as in the Mendelssohn Scherzo; it may be dark, as at the beginning of Liszt's *Les Préludes;* it may be rich and full, as at the beginning of Brahms's Symphony No. 1. It may be thin, as in a folk song accompanied by a guitar; it may be intensely rich, as in a *rock* piece amplified electronically. Often we describe tone colors more specifically, for example, as the brilliant, sharp-edged sound of the trumpet; the warm, full, and somewhat muffled sound of the French horn; the penetrating, somewhat nasal quality of the oboe; the sharp twang of the Japanese *koto*, a plucked string instrument.

The following chart incorporates the criteria of musical sound described above. After determining the degrees of pitch, strength, and the qualities of color, give some thought to what they may express to you, individually and all three combined.

QUALITIES OF SOUND

a. *Pitch: low* _____ *high*

b. *Strength: soft* _____ *loud*

c. *Color: dark* _____ *bright*

thin _____ *rich*

special qualities _____

MOVEMENT Musical movement has (1) pace, (2) regularity, (3) articulation.

Pace: The pace of musical movement can suggest states of feeling. Quick
slow, fast movement may be linked to vigorous physical activity, excitement, agitation, exuberance. Slow movement can suggest concentration, reflection, feelings deeply stirred, relaxation, calm.

Turning again to the pieces mentioned above, we can easily see that the quick pace of the Mendelssohn Scherzo links in with its high, soft, and bright sound to project the playful mood. The Brahms Symphony No. 1 supports its full, loud, and mixed sound with a slow pace. Country music, as well as rock and roll, rides on a deliberate, rather slow pace that provides room for words to be clearly declaimed and for nuances which typify this style.

Regularity of Musical movement is regular and even when it maintains a given pace.
Movement: It is irregular or uneven when the pace changes or is uncertain. The
even, uneven Mendelssohn Scherzo maintains a steady, quick pace from beginning to end, carrying the listener lightly and comfortably on its balanced flight. Liszt's *Les Préludes,* on the other hand, draws the listener into its searching mood by beginning with a tentative, rather uneven pace. In the first few moments of Brahms's Symphony No. 1, you will note

the firm, steady, slow pace in the lowermost instruments set against an irregular motion in the high instruments. This tug-of-war between the two pitch levels adds much to the power of the opening of this symphony. In an entirely different mood, jazz does much the same thing, creating interest by setting slight irregularities in the lead voices above a regularly moving support.

Articulation of Articulation of movement refers to the connection of tones, whether
Movement: they flow together or are separated. For example, if you hum the song
continuous, "Home, Sweet Home," the tones will flow into each other without a
separated break, creating a smooth, gentle effect. But if you pluck out the melody on a guitar, the separation will give the tune a crisp, piquant quality. The tones of the Mendelssohn Scherzo are lightly separated to impart a dancelike effect; the melody at the beginning of Liszt's *Les Préludes* flows to maintain the serious manner. In the Brahms Symphony we hear both types of movement: separation in the low voices, flow in the high, an additional effect of power.

The following chart may be used to evaluate qualities of movement; here, too, give thought to the expressive values conveyed, individually and combined.

QUALITIES OF MOVEMENT

a. *Pace: slow*_____*fast*

b. *Regularity: regular*_____*irregular*

c. *Articulation: continuous*_____*separate*

Before we proceed to arrival in music, we should discuss several other aspects of musical movement that help set the mood. One is *intensity,* the degree of effort or energy suggested. The Mendelssohn Scherzo has a low level of intensity; it has a relaxed sense of movement. The Brahms Symphony has a high level of intensity, a great outpouring of strongly focused energy. Another aspect of musical movement is *contour,* the shapes created by the rise and fall of pitch, changes in strength, color of sound, in pace, regularity, and articulation of movement. Every piece of music has its own contours along these lines, and we can get some idea of how the piece is formed by following one or more of these criteria. For example, in the first two minutes of the Brahms Symphony there are several striking shifts in strength of sound from loud to soft and back again, while the pitch levels move in great sweeps upward and downward. While the contour of the strength of sound changes steeply and abruptly, the melodic contour has a gradual shift. In the Mendelssohn Scherzo pitch levels rise and fall gradually, while the strength of sound tends to remain on a low level except for a series of three striking increases in the middle of the piece.

POINTS OF ARRIVAL

Points of arrival are like points of punctuation in language—commas, periods, semicolons, question marks, and exclamation points. As we listen to either music or speech, we expect some pause or effect of arrival when a statement is completed, partially or fully. Naturally, such points of arrival differ greatly in their purposes; some are merely touching points along a line of action, while others serve to bring a statement to a full close. Here we shall deal with points of arrival in fairly large sections of a composition. The effect of arrival in music varies according to the impression of *finality, clarity,* and *emphasis.*

Finality of Arrival

Points of arrival differ in their effect of completion. Only a few give a full sense of finality; these are generally heard at the ends of long sections. Some sentences in language come to a full close, yet the train of thought has not yet run its full course; we must continue to the end of the paragraph or even the chapter. Likewise, musical points of arrival are arranged so that only the last in a composition achieves complete finality. In the song "The Farmer in the Dell":

> The farmer in the dell (comma) the farmer in the dell (comma)
> Hi, ho, the deigh-rio (comma) the farmer in the dell (period)

only the last note of the melody gives us a final sense of arrival. Intermediate points of arrival, since they have a partial sense of completion, help us to keep our bearings in the musical movement, and they build expectations for the final point. Listening to the Mendelssohn Scherzo we can hear many nonfinal points of arrival, but only a few that round off the train of thought; compare the final effect of the last few notes with all the points of punctuation-arrival spread throughout the piece. In the Brahms Symphony, there is an unmistakable point of arrival about thirty seconds into the piece, but it clearly demands continuation.

Clarity of Arrival

Points of arrival connect as well as separate, rather like joints in a piece of furniture. Sometimes these points are *clearly marked* in the song "The Farmer in the Dell." On the other hand, some music deliberately avoids *clarity* of arrival in order to maintain a continuous flow; the first prelude in Book I of Bach's *Well-Tempered Clavier* keeps moving without clear punctuation from beginning to end; although it is a short piece, its sustained, even, unbroken movement shaped by a slowly descending pitch contour builds a strong thrust toward its final and only clear point of arrival.

Manipulation of the effects of arrival can build expectation, create surprise, raise questions, and inject humor. Johann Strauss plays with effects of arrival in his *Perpetuum Mobile,* and Glenn Miller, in his jazz classic *In the Mood,* makes several tries at a final ending; by continuing the music softly after these attempts, he underlines the humor of the jaunty principal idea. When finality of arrival is deliberately weakened, a sharp cut-off avoided, the mood of the piece continues after the piece is ended; this is a very moving effect for the listener, as in the song by Judy Collins, "Since You Asked."

Emphasis of Some music builds strong expectations for an approaching point of *Arrival* arrival, reaching that point with great emphasis; this takes place at the beginning of the Symphony No. 1 of Brahms. The Mendelssohn Scherzo, on the other hand, touches most of its points of arrival very lightly, with little emphasis. Each of these procedures contributes to the expressive qualities of the respective pieces; the Brahms piece will constantly build drives to hard-won goals, while the Mendelssohn piece moves liltingly and cheerfully from one lightly touched point to another.

CRITERIA FOR EVALUATING EFFECTS OF ARRIVAL

a. *Finality: final* _____ *nonfinal*

b. *Clarity: clear* _____ *unclear*

c. *Emphasis: gentle* _____ *strong*

Phases of When sound moves to a point of arrival, it completes a *phase of* *Movement: movement.* From beat to beat, or on a larger scale through short *short, long;* fragments of melody, small phases of movement are linked together in *equal, unequal* chains to create larger phases. These can be compared to phrases, *in length;* sentences, and paragraphs in language. They are the units of musical *approach to* form. They can be short or long, equal or unequal in length; and the *point of arrival* sense of movement toward the point of arrival can be steady, or build up, or drop in intensity. In language, an example is the nursery rhyme:

"Mary had a little lamb. Its fleece was white as snow." Here we have two short, complete sentences at first—short phases of movement, equal to each other, with relatively final points of arrival. The effect of balance, of symmetry is clear. Hemingway preferred short pithy sentences (short phases of movement), while Proust and Melville are noted for their extremely long and complex sentences. Joyce, in his "stream-of-consciousness" style, ran phases of movement together, totally avoiding clear points of arrival in his prose.

The Mendelssohn Scherzo, a quick, dancelike piece, has rather short phases of movement that tend to be equal in length, with a sense of balance or symmetry among the phases of movement; the Brahms Symphony begins with a very long phase of movement that builds in intensity to a climactic point of arrival; this is followed by a group of short phases, relatively equal in length, with a slight drop in intensity. The contrast between these two lines of action creates a large-scale contour among the phases of movement and helps build the shape of the piece.

PHASES OF MOVEMENT

a. Length: short _____ *long*

b. Balance: equal _____ *unequal*

By way of summing up we shall examine two compositions: the Ostinato from Book Six of Bartók's *Mikrokosmos* and the second movement of Beethoven's Symphony No. 5.

✗ BARTÓK

1. Quality of Sound
    a. *Level of sound.* Middle to high; occasional sections on low level for contrast; now and then abrupt shifts from high to low and vice versa, crossing over a steady middle-level flow.
    b. *Amount of sound.* Relatively small at beginning, increasing gradually and dropping off several times; section of considerable fullness toward end serving as kind of climax.
    c. *Strength of sound.* Contrasts between loud and soft, sometimes sharp, sometimes gradual; some soft, full-sounding places contrasted with thin, loud passages.

 d. *Color of sound.* Wide range from dark to brilliant; sharp contrasts in color; use of many different special effects drawing upon the flexibility and the numerous resources of the piano.

2. Quality of Movement
 a. *Pace.* Quick; one section in middle somewhat slower.
 b. *Regularity.* Strict regularity within sections, except for one or two places that seem to be held back momentarily.
 c. *Articulation.* Emphatic; occasional contrasting lyric manner.
 d. *Intensity.* Basically a driving, energetic manner; sometimes a sense of easy, regular, somewhat relaxed movement; at other times a more intense, strained effect, generally when color is most brilliant and sound is at its strongest.

3. Effects of Arrival
 a. *Finality.* Effect of ending very strong due to repetition of passages denoting arrival.
 b. *Clarity.* Generally clear points of arrival, often marked by changes in level and color of sound.
 c. *Emphasis.* Generally quite strong because of separation of passages; some intermediate points very light.

4. Phases of Movement
 a. *Length of phases of movement.* Rather short phases at the beginning; longer toward the end; no regular relationships of length; grouping into larger phases of movement very clearly defined.
 b. *Approach to points of arrival.* Simple articulations at beginning of piece; toward the end a strong sense of drive to points of arrival.

 The quick, energetic pace and the driving quality of movement in this piece suggest some kind of vigorous, well-patterned physical movement, probably a dance. Working against this steady basic flow, certain striking contrasts of color and pace increase interest and intensify movement. Toward the end a climax to the dance is suggested by strong and repeated effects of arrival.

× BEETHOVEN

1. Quality of Sound
 a. *Level of sound.* Wide range through the entire piece. Each section on a given level. Occasional sharp contrasts between sections. Low level at beginning to set the lyric, thoughtful mood of the piece.
 b. *Amount of sound.* Wide variation in amount of sound. Often only a few instruments playing; occasionally full orchestra for

substantial period of time. Consistent alternation between full and thin sound.

c. *Strength of sound.* Almost completely identified with amount of sound. Soft for few instruments, loud for many.

d. *Color of sound.* Wide range, from mellow to brilliant, from dark to light. Use of many different instrumental colors in salient passages. Sharp contrast of trumpet fanfares with all the rest of the orchestra.

2. Quality of Movement
   a. *Pace.* Slow, but with a swinging sense of movement.
   b. *Regularity.* Regular, except for occasional moments of pause.
   c. *Articulation.* Continuously flowing, lyric, even. Deviations from this manner occasionally, associated with greater strength and amount of sound.
   d. *Intensity.* Generally rather calm; at times a driving, bold manner; at other times a sense of hesitation or suspense.

3. Effects of Arrival
   a. *Finality.* Clearly-conclusive points of arrival for larger sections of piece; reinforcement at end of piece.
   b. *Clarity.* Almost all points of arrival clearly-defined.
   c. *Emphasis.* Rather large number of emphatic points of arrival; some gentler.

4. Phases of Movement
   a. *Length of phases of movement.* Well-defined, rather short phases of movement, marked by clear points of arrival. Some phases spun out to greater length.
   b. *Approach to points of arrival.* Simple articulations and gentle rounding off contrasted with occasional strong and dramatic drives to important goals.

   The slow yet easily moving pace of this composition, together with its rich, varied, and luminous qualities of tone color, suggest at first a deliberate dance or song. The new element introduced by the fanfare, however, combined with the moments in which a suspension of movement seems to occur, raises the expressive level of this piece far above that of a dance or song. There is a long-range feeling of growth and expansion. Many different ideas and values are incorporated.

   In this chapter we have dealt with experiences that can be shared by all listeners, whether or not they can read music, play an instrument, or are familiar with the technique or history of music. These experiences involve our feelings; sound creates a mood; movement suggests emotion or physical action; arrival rounds off the experience and enables us to grasp it, then to move on to another phase. We could stop at this point and still have a satisfying experience with music, strong and immediate. But music is an art and a science as well as a way of stirring the feelings. There is much pleasure to be gained from seeing how musical elements fit together in different ways, very much like the pleasure we have in understanding a game fully or playing it skillfully. The delight in appreciating various kinds of musical order can then merge with the lift that comes with the emotional response to provide the listener with a truly full musical experience. The following chapters of this book are concerned then with filling in the framework of the basic musical experiences explored in this first chapter.

CHAPTER TWO

MUSICAL ELEMENTS AND THEIR RELATIONSHIPS

I n Chapter 1 we were concerned with general impressions. Music was loud or soft; it moved quickly, slowly, vigorously, or gently; it had brilliant or dark color; it arrived with a flourish, or perhaps it did not seem to arrive at all. These impressions can evoke various emotional reactions. In this chapter we shall look into the ways in which sound, movement, and arrival are organized to create a sense of order, which links in with the expressive values of music.

Before we look into musical elements and their relationships, it will be helpful to become acquainted with some of the features of musical notation. Musical notation is a kind of shorthand. It specifies the pitch of notes, their length, the degree of loudness with which they are to be performed, their articulation, and the speed at which a piece is to be played.

NOTATION

PITCH

The pitch of tones is indicated on a five-line graph called the *staff*. Signs called *clefs* are placed at the left-hand edge of each staff to be used as guides for the specific locations of tones. Three clefs are used: (1) the F or *bass* clef, on the *fourth* line upward on the staff, which locates the note F *below* middle C (see Example 2-1); (2) the C clef, which may be placed on any line and which locates the note middle C; (3) the G or *treble* clef, which locates the note G *above* middle C and is placed upon the *second* line of the staff. Other notes are reckoned upward and downward from the clef tones; each line or space on the staff represents a specific pitch level depending upon the clef sign being used. Example 2-1 shows a staff with the three clef signs, a section of a piano keyboard, and the notes on the staff that correspond to the *white* keys of the piano. Note especially the *arrows* that locate the clefs on the staff.

EXAMPLE 2-1. *Clefs and their positions on the piano keyboard*

a. Staff and clefs

b. Section of piano keyboard

c. White notes of keyboard

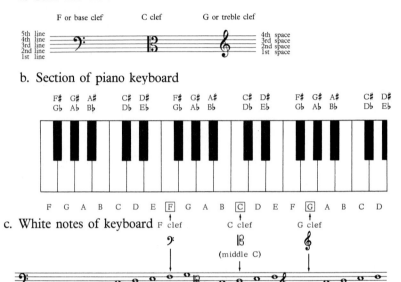

If you play the white notes moving upward (to the right) starting on any key, singing with the piano note, you will notice that the distances between the tones (*intervals*) are of two different sizes. Those between E and F and B and C are *smaller* than the others. The smaller intervals are called *half steps;* the larger are *whole steps.* The black keys provide half steps between the white whole steps. A line of tones moving upward or downward stepwise is called a *scale.* By combining white and black notes in various ways, many different scales can be created; each of these has its own special character. Throughout the ages composers have used specific scale arrangements at different times; these have had profound effect upon the style and expressive qualities of their music and will be discussed in the chapters to follow.

TIME Example 2-2 explains the relative lengths of various notes. In performance, a time value is established for one type of note, according to *tempo* instructions given by the composer. The other values are then played as multiples or dividends of that tone. For example, if a half note is supposed to be two seconds in length, a whole note will require four seconds, a quarter note one second, and an eighth note one-half second. The following example illustrates the relative lengths of the notes, based upon a half note of two seconds in duration:

EXAMPLE 2-2. *Relative duration of tones*

EXAMPLE 2-3. *Lengths of dotted and nondotted tones*

At the beginning of a piece, to the right of the clef on the first staff there is a figure that looks like a fraction, such as $\frac{4}{4}$, $\frac{6}{8}$, etc. These are *time signatures;* they designate the number of notes of a given value that are to be included in the time unit called the *measure.* Measures are marked off by *bar lines.* Thus a time signature of $\frac{4}{4}$ specifies that each measure in the piece will be four quarter notes in length (unless the time signature is changed in the course of the piece); this length may be made up from notes of various lengths—half notes, quarters, eighths, etc.—but all the notes in a measure will add up in length to four quarters. Often a piece may begin with one or more short notes before the first full measure, as in Examples 2-4*a* and *b.* Example 2-4 illustrates some of the more commonly used measure types or *meters,* based upon the patterns of familiar melodies.

EXAMPLE 2-4. *Measures*

a. Home, Sweet Home

Be it ev - - er so hum - - ble, there's no place like home

b. Oh, Susanna

I | came from Al - a - | ba - ma with my | ban - jo on my | knee

c. America

My   coun - try, | 'tis   of thee, | Sweet   land   of | lib - er - ty

d. Silent Night

Si - lent night! | Ho - - ly night! | All   is calm, | all   is bright.

The following exercise may be helpful as a simple application of the notation principles described above. First, play the notes given on the first staff, using the picture of the piano keyboard as a guide:

EXAMPLE 2-5. *Notation of "Jingle Bells"*

a. Pitch

Then, tap out the following patterns of note length:

b. Note lengths

Finally, put the two together to play part of the familiar song "Jingle Bells":

c. Pitch and note lengths combined

Silence is also part of music. A line of tones may be interrupted by moments of silence called *rests*. These correspond in length to the note values given in Example 2-2. They are notated as follows:

EXAMPLE 2-6. *Notation of rests*

The information on musical notation given above may be used in several ways. Even if you do not read music, you can look at a page to get some idea of the shape of the lines, their rise and fall, and their general contour; this applies to the excerpts from musical scores quoted in this book. If you wish to explore for yourselves the effects created in the simpler examples that illustrate basic procedures, you may use the keyboard, for which these examples have been arranged. Even if you have never played a musical instrument, it can be an exciting and rewarding experience to produce a simple passage at the piano, bringing to life the effects symbolized by the notation.

With the help of the clues to notation described above we can now investigate the *elements* of music. Sound, movement, and arrival are organized by these elements; they fall into four groups:

Rhythm—organization of musical time
Melody—musical line
Texture—interaction of musical lines
Harmony—specific relationships of musical tones

Coordinating these elements with the criteria of Chapter 1:

Sound includes: range, dynamics, texture, tone color, harmony
Movement includes: rhythm, melody, texture, harmony
Arrival includes: rhythm, melody, harmony

SOUND

RANGE

The total range of available sound is very large; it extends both above and below the piano keyboard. Among the familiar instruments, only the piano, harp, and organ can travel through most of this range. Electronic instruments can reach extremely high, creating sounds that become inaudible to human ears; or they can reach extremely low, so that the sound is felt more as a physical vibration than as a definite pitch.

The human voice and most musical instruments operate within a segment of the broad musical "space." For example, in a chorus, each part—high and low women's and men's voices—covers a segment of twelve or thirteen of the white notes on the piano. These voice ranges and their names are illustrated in Example 2-7.

EXAMPLE 2-7. *Voice ranges*

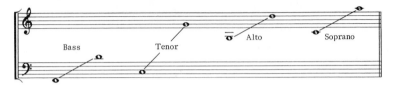

As you can see, voice ranges overlap. This overlap applies also to instruments of the orchestra, which have considerably greater ranges than voices do; they are deployed in the orchestra quite like voices, that is, as soprano, alto, tenor, and bass, in the following manner:

SOPRANO	ALTO	TENOR	BASS
Piccolo	Oboe	Clarinet	Bassoon and contrabassoon
Flute	Clarinet	Bassoon	Trombone and bass trombone
Oboe	Trumpet	Horn	Tuba
Clarinet	Violin	Trumpet	Cello
Trumpet	Viola	Bassoon	String bass
Violin		Cello	Timpani

Referring to the compositions given in Chapter 1 to illustrate levels of sound, we can now say that the Mendelssohn Scherzo emphasizes the soprano range, the Liszt example moves through the bass and tenor ranges as it begins, and the Brahms Symphony No. 1 covers all ranges, from deep bass to extreme soprano. In addition, we find that Berlioz's *Symphonie fantastique* is particularly striking in the manner in which it presents various instruments and instrumental groups in their characteristic ranges.

DYNAMICS Much of the expressive quality of a musical passage is created by *dynamics,* the degree of loudness or softness of sound. The dynamic range of music is indicated by terms, as given below, taken from Italian:

pp	pianissimo	very soft
p	piano	soft
mp	mezzo piano	moderately soft
mf	mezzo forte	moderately loud
f	forte	loud
ff	fortissimo	very loud

FIGURE 1. *String family: violin, viola, violoncello, string bass or contrabass. (Courtesy of the Conn Corporation, Elkhart, Indiana.)*

FIGURE 2. *Woodwind family: piccolo, flute, oboe, English horn, clarinet, bass clarinet, bassoon. (Courtesy of the Conn Corporation, Elkhart, Indiana.)*

17

FIGURE 3. *Brass family: trumpet, French horn, trombone, tuba.
(Courtesy of the Conn Corporation, Elkhart, Indiana.)*

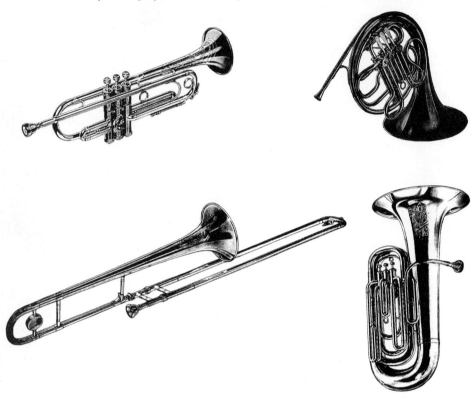

Sometimes, to dramatize their point, composers have indicated degrees of softness or loudness beyond this range, using the signs *ppp* and *fff*.

One extremely important aspect of dynamics is the steady increase or decrease of strength. These procedures, called *crescendo* (increasing) and *decrescendo* (decreasing), and often indicated by the following signs:

crescendo   decrescendo

are directed to the ebb and flow of emotional tension and excitement in music. For example, we can get a clear profile of the change in feeling in the first few minutes of Beethoven's Symphony No. 5 by sensing the dynamic range. After a very loud and short beginning, the music drops to a very soft level and builds with a crescendo to a very loud point of arrival; this procedure is repeated twice again, the final point of arrival being very clear, emphatic, and final. Example 2-8 sketches this dynamic profile; notice that each phase of movement is longer than the preceding and that the *ff* sections are increasingly broader. The effect of buildup and eventual triumph, so characteristic of Beethoven's

FIGURE 4. *Percussion instruments: timpani, bass drum, snare drum, bells (glockenspiel), marimba. (Courtesy of the Conn Corporation, Elkhart, Indiana.)*

music, is so strong here that it is easy to see why this symphony was a symbol of victory in World War II, apart from the fact that its opening four notes—short-short-short-long—are the same as the Morse code signal for V, which in those days stood for Victory.

EXAMPLE 2-8. *Profile of dynamics: Beethoven, Symphony No. 5 in C minor, first movement*

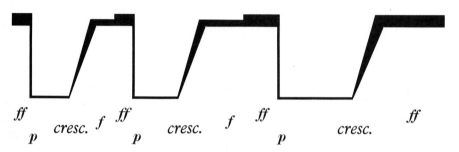

ff
p *cresc.* *f* *ff* *p* *cresc.* *f* *ff* *p* *cresc.* *ff*

TONE COLOR, TIMBRE
Tone color or *timbre* gives a characteristic flavor to musical action and is an important means for conveying expressive values. Often music is recognized first by its typical tone color—the heavy, rich sound of rock music with its peculiar flavor of electronic amplification, the light brilliance of a Vivaldi concerto, the subtle misty changes in a Debussy Prelude; watching a Japanese movie, we are brought immediately into its world by the twang of the *koto*, a plucked string instrument. The Mendelssohn Scherzo has a light, rather "velvety" tone color, thanks to the flutes that carry the line, while the Brahms Symphony has a full, heavy quality built from mixtures of individual tone colors—high strings, massive middle brass, and thunderous timpani.

Each instrument and each voice has its own particular color by which it can be recognized; different people singing the same tone might in turn sound nasal, rich, thin, clear, muffled, uncertain, firm. Much the same distinction appears among musical instruments; not only would an oboe and a saxophone give entirely different qualities to the same tone, but different instruments of the same type—a cheap violin and a precious Stradivarius—would be worlds apart in richness of tone color.

HARMONIC COLOR
Another important resource for musical expression is *harmonic color.* This refers to the effects created by combinations of tones sounded together, i.e., *chords.* For example, the Prelude to Wagner's music drama, *Tristan and Isolde,* has very rich harmonic color; each chord has a rich, full, and restless effect. On the other hand, the tone combi-

nations in the first movement of Bach's Brandenburg Concerto No. 2 seem consistently bright and firm. The instruments chosen in each case reinforce these effects; Wagner features violoncellos and the low registers of the oboes and clarinets at the beginning to set the mood of tension and uncertainty, while Bach focuses attention upon the violins, flutes, and oboes to highlight the takeoff for his exuberant exercise.

The types of chords used by a composer create a climate of harmonic color that affects all other kinds of musical action. Each era in Western music and each of the exotic musical cultures has its own preference for harmonic color. As we proceed in the survey of musical styles, this point will be further explored.

TEXTURE *Texture* is a term applied to the overall effect created by combinations of sound—pitch, dynamics, timbre, the number of tones sounding together, the number of performers, and the ways in which the voices or parts work with or against each other. Texture can be compared to the quality of a piece of cloth—the material used for thread, its size, color, direction and tightness of weave, patterns—in other words, the total picture.

When we evaluate musical sound for its texture, we correlate the various separate criteria already discussed. We note the spread of the pitch range, whether a given chord has many or few notes, the similarity or differences in tone color of the voices or instruments, the number of performers assigned to each line, the level of dynamics. Thus, the opening chord of Brahms's Symphony No. 1 has a very wide range, filled in from top to bottom, with a mixture of instrumental tone colors, and a large number of performers on each level playing *forte;* in terms of sound, this texture is rich, full, heavy, and mixed. The Mendelssohn Scherzo, on the other hand, separates high and low levels of pitch, features the sound of flutes, has a small number of notes in the opening chord, with one instrument each to the leading parts, and the entire effect is controlled by a low dynamic level. Typically, popular ballads and country music have a very light texture, voice accompanied by guitar; these are two highly contrasted tone colors set off clearly from each other.

The number of performers has a marked effect upon texture. Consider the difference in tone quality, in the sense of fullness and space, when one person sings a tone or an entire roomful of people sing the same tone. The Brahms Symphony demands many string players to each part to achieve its effect of grandeur; likewise, a magnificent chorus such as the "Hallelujah" from Handel's *The Messiah* was undoubtedly conceived for a massive group of voices.

Music with one performer to a part is called *chamber music* because it was traditionally performed in a room, a chamber, or small theater. Music with several performers to a part is called *orchestral* music if it includes strings (no voices); *band* music involves a group of wind instruments; *choral* music is written for voices. Orchestral, band, and choral music are differentiated from chamber music because they assign several performers to given parts. Some parts, however, may be played by a single or *solo* instrument or voice; in the orchestra, these single parts are generally assigned to woodwind and brass instruments, but in the larger orchestras woodwind and brass parts are often *doubled*, given to two or more players, in the *forte* passages.

To help you evaluate the use of elements of sound in a composition, the following chart is given. Some of the items in this chart and those given later in this chapter involve *approximate* effects, while others are *precise.*

SOUND

1. *Range (use chart on page 3)*
2. *Dynamics (use chart on page 3)*
3. *Instruments (identify)*

   a. *Wind (type)* _____

   b. *Brass (type)* _____

   c. *Strings (type)* _____

   d. *Percussion (type)* _____

4. *Texture (check proper line)*

   a. *Full* _____

   b. *Thin* _____

   c. *One to a part* _____

   d. *Several to a part* _____

MOVEMENT *Rhythm* refers to the organization of musical time by means of move-
AND ment and arrival. This is the most general meaning of rhythm and
ARRIVAL covers everything from a group of two tones to an entire composition.
RHYTHM More specifically, rhythm means the *manner* in which a piece
moves—its pace, regularity, articulation, and intensity of movement.

Sometimes, the term rhythm is used to describe a very striking, lively quality of movement, as in the Gershwin song "I Got Rhythm," where both the words and the music have a catchy, swinging verve.

As an element of music, rhythm involves (1) beat, (2) tempo, (3) meter, (4) note values, (5) accent, (6) motives, i.e., rhythmic patterns, and (7) larger rhythmic groups—phrases, periods.

Beat We all find ourselves at one time or another tapping our feet to music. In doing so, we are responding to the *beat* of the music. The beat is a pulse or stroke that recurs continuously and regularly; it is the heartbeat of the music, a sign of life that provides a clue to the quality of movement—fast, slow, regular, irregular, strong, gentle. Most of the music familiar to us—popular songs, dance music, the standard concert literature of the eighteenth and nineteenth centuries—maintains a clearly defined beat as a basis for its movement. Other styles—some Oriental music, Gregorian chant, and a considerable body of twentieth-century music—do not use a well-defined beat as an integral element. For most listeners trained in the Western tradition, the beat is something to hold on to, a thread of action that connects whatever events may be taking place. This applies both to the steady beat in the first movement of Bach's *Brandenburg* Concerto No. 2 and to the powerful, unrelenting beat of country and rock music.

Tempo Beats succeeding each other at a given rate create *tempo,* the technical Italian word used to designate the pace of music. Some of the conventional Italian terms used to specify tempo are given below:

presto—very quickly
vivace—lively
allegro—quickly
allegretto—rather quickly (slower than allegro)
andantino—rather slowly or leisurely
andante—moderately slow, moving (slower than andantino)
adagio—slowly
largo—broad and slow

Tempo is something of a subjective matter. Mozart specified allegro as the tempo for the first movement of his Symphony No. 40 in G minor; yet if you listen to the version conducted by Otto Klemperer and then to the one conducted by Erich Leinsdorf, you will immediately notice the marked difference in pace between the two versions and the differences in expressive qualities implied. The Klemperer version is heavier and has a deeper quality of feeling than the more buoyant Leinsdorf reading. This demonstrates the critical role of the performer in establishing the tempo of a piece, a condition that is present every time a piece is performed.

Gradual change in tempo, accelerating or slowing down, has a marked effect upon the expressive quality of the music. We have all heard performances that take on greater excitement and brilliance by quickening of tempo; conversely, some performers try to make greater expressive impact by slowing down at certain points. Such changes in tempo are often designated by the terms *accelerando* (speeding up) and *ritardando* (slowing down).

Meter; Meter and note values have already been illustrated (see page 12).
Note Values Basically, there are two kinds of meter, *duple* and *triple*. A measure that has two beats is in simple *duple meter;* a measure containing three beats is in simple *triple meter*. Example 2-4*b* represents simple duple meter; Example 2-4*c* represents simple triple meter. When a measure contains a number of simple groups, it is said to be in *compound* meter. For example:

2 groups of 2 beats form a 4-beat group (see Example 2-4*a*)
2 groups of 3 beats form a 6-beat group (see Example 2-4*d*)

In addition, we occasionally find three groups of two beats and three groups of three beats; however, the majority of compositions are set in the two simple and two compound meters described above.

Duple and triple meters have their distinctive qualities of movement. Duple has a shorter thrust, more power than triple, while triple has a more swinging, generally lighter effect than duple. Thus, a march like Sousa's "The Stars and Stripes Forever," set in quick duple time, calls for a quick, striding step, while a waltz such as Strauss's "The Blue Danube," in quick triple time, moves with a sweeping, gliding effect.

Note values are linked to qualities of movement. Both the Mendelssohn Scherzo and the quick section of the Brahms Symphony No. 1, first movement, following the slow introduction, use triple meter (Mendelssohn $\frac{3}{8}$, Brahms $\frac{6}{8}$). The Brahms Symphony uses notes of long value, interspersed with a few shorter notes; the Mendelssohn does exactly the opposite, using a great many short notes. Apart from the different tempos, the note values contribute to the heavy style of one and the lightness of the other.

Accent *Accent* means emphasis. When we listen to groups of beats, we tend to feel that the first of each group has a greater emphasis than the others, as: **1** 2 / **1** 2, or **1** 2 3 / **1** 2 3. These first beats are called *strong* beats; intrinsically, they have greater importance, greater accent than the others, which are called *weak* beats; this is true even though there is no difference in the strength with which the notes are played.

Accent can be made stronger by increased loudness or increased length. The former is called accent of *stress* or *dynamic* accent; the latter is called accent of *length* or *agogic* accent. Both effects join to give the first note of the finale of Beethoven's Symphony No. 3 a tremendous impact of accent.

Accent can shift by dynamic or agogic means from the normal strong beat to a weak beat, marking the weak beat for special attention, as:

1 **2** / 1 **2** / 1 **2** or
1 2 **3** / 1 2 **3** / 1 **2** 3 or
1 2 **3** / 1 2 **3** / 1 2 **3**

Note how the shifts of accent in the following example from Beethoven's Symphony No. 3 build a tremendous accumulation of rhythmic momentum, whose energy is finally discharged at a climactic point of arrival.

EXAMPLE 2-9. *Beethoven: Symphony No. 3, first movement*

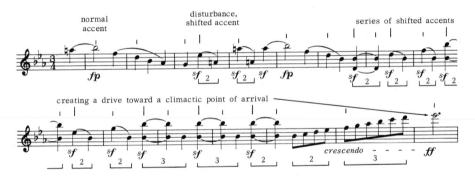

Another way of disturbing the normal flow of the beat is to begin a note slightly before the beat or after it, then hold it for an instant beyond the beat. (See Example 2-10b.) The effect is to give the movement a lift, a bounce. In the first line of the song "Buffalo Girl," the shifted stress on "come *out* tonight" gives the melody a snappy turn. Much African music is built on the play of shifting accents, irregular groups of beats in highly sophisticated complex patterns. Play with the normal flow of beats is the very touchstone of jazz throughout its history. Stravinsky achieved an odd, parodistic effect, suggesting the eccentric movements of a puppet show, at the beginning of the Soldier's March in his *L'Histoire du Soldat;* he sets a normal beat in the lower instruments against irregular accents in the upper parts. Generally speaking, shifts of accent are called *syncopation*.

Rhythmic When notes of various values are connected, they form distinctive
Motives patterns, *rhythmic motives*. For example, the first line of the song
"Jingle Bells" has four patterns: short-short-long, short-short-long,
short-short-short- short-long; each of these four patterns is a rhythmic
motive. We might recognize the song even if these patterns were
tapped out without the tune; these motives determine the quality of
movement and the lively manner of the song. The four notes at the
beginning of Beethoven's Symphony No. 5 constitute probably the
most famous motive in all music, especially since it was used as the V
for Victory symbol in World War II. A rhythmic motive thus is a kind
of motto that helps to set the style or expressive quality of a passage or
even of an entire piece, as in the eight-note figure of the first prelude of
Bach's *Well-Tempered Clavier,* Book I. Rhythmic motives are particularly well defined in dance music, partly to set the pattern for the
dancer's steps, partly to keep the movement steady, regular, and
clearly marked. Example 2-10 illustrates rhythmic motives.

EXAMPLE 2-10. *Rhythmic motives*

a. Waltz

b. Ragtime

c. Polka

d. Mendelssohn, Scherzo from *A Midsummer Night's Dream*

Larger Larger rhythmic units, *phrases* and *periods,* are formed by connecting a
Rhythmic series of rhythmic motives, just as motives themselves are formed by
Units: groups of notes. The difference between a phrase and a period lies
phrase, period partly in length, partly in the effect of arrival. A phrase is like a partial
statement in language, a clause in a sentence. It is rarely more than
four to six measures in length; it may or may not have a final point of
arrival, but is sensed only as a *part* of a complete statement. A period

is like a complete sentence; it ends with a strong, clear, and generally conclusive point of arrival, and is most often made up of two or more phrases.

The clearest layouts of phrases and periods occur in songs and dances. Much of the appeal of such pieces comes from the sense of inner balance, where the phrases are of the same length, and they are arranged by twos or fours to create periods. Example 2-11 illustrates this arrangement, designated as *symmetry:*

EXAMPLE 2-11. *Phrase and period symmetry:* "Oh, Susanna"

"Oh, Susanna" has perfect symmetry in its phrase and period arrangement; there are two periods, each made up of two phrases. This arrangement is very pleasing and satisfying in short songs and dances, but can become dull and boring in longer pieces. Interest grows and feeling intensifies when symmetry is disturbed. Brahms, in the opening of his Symphony No. 1, plays symmetry against irregular patterns to create a high level of tension. If you count with the beats of the timpani, you will sense regular groups of six for seven measures; then, at the eighth measure, an extra three beats are added to increase the drive to the point of arrival. These three extra beats disturb the symmetry, adding power to the movement. Above this steady beat the upper voices soar in an irregular rising and falling flight, in which we cannot sense a clear symmetry. The two types of motion create a gigantic tug-of-war. Symmetry, in this kind of music, is not a goal, but a resource to build a larger design.

Rhythmic phrases and periods differ greatly in length and internal arrangement, just as sentences do in language. The way in which the composer shapes phrases and periods in a piece tells us something about its expressive objective—a neatly trimmed, comfortable symmetry, as in the Mendelssohn Scherzo, or a compelling thrust, built of long, often nonsymmetrical arrangements, as in the Brahms Symphony No. 1. On the largest scale, the entire form of a piece represents rhythm; certain sections act for movement, others for arrival; together they create extended rhythmic units.

RHYTHMIC EVALUATION CHART

(Some of these overlap; check one in each group.)

1. Beat

   a. Regular _____

   b. Changing _____

   c. Emphatic _____

   d. Gentle _____

2. Tempo
   a. Presto, vivace, allegro, allegretto, andantino, andante, adagio, largo

   b. Steady _____

   c. Changing _____

3. Meter (establish basic beat)

   a. Duple _____

   b. Triple _____

4. Accent

   a. Strong _____

   b. Light _____

   c. Regular _____

   d. Shifting _____

5. Motives

   a. Clearly defined _____

   b. Not clearly defined _____

6. *Phrases*

   a. Symmetrical (equal in length) _____

   b. Nonsymmetrical _____

MELODY The memorable moments in music are often furnished by melody. The "Blue Danube Waltz," "Yesterday," "America the Beautiful," the "Ode to Joy" in Beethoven's Symphony No. 9, "Stardust"—these are melodies known and loved by millions.

Contour In its simplest definition, melody is a line of tones. Like all lines, melody has a shape, a *contour*. It may rise or fall; it may remain for a short time on a level; it may have a rounded or jagged contour; it may have a wide or narrow range. Each of these patterns contributes to musical meaning and expression, much as the gestures of a dancer or actor convey a mood on the stage. Or, as you listen to a melody, you might also imagine that you are observing an artist sketching a figure. The path of the artist's pencil gradually builds a meaningful pattern, an image, much as a line of tones builds a melodic shape.

When a melodic line rises steadily, it can suggest increasing energy or growing tension; when it drops steadily, it can suggest relaxation or a sense of settling. A melody that is more or less level, or has a narrow range of pitch, may suggest steadiness and evenness of movement. Abrupt rise or fall, particularly between high and low pitches, indicates a bold, vigorous, or perhaps strenuous quality of movement, especially if the pace is quick. When the melodic tones are connected, that is, next to each other in pitch, the melodic movement is described as *conjunct*. When gaps in pitch appear between successive melodic tones, the melodic movement is described as *disjunct*. Example 2-12 illustrates some melodic shapes.

EXAMPLE 2-12. *Melodic shapes*

a. Rising

Moderato

b. Falling. Beethoven: Sonata in F minor, Op. 2, no. 1, first movement

c. Remaining on a level. Beethoven: Symphony No. 5, third movement

d. Turning around one or two points: Schubert: Symphony in B minor, first movement

e. Connected or *conjunct*. Beethoven: Symphony No. 9, "Ode to Joy"

f. Disconnected or *disjunct*. Bach: Concerto for Two Violins in D minor, first movement

Note, in the above examples, how the changes in direction, the rise and fall, tend to compensate for each other. Such motion contributes to the *sense of balance* in the melody, in addition to its primary role in creating the melodic contour.

As a melody continues, it may arrive at a high point, or *apex*. This is a moment of high expressive intensity, a climax. In the beautifully lyric song of the Beatles, "Yesterday," the melody rises to an expressive apex on the words "so far." An entire composition can be shaped to rise to a grand melodic apex that gives a large-scale contour to the form of the piece; this takes place in Wagner's Prelude to *Tristan* and in the second fugue of Bach's *Well-Tempered Clavier*, Book I, in C minor. Example 2-13 shows how a melody can build to an expressive climax through a series of constantly higher apices.

EXAMPLE 2-13. *Melodic apices. Beethoven: Symphony No. 5, Op. 67*

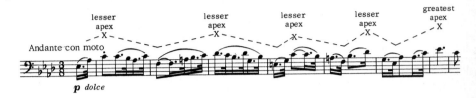

Melodic Melodic contour is built through a succession of *melodic intervals.* An
Intervals interval is the *distance in pitch* between two tones and a *quality of
sound* created by these two tones.

   The keyboard is useful for getting acquainted with the more
common intervals. At the piano, play the note C as indicated in
Example 2-14. The white note immediately to the right of C is D; the
interval connecting these two tones is called a *second.* Each interval is
named according to the number of degrees on the musical staff which
it includes.

EXAMPLE 2-14. *Common musical intervals*

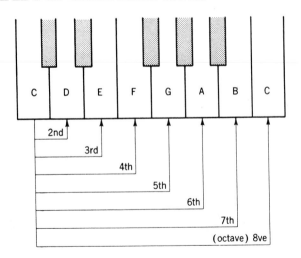

Listen carefully to each interval: you will notice that each has a characteristic quality of sound. Thirds and sixths sound full and rich; fourths and fifths have a rather open feeling; sevenths and ninths seem unsteady and tense; seconds are rather smooth and neutral in effect. These values affect the nature of the melodies of which they are part.

Since intervals differ in size, they differ in the impression of movement which they can give in a motive. For example, listen to the beginning of Mozart's *Haffner* Symphony:

EXAMPLE 2-15. *Mozart:* Haffner *Symphony*

The bold effect of this music is created by extremely large intervals in the melody. Certainly this is a most arresting way of introducing the brilliant and festive piece to follow.

The effect is quite different at the beginning of "Yesterday," where the closely spaced intervals link in with the mood of sadness pervading this song, which has become a classic in today's popular music.

Melodic Melodic contour combines with rhythmic motives to create *melodic*
Motives *motives.* A melodic motive gives us a clear indication of style and mood in a nutshell. For example, the first six notes of the song "Good Night" from the *Music Man* have the same general contour as the beginning of the march tune "Seventy-six Trombones" from the same musical. The slow, smooth triple meter of the song, in waltz time, cues us in to its sentimental mood, while the jaunty, incisive, quick duple time of the march sets the foot to tapping and lifts the spirit.

Melodic motives are the most easily recognized elements of musical form. Once you hear a motive, you can recognize it later in the piece, and this helps you to keep your bearings as far as the form is concerned. A motive can be *repeated* exactly, or it can be *varied* in many ways and yet retain its similarity to what was heard before. *Contrast* can be introduced among motives for the sake of variety or to create a kind of melodic tug-of-war that can intensify the ongoing action.

Example 2-16 is concerned entirely with *repetition* and *variation.* Beethoven states the motive of four notes, *repeats* it at lower pitch, then restates it eleven times in *varied* forms to build a period which rises steadily to a point of climax. The one motive has been used exclusively here to "spearhead" the direction of the larger melodic line.

EXAMPLE 2-16. *Beethoven: Symphony No. 5, first movement*

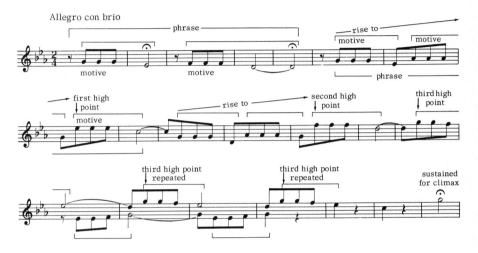

Sharp contrast occurs between the motives in the following example:

EXAMPLE 2-17. *Mozart:* Jupiter *Symphony, beginning*

The whole orchestra begins with a flourish of three bold strokes; this is followed immediately by a reply which offers, in contrast, the merest fragment of a soft lyric melody. The back-and-forth of "vigorous" and "singing," twice stated, lets loose a rush of powerful musical action that pulls to a halt only fifteen measures later. Contrast here is a springboard for an exciting flight.

In listening for melodic motives, note the number and variety used. For example, the first movement of Beethoven's Symphony

No. 3 uses many different motives (or *figures*), often highly contrasted.

Other works deal with just a few similar motives, constantly manipulating them, as in the first movement of Bach's *Brandenburg Concerto No. 2.* Still again, the melodic material may be so consistent and continuous that we can hardly speak of separate motives, as in the plainsong *Alleluia, Masterpieces,* no. 2. In each case, the goal of expression is reflected in the play of melodic motives. Beethoven's music is charged with tremendous tension and conflict; Bach's has a playful vigor; the plainsong has a floating, remote quality.

The motive in music does not represent a fully developed musical idea, yet its very brevity, coupled with its distinct manner, enables it to fill a very powerful role in carrying forward musical movement. Each time you hear a familiar motive reappear or encounter a new motive, you sense that the music has gained fresh melodic momentum.

*Melody—Types
of Material* Melody takes many forms and serves different purposes. It may be simple and clear, as in a familiar song; it may be complex and elaborate, as in the brilliant passage work of a concerto or in the improvisations of an Indian raga. It may be laid out in short, symmetrical phrases and periods, as in a song; or it may be made up of many motives linked to form long, asymmetrical periods as in the first movement of Mozart's *Jupiter* Symphony or the second movement of Bartók's *Music for String Instruments, Percussion, and Celesta.* Much music of our time does not fashion melody as a clearly linked succession of tones; it isolates individual tones or small groups, separating them by wide gaps in pitch or by changes of tone color as in Webern's *Five Pieces for Orchestra.* Nevertheless, there is melodic connection between the tones, and the shapes imply striking, intense gestures.

A complete, self-sufficient melody is generally called a *tune.* The important melodic materials of larger compositions, complete or fragmentary, are called *subjects* or *themes;* they represent topics for musical discourse throughout the piece, much as the subject of a discussion in language is given at the beginning of a speech or essay and referred to throughout the presentation. In an extended work, a section which presents a distinctive theme or tune is felt as a relatively stable part of the work, a kind of plateau in the contour of the action. When melodic motives are worked over, that is, *developed,* greater intensity of movement is felt. In works of large scope these procedures tend to alternate, but one may predominate over the other. For example, development of melodic motives seems to take place most of the time in the first movement of Beethoven's Symphony No. 5, while in the second movement of this work the composer is concerned principally with framing tuneful melodic material.

MELODIC EVALUATION CHART

(Check one in each group.)

1. Contour

    a. Principally rising _____

    b. Principally falling _____

    c. Balance of rise and fall _____

    d. Principally conjunct intervals _____

    e. Principally disjunct intervals _____

2. Motives

    a. Repeated _____

    b. Varied _____

    c. Contrasted _____

	repeated	*contrasted*	*repeated*
d. Arrangements (for example: a	*a*	*b*	*a*)

    _____

3. Treatment of melody

    a. Tune or tunelike _____

    b. Play of figures _____

TEXTURE The total effect of sound and movement in nearly all music is the result of a number of lines (voices or parts) working together to create *texture.* In discussing elements of musical sound we have already dealt with texture, comparing it to the way a piece of cloth is put together. Texture, as it involves movement, deals with the total effect of action as voices take different roles. These roles include:

1. A principal melody
2. A supporting bass line
3. A middle part, less prominent, that fills in the sound

4. Melodic lines working *against* each other
5. A supporting line moving in the same pattern as the principal line but at a different pitch

The textures created by these roles are of two general types: (1) *homophonic,* in which a single principal melodic idea is presented, and (2) *polyphonic,* or *contrapuntal,* in which two or more important melodic lines are heard at the same time.

Homophonic Probably the most familiar texture in music is one in which a melody
Texture is performed to a simple support. This is typical of most popular music, which supports the voice with light chords struck regularly on a guitar. This texture is called *melody and accompaniment.* The accompaniment itself can use various patterns—struck chords, sustained tones, or a pattern of light, quickly moving notes that is steadily repeated, as in Example 2-18, where the simple figure creates a light and flowing sense of movement:

EXAMPLE 2-18. *Mozart: Sonata in C major, K. 545, second movement*

← Melody

← Accompaniment

(Note different patterns of movement in
melody and accompaniment.)

Example 2-19 is also homophonic, since the heavy chords support a powerful melody in the uppermost voice. But notice that all voices are moving in the same rhythmic pattern, to reinforce the melody, rather than set it off. This kind of texture may be called *isometric,* from "iso," meaning "equal," and "metric," meaning "measured."

EXAMPLE 2-19. *Beethoven: Symphony No. 5, last movement*

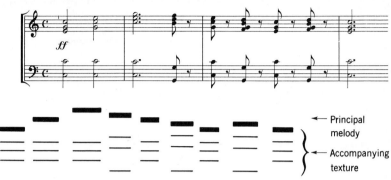

The accompanying voices carry out the same rhythmic
action as the uppermost voice, the melody.

When a single voice or instrument, or a group of performers, sings
or plays a melody without accompaniment, the texture is designated as
monophonic, meaning "one-voiced."

Polyphonic When several voices play clearly separate lines, each with some degree
Texture of melodic importance, the texture is called *polyphonic* (meaning
"many-voiced") or *contrapuntal.* The most easily grasped kind of
polyphonic texture is created by *imitation.* In imitation, one part
begins with a melody, and after a few measures a second part enters
with the same melody, while the first continues to spin out its line.
Imitation may involve as few as two and as many as five or six separate
parts. A familiar type of imitative polyphony is the *round,* such as
"Row, Row Your Boat." In singing such a piece, each performer feels
that his part works against the others in a neatly fitted texture; he thus
gains vivid satisfaction in musical participation. Imitation can also be
used to build a tight, continuous line of action in broadly scaled,
complex pieces. Example 2-20 illustrates this procedure in a Prelude
by Bach; note the sense of drive and accumulation built as the voices
enter successively.

EXAMPLE 2-20. *Imitative polyphony: Bach, Prelude in E♭ major,
Well-tempered Clavier Book I*

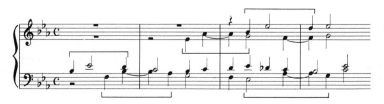

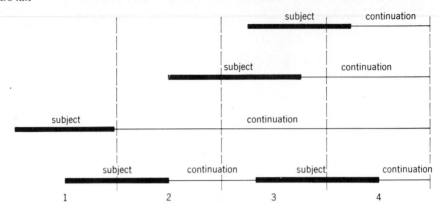

Counterpoint *without* imitation can give the impression of two different kinds of melodic action neatly fitted to each other while they retain their own character. One of the most delightful examples of this can be heard in the final strain of Sousa's "The Stars and Stripes Forever"; the trombones give us the wonderful tune in their full-throated middle register while the piccolos dance in the stratosphere with their sprightly jumping figures, a marvelous counterpoint of color, register, rhythm, and conjunct versus disjunct melody. In a more serious vein, the three lines at the beginning of Brahms's Symphony No. 1, rising, falling, and level, embody this kind of counterpoint, the nonimitative, called *free* counterpoint.

Homophonic texture lends itself to clear punctuation and regular movement, governed by the leading voice. In polyphonic texture, the overlapping of voices disguises punctuation, and therefore promotes a continuous flow.

A great deal of music uses elements of homophonic and polyphonic texture together or side by side. For example, the opening of the Symphony No. 1 by Brahms has two important melodic lines in the upper voices, one line descending, the other rising, linked in tight polyphonic action. Underneath, the steady beat of the accompanying bass repeats the same note; it adds a firm homophonic-style support to the upper voices. Notice also that while there are but three important melodic lines, the entire orchestra is deployed to reinforce these lines; this procedure is called *doubling* of voices or parts. (See page 22.) When the principal melody is handed around among the performers in a group, or among various parts, the process is designated in this book as *give-and-take*. This has something of the aspect of a game in which players take turns. Jazz thrives on this textural layout; Dixieland music could not exist without it. The exchange can be very clear, as in Dixieland, or it might be very subtle, when an accompaniment figure takes on more than minimal interest, and perhaps may even suggest an imitation of the principal melody, as in Example 2-21:

EXAMPLE 2-21. *Beethoven: Sonata for Piano in B♭ major, Op. 22,
second movement*

TEXTURE EVALUATION CHART

(Check one in each group.)

1. *Homophonic*

   a. *Solo* _____

   b. *Melody-accompaniment* _____

   c. *Isometric* _____

2. *Polyphonic*

   a. *Imitative counterpoint* _____

   b. *Free counterpoint* _____

3. *Give-and-take* _____

HARMONY In listening for melodic interval qualities, we heard that each interval had its own characteristic sound. The differences in sound among intervals is the basis of *harmony.* Harmony deals with (*a*) effects created when tones are sounded together *or* arranged in a series and (*b*) the use of these effects for sound, movement, and arrival. In the following section, these basic aspects of harmony will be discussed: (1) consonance and dissonance, (2) chords, (3) tonal center, (4) cadences, (5) modulation.

Consonance *Consonance* and *dissonance* refer to the way we hear intervals and the
and way we hear chords. Consonance means "sounding together," and
Dissonance dissonance means "sounding against." To test for consonance and dissonance, play various two-, three-, and four-note combinations at

the keyboard, using middle C as the bottom note. Combinations such as C-E, C-G, C-A, C-E-G, C-G-C will sound blended, together, giving a sense of stability and rest. Other combinations, such as C-D, C-B, C-D-F, C-E♭-G♭, C-F♯-B will sound edgy, separate, as if the notes were not smoothly fitted together, giving a sense of instability, of a *need to move onward*. By themselves, consonant intervals suggest arrival; dissonant intervals suggest movement. The sweetness of the song "Silent Night" is largely due to the large proportion of consonant chords that support the melody; the drive at the beginning of Brahms's Symphony No. 1 is powerfully reinforced by the incorporation of a number of strongly dissonant chords.

Chords   A chord is a group of three or more notes sounded together. In our Western music, since about the year 1400, the principal chords have contained three different notes and have been built by placing one third above another. These chords are called *triads,* meaning a group of three. There are four standard triads, each having a different arrangement of major (two whole steps) and minor (one and one-half steps) thirds. Example 2-22 illustrates these triads—the major, minor, augmented, and diminished. As you play these, note that each triad has its own characteristic sound; the major is bright in relation to the others; the minor has a darker quality; the diminished triad has a tight, dissonant quality, while the augmented has a rich, unstable effect.

EXAMPLE 2-22. *Triads*

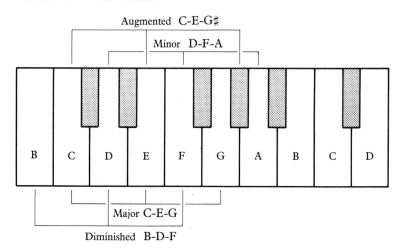

These chords, of course, can be built upon any note; their thirds are arranged as follows:

major triad	*minor triad*	*diminished triad*	*augmented triad*
minor third	major third	minor third	major third
major third	minor third	minor third	major third

Major and minor triads can act for arrival, although they can promote movement as well; diminished and augmented triads, since they are unstable, act for movement.

To distinguish the qualities of these triads, sing the notes in turn, or together in a small group. Also, listen for them in musical compositions. For instance, the sweet sound of a song like "America, the Beautiful" is based upon the many major triads it uses, while the darkness of the second movement of Beethoven's Symphony No. 3, a funeral march, is due largely to its minor triads.

Chords with more than three different tones are called *seventh* chords, *ninth* chords, *eleventh* chords, and *thirteenth* chords, according to the interval—seventh, ninth, etc.—above the bottom note of the chord. These are all dissonant, and of these, seventh chords have been by far the most useful to promote harmonic motion.

Tonal Center   When tones are sounded, whether simultaneously or in succession, there seems to be a tendency for *one tone to assert itself* in our hearing more strongly than others, to establish itself as a point of reference. This can be illustrated simply. Hum to yourself a familiar song such as "My Old Kentucky Home" or "America." Stop humming just before the last note. The song is halted short of its goal. No matter what you do rhythmically or melodically, the sense of arrival necessary to round off the piece is missing *unless you sing the last note;* this tone, the last note, is a point of reference for the whole piece. It has established itself as a *tonal center.*

There are two principal ways in which a tonal center can be fixed:

1. By *prominence.* The note is heard often, at the beginning, in the middle, and at the end of a melody. Prominence causes the note itself, as a level of pitch, to stand out.
2. By *interval relationship.* Intervals or chords are so arranged that the forward movement points to a specific tone as an expected point of arrival.

Example 2-23 illustrates these methods. In Example 2-23*a* the melody circles around the tone E, touching it seven times; its prominence establishes it as a point of reference, a tonal center. This method of fixing or defining a tonal center was used in medieval church music, and it is presently used in many folk songs, popular songs, and in much exotic (that is, non-Western) music. In Example 2-23*b*, the tonal center C is strongly felt at the end; it appears only twice during the melody, but the last four notes seem to "tie a knot" around C by means of their interval relationships, fixing it in our hearing very strongly as a tonal center. This is the basis of the method used in Western music from the fifteenth century to the present. In prominence, the melody *floats* around its tonal center; in interval relationship, it is *anchored* to its tonal center.

EXAMPLE 2-23. *Definition of tonal center*

a. Prominence

b. Interval relationship

Example 2-23*b* uses the notes of the familiar *major* scale. The interval relationships in this scale form the basis of the Western harmonic system. Example 2-24 illustrates this scale.

EXAMPLE 2-24. *Major scale*

Singing this scale, we accept the first note as a point of departure; we reach a satisfactory point of arrival only at the upper C. The two C's represent a tonal center, called a *tonic* note. The other notes move between the two C's and require them as anchorage; conversely, these C's need the other notes for clarification and support. Note especially the half steps between 3 and 4, 7 and 8. Play them as follows: $\frac{7}{4}$ to $\frac{8}{3}$; note the progression from instability to stability, the two intervals fitting together as if they were gears. This progression is a special property of the major scale; it is a powerful means for defining a tonal center.

Other dissonant or unstable intervals—seconds, sevenths, ninths, fourths—also can lead the ear to a specific stable interval, a *resolution*.

In the course of a phrase or period, the pairing of unstable-stable intervals or chords promotes harmonic movement and builds an expectation for arrival. Example 2-25 illustrates progressions of this type in the major scale.

EXAMPLE 2-25. *Progressions in major scale alternating instability and stability*

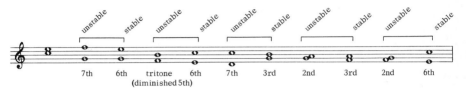

When a tonal center is defined by consistent use of instability-stability relationships, it is called a *key*. Therefore, Example 2-25 is in the *key* of C major.

A companion key to the major, more colorful in sound, but less strong in its ability to define its tonic, is the *minor* key. The terms major and minor refer to the size of the third between 1 and 3 of the scale; in the major scale, the third is large, a major third (see page 31); in the minor key, the third is minor. To hear the difference between a major and minor third, play or sing C-E; then play or sing C-E♭. Note the darker, tighter effect of C-E♭, the minor third. The third, in each case, gives the characteristic color of the key. Example 2-26 gives three versions of the minor scale:

EXAMPLE 2-26. *Minor scales*

Natural

Harmonic

Melodic

Note, in the *natural* version of the minor scale, that the half steps lie between 2-3 and 5-6. As you sing this scale, clearly there is no tight connection between 7-8 as there is in the major scale. To give the minor scale a firm arrival at its tonic, it has been customary to *raise* the 7th note, so that it forms a half step to 8. This version is called the *harmonic* minor scale, because it accommodates the need for harmony to move to its tonic. When you sing this scale, you will find an awkward, over-large interval between 6 and 7. Therefore, in order to accommodate smooth melodic connection, 6 is sometimes raised, creating the *melodic* minor scale. This is easier to sing than the harmonic scale. Note that the third, the defining note for the minor scale, remains the same in all versions; depending upon circumstances, all three versions can be used interchangeably.

Music of the eighteenth and nineteenth centuries uses the *harmonic* version predominantly, as in the subject of the Fugue in C minor, *Well-Tempered Clavier*, Book I, of Bach; now and then the natural and melodic versions will be used for smooth melodic flow. The *natural* version has come into its own in the twentieth century. Its lyric, plaintive, less assertive quality has been taken up in many popular songs of the mid-twentieth century. (See Debussy's Prelude "Footsteps in the Snow," Example 8-4.)

One of the most impressive contrasts between a minor and a major key occurs at the beginning of the last movement of Beethoven's Symphony No. 5. The passage that closes the third movement has been in a minor key; a quick buildup in strength and intensity of sound along with a gradual rise in pitch to a climactic point leads directly without break into a broadly massive, brilliant major sound, played by the full orchestra at maximum strength. Here, the minor key provides a dramatic staging of the entry of the major.

Each note of a key can become the lowermost note of a chord built upward in thirds. Example 2-27*a* shows the triads of the key of C major with the names and the Roman numerals assigned to them. Example 2-27*b* shows how the notes of the C major triad, C-E-G, can be distributed at various levels; *no matter how the notes are arranged, this chord is heard as I of C major.* (*Root position* occurs when the lowermost note of a triad is in the bass; when the bass takes the middle note of a triad, the chord is in *first inversion;* when the bass takes the uppermost note of a triad, the chord is in *second inversion.* Note that the firmest effect is created by the root position; therefore, root position reinforces effects of arrival.)

EXAMPLE 2-27. *Triad relationships*

a. Simple triads

I	II	III	IV	V	VI	VII	I
tonic	supertonic	mediant	subdominant	dominant	submediant	leading tone	tonic

b. Distribution of notes in the C major triads

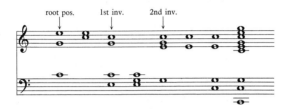

If we place another third above each of these triads to make a seventh-from-the-bottom note, for example, C-E-G-B, or G-B-D-F, the chord becomes a *seventh* chord and takes on dissonance.

For a given key, the triads I, IV, and V and the seventh chord on V play the most important roles in shaping its harmonic progressions. In the song "Silent Night" the sequence of chords is:

Silent night . . . All is calm, All is bright. Round yon . . .
  I   V   I   IV

mother . . . Holy Infant . . . tender . . . Sleep . . .
  I   IV   I   V

peace . . . heavenly . . . peace.
  I   V   I

This progression gives a very clear and intense impression of the major key.

Cadences Cadences are harmonic points of arrival, comparable to commas, semicolons, colons, question marks, exclamation points, and periods in language. They mark the end of a phrase or sentence. In Example 2-28 note the various effects of arrival marked by the brackets:

EXAMPLE 2-28. *Cadences*

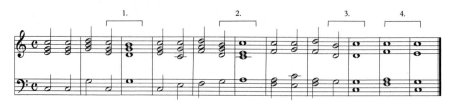

Each of these four points of harmonic arrival represents one of the traditional cadences used in the Western system of harmony. They are:

1. The *authentic* cadence, which provides a final effect of arrival; in its simplest form it consists of the dominant chord, V, as marked in Example 2-27a, moving to I. This is equal to a period in language. The third of the bracketed progressions in Example 2-28 is an authentic cadence.
2. The *half cadence,* a pause or break in the musical action; it consists of a stop on V and is similar to a comma or semicolon. The first bracketed progression in Example 2-28 is a half cadence.
3. The *deceptive cadence,* which "deceives" the ear by substituting some other chord for the tonic in the authentic cadence; generally, VI is the substitute chord. The second bracketed progression in Example 2-28 is a deceptive cadence.
4. The *plagal cadence,* in which IV moves to I. This progression is familiar to us as the "amen" of a hymn, and is sometimes called a "church" cadence. It has a gentle, settling effect, something like an afterthought. The fourth bracketed progression in Example 2-28 is a plagal cadence.

Modulation *Modulation* means *change* of tonal center. Play or sing Example 2-29a; the tonal center is clearly the note C. Then play Example 2-29b; sense the change of tonal center when the note F♯ appears, leading to the note G as the tonic. Then play Example 2-29c; after the arrival at G, F♯ is replaced by F, and the tonal center shifts back to C.

EXAMPLE 2-29.

a. Tonal center remains on C

b. Tonal center shifts to G

c. Tonal center shifts to G, then back to C

In the Christmas carol "Adeste Fideles" (O Come All Ye Faithful), the music arrives at a new tonal center on the word "Bethlehem"; it returns to the original tonal center, the home key, at the refrain "O come, let us adore him" and remains there for the rest of the song.

The effect of modulation is to give a harmonic shape to a piece. In Example 2-29*a* the harmonic contour is:

C –––––––––––––– C

In Example 2-29*c*, the harmonic contour is:

Modulation can impart a subtle sense of shift in *harmonic position,* as in the examples given above. It can also provide a striking effect of *harmonic color.* In the second movement of Beethoven's Symphony No. 5, there is a surprising change of key after the opening songlike melody has run its course; a passage of total harmonic instability then follows to lead to a brilliant and powerful melody in a new key. Note how Beethoven combined all elements to create a "blockbuster" effect. The key color shifts from dark to light; the rhythmic movement changes from gentle legato to bold detached; the scoring changes from low strings to high brass. Example 2-30 illustrates this passage:

EXAMPLE 2-30. *Beethoven: Symphony No. 5, second movement*

As embodiment of the basic criteria, modulation from one key to another represents movement; settling or confirming the new key by means of a cadence represents arrival.

The elements of harmony discussed above—consonance, dissonance, tonal center, major and minor scales and keys, cadences, and modulation—represent the basic features of traditional Western harmony, especially of the eighteenth and nineteenth centuries. This harmonic system has worked like a beautifully tooled, well-oiled machine, capable of producing a vast number of different objects through permutations and combinations of processes that fit well together. But it has its limitations. When we come to the music of our present century, we shall see how other harmonic systems work and what possibilities they have for musical expression and form.

HARMONY EVALUATION CHART

(Check one in each group.)

1. *Consonance-dissonance*

   a. *Consonant interval or chord* _____

   b. *Dissonant interval or chord* _____

2. *Triads*

   a. *Major* _____

   b. *Minor* _____

   c. *Diminished* _____

   d. *Augmented* _____

3. *Definition of tonal center*

   a. *By prominent tone* _____

   b. *By cadential relationships* _____

4. *Cadences*

   a. *Authentic* _____

   b. *Half* _____

   c. *Deceptive* _____

   d. *Plagal* _____

5. *Modulation*

    a. Change of tonal center or key _____

    b. No change of tonal center or key _____

PERCEIV- We hear musical form on various levels. At first, we may note interest-
ING ing details and effects. As the piece moves on, a series of impressions
MUSICAL will be stored up; some of these appear to be more salient or important
FORM than others, acting as landmarks along the way. Listening again, and
more closely, we can perceive the relationships between individual
parts of the piece, and the organization of these parts to achieve
movement and arrival on a large scale.

    Listening for musical form is very much like watching a play. At
first we are impressed by the settings, the appearance of the players, or
striking moments and lines. Then we follow incident upon incident,
watching the unfolding of the plot, so as to grasp the step-by-step
continuity. In a well-constructed play we are led to important points
of climax in an effective manner; formally, these points may balance or
match each other. Finally, our experience is brought to some recognizable point of completion as the play ends. Later we relive certain
moments and reflect upon the various issues presented in the play; we
evaluate the author's, director's, and actors' skill in moving our emotions or delighting us with their offering. In musical form, as in drama,
we first note details, then develop a perspective of the entire work, and
finally, make it our own with our personal evaluation.

    As you listen for musical form, you will find that asking the
following questions can help to make the action clear:

1. What is taking place now?
2. What will happen next?
3. How does the present action relate to what has gone before?

In answering these questions, keep in mind that musical action works
according to the following plan:

STATEMENT answered by COUNTERSTATEMENT

    Statements and counterstatements link together in a continuous
chain. Each link is separate; yet the entire length and shape of the
chain gives the listener a single impression of the outline or form of

the whole. Here are some ways in which statement and counter-statement relationships are created in musical form:

STATEMENT	POSSIBLE COUNTERSTATEMENTS
Motive	1. Repetition, or
	2. Variation, or
	3. Contrast
Melody	1. Repetition of melody, or
	2. Contrasting melody
Half cadence	Authentic cadence
Tonal center or key	1. Contrasting key, or
	2. Return to home key as counterstatement to contrasting key
Phrase	1. Answering phrase of comparable length, giving rise to symmetrical construction, or
	2. Answering phrase or phrases of markedly different length, giving rise to nonsymmetrical construction

Of all types of counterstatement, *repetition* is the clearest and easiest to grasp. Immediate repetition impresses an idea or progression strongly upon the listener; repetition later in a piece acts as link between the two statements of an idea, adding coherence to the form.

Variation as a counterstatement has the effect of growth, of change in a musical idea. The original idea can still be recognized, but some change in the shape, color, pitch, time values, amount or strength of sound presents the material in a new light.

Contrast provides a striking highlight in a counterstatement, throwing musical ideas into sharp relief against each other; contrast often increases the intensity of movement through the unexpected. Repetition tends to act for arrival in a form while variation and contrast promote movement.

To illustrate statement-counterstatement relationships in a familiar song, take "Home on the Range." The four phrases of this melody are arranged as follows:

	repetition (slight variation at end)	*contrast*	repetition of A′
A	A′	B	A′
Oh, give . . .	where never . . .	home home . . .	where never . . .

All four sections are equal in length. The first two make one period, the next two a second period; each of the four sections also divides into two equal parts. Thus we have a sense of perfect balance, of *symmetry* in this song. Other elements contributing to its shape and unity are: (1) unity of key (it remains in one key), (2) a steady gentle rhythmic flow, (3) the melodic apex on the word "home." All of these frame the sweet sadness of this old and familiar tune.

Statement-counterstatement relationships can be effective on a broad scale. When the opening theme of Brahms's Symphony No. 3 returns at the end of the symphony, you can sense an especially effective closure of the form, as if the music had come full circle. This *recall* is particularly striking because the counterstatement at the end is a variation, not a repetition. The opening version of the theme is heavy, bold, sweeping, with a restless harmony and rhythm; the final version, the recall, is quiet, stable, set with a light, shimmering orchestral color, securing the effect of final arrival.

Layouts The continuity of musical form involves two types of arrangement: (1) a *sectional* layout, (2) a *continuous* flow of action. Music with well-defined sections tends to highlight attractive tunes, as in Sousa's "The Stars and Stripes Forever." You can easily sense the definition of each relatively short section of this piece, especially since sections are repeated in performance. Music with more continuous action, with irregular punctuation, tends to emphasize rhythmic thrust, tone color, harmonic effects, or a play of melodic figures that do not form into a well-rounded tune, as in an Indian raga or the second movement of Bartók's *Music for Strings.*

Sectional and continuous arrangements often intermingle. An important theme in a large piece can be set off as a well-defined section, so that it becomes an *area* of arrival for the continuous action that preceded it; or it can stand as a point of departure for subsequent action. Such an alternation of sectional and continuous layouts characterizes the last movement of Mozart's *Eine kleine Nachtmusik,* where continuous action provides an effective foil for the delightful tunes in this piece.

With the materials explored in Chapters 1 and 2, we are ready to enter areas of musical style. We begin with medieval music for the following reasons:

1. Medieval music is the starting point for the history of Western music. As we move forward through the various styles and eras of our musical heritage, we can understand each phase better if we know it both for what it is and for the ways in which it grew from earlier music and evolved into a later style.

2. Medieval music provides an easily grasped point of departure—the single-line melodies of medieval church song; these melodies can be sung, and their features can be quickly noted. Then we can see how our Western musical language was built through melodic, rhythmic, harmonic, and textural additions to these melodies.

CHAPTER THREE

MEDIEVAL MUSIC

Picture the interior of a medieval church—the great space marked out by the stone walls and ceiling and the dim light made by the flickering candles. Imagine monks intoning a prayer to a slowly undulating melody, whose tones reverberate and mingle as they pervade every corner of the space. A mood of contemplation, of exaltation, of removal from the everyday world is created. This must have been the effect produced by *plainsong,* medieval church song, an effect that can still be experienced today in churches that have retained some of the traditional musical worship of the Middle Ages. Example 3-1 is a fragment of a plainsong; as you sing it, note its even flow, its gentle contour.

EXAMPLE 3-1. *Plainsong "Miserere Mei" (Lord, have mercy upon me)*

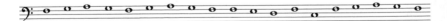

Plainsong is a means for intensifying and elevating the mood and meaning of a sacred text. Sacred texts, from the Scriptures or written during the Middle Ages, have a wide range of expression and meaning. Listen to nos. 2 and 3 in the recorded collection *Masterpieces of Music before 1750, Vidimus stellam* (We Have Seen the Star) and *Victimae Paschali* (The Paschal Victim). *Vidimus* is a song of jubilation. The star of Bethlehem has been seen in the East; it is a time for joy. Alleluias are sung; the music takes flight, breaking away from its text to intone many notes upon one syllable, in the style called *melismatic*. *Victimae* tells the story of Christ's sacrifice, death, and resurrection. The mood is sober, the movement deliberate, the action tightly con-

FIGURE 5. *Plainsong "Benedicamus Domino" in traditional notation from a liturgical songbook. (Courtesy of the Stanford University Libraries.)*

trolled by short phrases and many repetitions. Each syllable takes a different note, in the style called *syllabic*.

In the first number of the *Masterpiece* set, *Laus Deo Patri* (Praise God, the Father), you will hear a mixture of syllabic settings with short melismas. This has been called *group* style, the most commonly used in plainsong. This song is a prayer, given lift and intensity by its short melismas, but held to a serious deliberate manner by the syllabic sections.

Laus Deo has a number of features typical of plainsong which are listed below:

1. *Sound.* Male voices in middle to low register, with a striking change in color between the solo and the group of singers, giving a sense of background and foreground, as if the singers were on a stage. (See page 15.)
2. *Movement.* Moderately slow, gently flowing, with a free play between shorter and longer notes. A deliberate rise and fall of the melody within a narrow range of pitch. (See page 30.)
3. *Arrival.* Clear points of arrival articulating each short phrase of the text in a gentle manner. Tonal center defined by prominence—opening and closing tone. (See pages 41–42.)

The prominence of the tonal center, the notes clustering around it, and the recitation in the middle of the song upon a higher tone represent the harmonic system of medieval music, the *modal* system, made up of eight church *modes*. A mode is a scalewise arrangement of tones, each with its own combination of range and tonal center. Example 3-2 gives a plainsong-like melody set in four of these modes. As you sing them, note differences in quality; the Dorian melody corresponds to our minor mode, the Mixolydian to our major mode; the Phrygian melody, with its "low" second degree, has a marked melancholy quality, while the Lydian, with its "high" fourth degree, has a striking "edge" in the melody.

EXAMPLE 3-2. *Melody in medieval modes*

Dorian

Phrygian

Lydian

Mixolydian

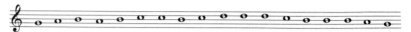

Church modes governed melody and harmony well into the seventeenth century, but later they fell out of use. People were so strongly conditioned to the major and minor scales that when church melodies were sung, they were changed to conform to major and minor scales. But in the twentieth century, the charm, the less assertive, somewhat floating quality of the old modes was again valued. Composers such as Debussy, Stravinsky, and Bartók wrote many melodies that used scales identical to those of the old modes. Today's popular music finds its sentimental strain very effectively expressed with modal melodies; one such melody is the Beatles' "Yesterday."

During the fifteen hundred years and more of its existence, from about the year 400 to the present day, plainsong has been the most significant factor in the musical life of the Roman church. Today it is the authorized musical language of that church. It has been a rich source for musical materials, an inexhaustible fund from which composers draw constantly. As an art form, it is highly polished, subtle, full of delicate shadings and nuances, and capable of a wide range of musical expression.

THE EVOLUTION OF POLYPHONY

Some time before the year 1000, it became the practice occasionally to add another voice as plainsong was sung. This is the birth of Western *polyphony*. (See page 37.)

Now, consider the implications of this practice for the history of Western music:

1. Polyphony created a new *sonority* value; it gave a new dimension to musical sound, increasing its evocative power.
2. Polyphony contributed to the evolution of *harmony*. The added voice could sing only certain prescribed intervals with the plainsong; some of these intervals were held to be consonant, others dissonant, and their arrangement and relationship represented an early system of harmony. (See page 39.)

FIGURE 6. *Nuns singing in praise of the Virgin and Child. Frontispiece from a liturgical songbook. (Courtesy of the Stanford University Libraries.)*

3. At first the added voice sang the same melodic lines as the plainsong, but at a different pitch; very soon, however, it began to change and move away from the plainsong pattern, thus creating *melodic countermovement.*

4. Polyphony enforced *rhythmic order.* Two or more voices singing

together had to sing the proper intervals at the right time. Thus a system of rhythmic notation was evolved in order to allow composers and performers to keep in touch with each other.

5. Polyphony *shifted* the focus of interest from the *text* to the *music*, especially if singers were intoning the same words at different times and in different melodic patterns.

6. Polyphony, by setting its characteristic processes of addition and elaboration in motion, continually opened up *new and fresh areas of form, style, and expression.* It caused changes in every aspect of music, and is responsible for music as we know it today.

Medieval polyphony grew by stages, by adding something to what was already present. These stages can be outlined as follows:

1. A plainsong melody could be sung in octaves, fourths, or fifths, with all voices moving *parallel* to each other. The plainsong melody was called the *cantus firmus* (the fixed melody) while the added voices were called *organal* voices, meaning that they *organized* the polyphony. Medieval polyphony, to the end of the thirteenth century, was designated as *organum,* and the simplest type was called *parallel* organum. While parallel organum retains the shape of the plainsong, it adds a richness of sound and a heavier quality of movement, so that the sense of melodic freedom is reduced. Sing Example 3-3, the plainsong melody of Example 3-1 set in parallel organum, and note the resonant effect.

EXAMPLE 3-3. *Parallel organum*

Cantus firmus

Added voice

2. The next stage in polyphony took place when the added voice broke away from strictly parallel motion with the plainsong and created its own melody. This was called *free organum.* A variety of harmonic intervals was created, adding interest in the way of harmonic color. Example 3-4 represents a *possible* setting of the plainsong of Example 3-1 in free organum; as you sing this example, sense the play of different harmonic intervals, and the more pronounced contrapuntal effect produced by the different melodic contours.

EXAMPLE 3-4. *Free organum*

Number 7 from *Masterpieces, Agnus Dei* (Lamb of God) illustrates free organum.

3. A further change, a drastic one, slowed down the plainsong to long notes, while the added voice took off on an elaborate melodic flight, a *melisma.* This was called *melismatic organum.* Since the cantus firmus, the plainsong, was held for a long time, it was called a *tenor,* meaning "that which holds." Melismatic organum must have been music for accomplished performers, perhaps soloists. Something of the same spirit of freedom and improvisation exists in jazz as soloists move off into a "break," an improvised solo. Number 8 from *Masterpieces, Benedicamus Domino* (Let Us Bless the Lord) illustrates melismatic organum.

4. In the next phase, a corner is turned. The elaborate melodic flight of melismatic organum is curtailed. The free rhythm of the added voice gives way to a precise arrangement of long and short notes, taken from the rhythmic patterns of poetry; it is laid out in simple triple meter, as for example: (See page 24.)

This style was called *measured organum,* a profound change for medieval music. It established regular *accent,* locating specific points of arrival, and laying the foundation for what much later was to become *measure;* it established a control for consonance and dissonance, locating consonance on long or *accented* notes, dissonance on short or *unaccented* notes. Rhythmic patterns began to take on the character of *motives* that could be repeated, varied, and traded off when there were two or more organal voices singing against the tenor. The continual statement and restatement of short motives piles up momentum, giving a vigorous, driving quality to this music, in contrast to the unpredictable flight of melismatic organum. Number 9 from *Masterpieces,* the *Alleluya,* illustrates measured organum. Note the behavior of the tenor, the lowermost voice, in the middle of the piece. The tenor drops its sustained-tone support to sing motives, then returns to its sustained tones to end the piece. This creates a form for the piece, a three-part A B A layout.

The organum period in medieval music lasted until about 1300 and is called the *Ars Antiqua* (the Old Art or Style). After 1300 the process of change and elaboration continued to create very complex works in the fourteenth century, especially in the play of rhythm and melody. This was called the *Ars Nova* (the New Art or Style). While it retained the basic harmonic language of the older style—use of fourths, fifths, and octaves as consonant intervals—it dissolved the firmness of measured organum with a rich tapestry of shorter notes and shifting meters. Probably the most important single element in this change was a different view of meter.

Ars Nova introduced *duple meter* as an important rhythmic element, greatly increasing the variety of note values available, and, even more important, mixing duple and triple meters in various lengths and patterns; syncopation also became an important rhythmic element. (See page 25.)

One of the monuments of Ars Nova music is Guillaume de Machaut's Mass, composed in the mid-fourteenth century. The *Agnus Dei* (Lamb of God) from this Mass is illustrated in Masterpieces, No. 13. It shows a vigorous, straightforward quality of movement, based principally on duple meter, particularly in the shorter note values. There are four different parts here, some sung, some played by instruments. Again, the sounds are predominantly the open intervals characteristic of medieval music. We can hear them reinforced by doublings and duplications, creating a larger amount of sound.

One special feature of Machaut's *Agnus Dei* is the well-delineated contrast between movement and arrival, harmonically speaking. Points of arrival are clear and emphatic. There is *leading-tone* action preceding the chords which act for arrival. You hear the clear resonance of the heavy caesuras and the edgy, frequently dissonant sound within the phases of movement. Harmony in this music is well defined by consonance and dissonance, assisted by the careful distribution of rhythmic motion and rest. Note also the effects of syncopation in the uppermost voice.

SECULAR MUSIC

Poetry, music, and dancing were cultivated as forms of entertainment by the medieval nobility. These arts were a reflection of the spirit of chivalry and of courtly love that flourished from the early twelfth century on. Among the topics of the poetry we find stories of love, war, adventure, along with less romantic themes—good living, fair weather, perhaps a thinly disguised bit of scandal, or some high-minded moralizing; in short, topics that we might find today in a musical comedy or television show.

Musically, the solo songs, the *monophonic* pieces, have much in common with plainsong, as we can hear in the trouvère song *Or la truix* (I Find It Difficult) and the minnesinger song (or minnelied) *Willekommen Mayenschein* (Welcome, May's Sun), *Masterpieces*, nos. 4 and 5. *Polyphonic* secular songs reflect the style of sacred music with which they are contemporaneous, i.e., organum; they are set in the rhythmic modes, and they have well-defined phrase structure marked by clear and rather evenly spaced points of arrival.

Dancing as well as singing was a popular diversion at court. In medieval dance music we can recognize, for the first time in Western music, the typical patterns that have shaped dance music to the present day. Rhythmic motives tend to be sharply defined, and phrases tend to be short, balancing each other, with clear points of separation; phrases may be repeated. In the *estampie*, no. 12 of *Masterpieces*, we see an early example of a standard dance form for Western music. Counting beats, we find a kind of half cadence at the eighth beat, and a final cadence at the sixteenth. Thus, two eight-beat (or eight-measure) phrases are *paired*. This arrangement continues throughout the dance. Each first phrase ends with an *open* cadence effect; each second phrase ends with a *closed* cadence effect. These pairings represent a clear relationship of *statement and counterstatement* in phrase arrangement, a pattern that will be used frequently in dance music during the following centuries. Example 3-5 shows this symmetrical arrangement in diagram form. (See page 27.)

EXAMPLE 3-5. *Diagram of estampie*

The open cadence in the estampie has the same punctuation effect that the half cadence will have in later styles, while the closed cadence serves the same purpose as the authentic cadence. (See page 45.)

**PERFORM-
ANCE OF
MEDIEVAL
MUSIC** The performance of medieval music involved voices, instruments, and combinations of voices and instruments. We find substitutions of a voice for an instrument, or vice versa. Thus, there are motets expressly indicated for instrumental performance. We are still investigating the performance practices of medieval times, but we do know that it was

FIGURE 7. *Strassburg Cathedral* (*from an eighteenth-century engraving*). *An example of the Gothic style in architecture.* (*Courtesy of the Stanford University Libraries.*)

considered adequate if each part had a representative performer of some kind. Therefore, contrasts and variations in tone quality, not only in different pieces but in different performances of the same piece, may well have occurred. Indeed, in view of the general transparency of the texture and the consistency of style, such variations in performance may have been quite welcome.

Early instruments included plucked and bowed string instruments, wind instruments, keyboard instruments, and percussion. There was a tremendous variety within these groups; they were not at all standardized as at present. Recordings show a freshness and lightness of tone quality that well suits the performance of one-, two-, or three-voice music.

Throughout medieval music, from the time that voices began to sing together, the general harmonic quality of sound remained constant. Points of arrival, for both large and small phases of movement, were characterized by the sound of open intervals, principally the fifth and the octave. These gave a maximum impression of stability. Open intervals also fairly saturated the entire harmonic language. Between points of arrival, mixed in with the fourths, fifths, and octaves, there was a considerable amount of dissonance, brought about by the incidental clashes of melodic lines. Medieval harmony is thus characterized by rather sharp contrasts between the stable sounds of arrival and the active dissonances heard frequently between points of arrival.

Later medieval music, particularly of France during the thirteenth and fourteenth centuries, has been called *Gothic*. Parallels between music and Gothic architecture have frequently been drawn. If we consider that Gothic music and the Gothic cathedral took shape by the addition and juxtaposition of separate, distinct, and often clashing elements, and that these elements were focused on the central idea of the worship of God, then the analogy seems quite valid. Indeed, throughout Europe from A.D. 400 to 1400, the force of a central, all-powerful authority makes itself felt in every aspect of religion, politics, and art. Feudalism and the hierarchy of the church dominated men's thoughts and, indeed, their very lives. As we have seen, music reflected this state of affairs; the only music of which we have record is that performed in church or court.

SUMMARY Sacred music in the medieval period was based on plainsong. Addition and elaboration were the processes by which the art of music grew during this age. The stages were as follows:

1. *Plainsong* (from the early Christian era, before 500 A.D. to the present day). Syllabic, melismatic, group style.
2. *Parallel organum* (before 1000 A.D.). Addition of voices moving in parallel fourths, fifths, or octaves.
3. *Free organum* (around 1100 A.D.). Melodic freedom in the added voices.
4. *Melismatic organum* (1100 to 1150 A.D.). Slowing down of the cantus firmus; extensive elaboration in the added voices.
5. *Measured organum* (around 1200 A.D.). Poetic meter added to the

melismatic voices; rhythmic patterns in parts of the tenor, the plainsong voice.

6. *Motet* (after 1200 A.D.). Texts set to the added voices.
7. *Ars Nova* (after 1300 A.D.). Incorporation of duple meter; mixtures of duple and triple meters on various levels to create complex rhythmic patterns.

QUESTIONS

1. In what ways does plainsong fit music to text?
2. What were some of the effects of polyphony upon musical relationships?
3. Describe briefly the various types of organum.
4. How did dancing influence musical form in the medieval period?

CHAPTER FOUR

RENAISSANCE MUSIC

W e feel a strong kinship with the Renaissance. Its art and music are as alive for us today as when they flourished in the fifteenth and sixteenth centuries. Renaissance music strikes a warm and familiar note, especially for those who have sung in a choral group.

SOUND Renaissance music introduced a new quality of sound. Around 1425, thirds and sixths began to appear more and more in combination with the fourths, fifths, and octaves of earlier harmony. This was the moment in history when the traditional Western system of harmony began to take definite shape, when the *triad*, the mainstay of harmony for centuries to come (see page 40), became the principal element in the sound of music. The changes in style produced by this new sound were far-reaching, both for the Renaissance and for music of later ages.

The impetus toward the new harmonic language probably came from England. During the Middle Ages the English seem to have had a preference for singing in thirds instead of fourths and fifths. As a result of the Hundred Years' War (1337–1453), which was fought in France, English ways became known to Continental musicians, and they began to use the sonorities they heard in English music. The sweetness of this new style was so captivating that frequently whole chains of such chords were sung, decorating the plainsong in parallel movement.

You can discover for yourselves the effect of this technique, called *fauxbourdon* in the fifteenth century. At the piano select any white note. Play along with it the third above, and add to these the fourth

65

above the upper note. You now have a chord in which the interval between the outer voices is a sixth; also, the middle voice forms a third with the lowest voice. Such a chord is called a *sixth chord* (see Example 4-1). Keeping the voices strictly parallel, move up and down the keyboard. The effect is pleasant on the piano, but in voices its sweetness is much greater. Indeed, many popular singing teams today rely heavily upon the sixth-chord progression to give body and color to a simple melody. In fauxbourdon, we receive the impression that a single melodic line has widened into a consonant, rich, and sonorous stream of sound. Example 4-1 provides a simple illustration of sixth-chord style compared to its earlier counterpart, parallel organum.

EXAMPLE 4-1. *Sixth-chord style; parallel organum*

a. Melody set in sixth-chord style

Melody below

b. Melody set in parallel organum

Melody above

The result of this new taste in intervals was to *establish the triad as the basic harmonic element,* since the notes of sixth chords are those of the major and minor triads (see page 40). Within a short time, triads came to saturate the harmonic action entirely, driving out both the open sounds of medieval music and its striking dissonances.

Josquin des Prez's *Ave Maria* (Hail, Mary), no. 19 of Masterpieces, exemplifies the Renaissance sound based upon triads, as well as the melodic, rhythmic, and textural elements associated with this harmonic style. We can note the following characteristics:

1. A new quality of sound, different from that of medieval music; drastic reduction in the amount and the impact of dissonance; harmony based upon thirds and sixths, rather than fourths and fifths.
2. Many changes in the amount of sound
3. Very clear and distinct separation of voices with respect to range

4. Sustained quality of movement; moderately slow beat; avoidance of extremes of brevity or length in note values (compare melismatic organum); overlapping voice parts; joining of phases of movement; gracefully turned melodic material; imitation
5. Several very strong points of harmonic arrival

Note the compactness and fullness when all four voices are singing, and the difference in range when pairs of voices are set against each other. This gives the effect of a third dimension, an aural perspective delineated by the opposition of high and low, comparable to the visual perspective in Renaissance painting that creates an impression of near and far.

As an overall impression, we can say that this music seems to have a balance, a control, an evenness, a sense of parts fitted together in a perfectly integrated and smooth manner.

MOVEMENT   We can sense a steady, even flow, without strong accent, in Josquin's *Ave Maria*. This quality of movement is typical of Renaissance music; it is regulated by a gentle pulse or beat called the *tactus* (*tacti* in plural). The length of the tactus can vary according to the character of the piece or the tempo taken in performance, but it would generally correspond to a moderately slow quarter note in our present-day tempo system. The first note of the Josquin *Ave Maria* has a length of two tacti; the next two are each one tactus in length.

Movement in Renaissance music is maintained in part by its texture—a polyphonic web in which the various voices enter and drop out at different times, overlap in their phases of movement, and have a give-and-take among their long and short notes and their moments of silence. Counterpoint, in Renaissance music as well as in other styles, is made up of melodic lines moving against each other (that is, *counterline*) and by combinations of different rhythmic patterns (*countertime*).

ARRIVAL   The even, steady flow of Renaissance music often covers up points of arrival. One voice may arrive at the end of a phrase while another continues with its melody. To appreciate this effect, listen to the soprano in Josquin's *Ave Maria*. You will hear a clear ending when it finishes the word "Maria"; but the alto has begun its figure shortly before and moves on at the soprano's point of arrival to render the punctuation gentle and somewhat unclear.

Strong points tend to be widely spaced in the kind of music

FIGURE 8. *Hartmann Schedel: Landscape from* Liber Cronicarum, *1493 (The Nuremberg Chronicle). The architecture illustrates Romanesque and Gothic styles, while the overall design demonstrates the Renaissance treatment of perspective. (Courtesy of the Stanford University Libraries.)*

represented by Josquin's *Ave Maria.* Actually, there are only three points where all voices join to make a stop: (1) at the word "vivi" (living) about two-thirds through the piece, (2) at the word "regum" (King), and (3) at the end of the piece.

MELODY Like plainsong, Renaissance melody describes rounded patterns, in which the line dips and rises gradually with comfortable balance.

There are few large or striking leaps, and when they occur they are balanced by a stepwise movement in the opposite direction.

The opening of Josquin's piece serves well as an example of this melodic style. The subject begins with a small downward leap; as a counterstatement, the melody rises gradually beyond the pitch of the beginning, turns around the high point several times, and makes its way downward gradually. In this melody, as the music moves upward, rhythmic action becomes more lively with the appearance of shorter notes; with the descent, action quiets and longer notes again predominate. One can hardly find anywhere a more exquisite example of a melodic period that creates, out of the gentle ebb and flow of movement, such a perfect inner balance.

HARMONY Renaissance harmony contributed to the steady, moderately paced flow of its music by spinning out progressions of smoothly connected triads. The movement from one triad to the next was controlled by *conjunct voice-leading;* this involves stepwise movement among the various voices or, even more smoothly, holding over one or more voices without moving to a different one, a *common-tone* progression. Example 4-2 illustrates the typical chord progression of Renaissance music; play this on the piano, or, even better, sing it to get the flavor of this very suave harmonic style.

EXAMPLE 4-2. *Smooth chord connection; conjunct and common tones*

While all the chords in Example 4-2 are triads, they have different effects of stability. Chords 5, 8, and 12 are less stable, less firm than the others. By listening to the bass voice, you can hear that it regulates the effect of stability. When the bass has a *perfect fifth*, third, or octave with an upper voice, the chord sounds very firm; when the bass has a *sixth* with an upper voice, stability is less marked. *The power of the bass voice to control harmonic stability was one of the chief developments in Renaissance harmony, giving rise to the standard cadences of Western music* (see page 45).

Throughout Josquin's *Ave Maria* you can hear light cadences spaced every few measures, and a clearly final authentic cadence to end the piece; in these cadences, it is the *bass* that determines the type and the emphasis of punctuation. This role of the bass, established in the Renaissance, becomes even more pronounced in the seventeenth and eighteenth centuries, and is still a controlling factor in today's popular music. If, instead of listening to melody, you listen to the bass during one hearing of a piece, you will perceive how it controls the direction of movement and the effect of arrival.

DISSONANCE Against the flow of well-blended triads, a dissonant tone can have a powerful effect. Renaissance music made use of this harmonic resource, for expressive purposes and to intensify movement. However, dissonance was strictly controlled; it was assimilated into the steady flow of consonance in a subtle manner as follows: a tone was held over, *suspended,* from a preceding chord in one voice while the other voices moved to the next chord; then the suspended voice would move (*resolve*) to its proper note, always by step, and generally downward. Example 4-3 illustrates this procedure: it is particularly effective when sung.

EXAMPLE 4-3. *Dissonance treatment (suspension and resolution)*

7 - 6

Note that the suspension works against *both* the harmony and the rhythm; the suspended voice *holds,* while the others *move.* This overlap in movement promotes the smooth flow characteristic of Renaissance music. At the end of Josquin's piece we hear the top voice holding back just before proceeding from 7 to 8 of the scale. The effect of arrival is thereby strengthened.

Dissonance moves the harmony forward (see page 39); it also has the power to *move* the feelings by its instability and edginess. Renaissance composers exploited the dissonance of the suspension to highlight especially poignant or expressive moments in the poetry they were setting to music. For example, when Marenzio, in his *S'io parto, i'moro* (If I Leave Thee, I Die), no. 27 of *Masterpieces,* set the word "die," he gave it a strong expressive accent with a sharply dissonant suspension.

Another technique for creating special effects against the even flow of Renaissance harmony was *chromaticism.* In this technique, chords belonging to different scales were placed either next to each other or very close to each other, to give the impression of a colorful, somewhat unstable shift of harmonic meaning. In the Marenzio madrigal, at the words "and yet I must still leave thee," there is a chromatic relationship between the chords that begin and end the passage. This movement from one scale to another cleverly underscores the idea of departure. Such expressive and pictorial play upon music and words bespeaks the flexibility and richness of musical resources in the Renaissance.

Example 4-4 is a modified version of Example 4-2, introducing two chromatic chords, nos. 7 and 10. The striking point of color produced by each can easily be imagined as a setting for a particularly expressive word or syllable, especially if there is a slight pause in the flow of the music upon the chromatic chord or just before it, as a means for highlighting the change of harmonic color.

EXAMPLE 4-4. *Chromaticism*

The qualities of sound, movement, and arrival in Renaissance music described above apply chiefly to its vocal style. This style shares some general qualities with Renaissance painting. The sweetness and suavity of the sound are like the rich, vivid, and subtly shaded colors of painting, with a strong sense of presence, as if we could touch the object being depicted. Movement in Renaissance music has the same kind of balance and shape we find in the molding of figures, objects, and landscapes in painting, with a clear impression of exploring "real" space; the horizontal perspective in the paintings of Raphael, Titian, Correggio, and Michelangelo has its counterpart in the vertical perspective of Renaissance harmony as the bass is set against the upper voices.

Instrumental music in the Renaissance was regulated by the same principles of rhythm, harmony, and melody that governed vocal music, but the tone colors of various instruments and their techniques of performance produced different qualities of sound and effects of rhythm. Later in this chapter instrumental music will be discussed, but now we shall look at some principles of form established chiefly by Renaissance vocal music.

FORM Renaissance music took form according to a number of procedures: (1) addition and elaboration, (2) imitation, (3) distribution of cadences and tonal centers, (4) repetition and contrast, (5) two-part dance layouts.

ADDITION
AND
ELABORATION
Addition and elaboration, the processes by which medieval music evolved, were still at work in the Renaissance. The most important method—to take a preexisting melody and to elaborate upon it—is illustrated in Josquin's *Ave Maria*.

Josquin "borrowed" a plainsong melody, *Ave Maria, Gratia Plena* (Hail Mary, Full of Grace), to use as a framework for his piece. Each phrase of the plainsong is used in turn as the melodic basis of a section of the piece. The plainsong melody itself is altered rhythmically to fit to the general style, moving with the flow governed by the steady, moderately slow, gentle tactus.

Almost any available music could serve as preexisting material for addition and elaboration; among these were popular melodies like *L'Homme Armé* (The Armed Man) or entire compositions made longer, often with added voices and more elaborate melodic action.

Addition and elaboration were basic procedures in the instrumental music of the Renaissance. This point will be discussed in connection with instrumental music. (See page 83.)

IMITATION Renaissance music used imitation extensively to promote the flow of action, to achieve a sense of melodic unity, and to build out musical form. By the time that three, four, or five voices have entered in turn with a theme, a considerable section of a piece has been shaped, unified by restatements of the theme. You can hear how each imitative section typically arrives at a cadence, then begins again with a new subject or theme. The subjects themselves might be invented by the composer or taken from a preexisting melody, a plainsong or a secular tune. Josquin's *Ave Maria* borrows a plainsong, while Lassus' *Tristis est anima mea* (Sad Is My Soul), *Masterpieces* no. 23, has newly invented themes. Each set of imitative entries was called a *point of imitation*.

Imitation can be exact or *strict*, in which each voice sings precisely the same intervals as the preceding voice. A round such as "Row, Row

Your Boat" represents this procedure (see page 37). Strict imitation is also called *canon* or *canonic imitation;* it involves great ingenuity and was used often in the Renaissance to demonstrate the skill of the composer. *Free imitation* allows some freedom to change intervals and rhythmic patterns as the voices enter and continue; after the voices have entered, the music will spin out to a cadence in free imitation, while in strict imitation they will continue to imitate each other exactly.

Most of the imitation you hear in Renaissance music is free imitation. For example, in the Lassus motet, *Masterpieces* no. 23, each voice enters with the characteristic three-note motive which is the subject of the first phase of imitation; yet some of the voices sing a different version of the motive, and the first voice sings it upside down! Still we have no trouble in recognizing the basic motive in each entry. Working with such short flexible motives, the composer could handle his counterpoint very freely and constantly discover opportunities for fresh movement. *Not only was free imitation by far the most useful and prevalent type in the Renaissance, but it has dominated contrapuntal composition from that time to the present day.*

DISTRIBUTION OF CADENCES AND TONAL CENTERS In Chapter 2 we heard how modulation gives a harmonic profile to the form of a composition. The tones of a scale are like satellites surrounding the tonic. Within a piece, as the music arrives at cadences upon the satellite tones, a harmonic form is created. Thanks to its triadic harmony and its use of the bass as a harmonic guide, Renaissance music could make use of the various degrees of the scale as form-building elements. For example, in Josquin's *Ave Maria,* the tonic of the mode is *g*, which you can hear as the final note in the bass, while cadences within the piece arrive at the following tones:

Bb Bb g g Bb Bb d d g g D g

(Cadences on major triads are indicated by capital letters; on minor triads by small letters.)

To be sure, most of these cadences are very light; they do not interrupt the steady flow of the music, especially since one voice begins a melodic line as the others arrive.

REPETITION AND CONTRAST The steady, even flow of Renaissance music supports continuous spinning out of melodic material, so that in many pieces we hear no repetition of preceding sections. This procedure is described as being *through-composed.* Except for dance music and songs in which several stanzas are sung to the same melody, repetition in Renaissance music is not an important principle of form. When it does occur, it may be used for some special expressive purpose, as in the Marenzio madrigal *S'io parto* (If I Leave), *Masterpieces* no. 27; here the phrase *dolorosa partita* (sad departure) is heard twice at different places with virtually the same musical setting.

In a style as consistent and smoothly flowing as that of Renaissance music, contrast makes itself felt in a rather subtle and subdued manner. In Josquin's *Ave Maria* the play of delicate contrasts throws light and shadow, giving a profile to the various sections of the piece. The shift from one range to another, the change of motives from a relatively slow subject to one that is quicker, the change of meter from duple to triple and back again in the latter part of the piece, and the play of major and minor triads—these produce subtle effects of contrast that help to shape the form.

TWO-PART
DANCE
LAYOUTS

We have already referred to dance forms in medieval music (page 61). The two-part layout was extensively cultivated as a pattern for dance forms in the Renaissance and was, of all forms, the most precisely and neatly trimmed formal scheme at this time. It was also used in many short vocal pieces, sacred and secular, with the typical open and closed endings, respectively, for the first and second parts.

EXPRESSION

The carefully polished Renaissance style could be colored to express a wide range of moods and feelings. As a matter of fact, this era is the first in which there is considerable documentation about musical expression. Composers and theorists were as sensitive and careful about expressive nuances as they were about harmony, rhythm, melody, and texture. Expression ranged from the profound pathos of Lassus' *Tristis* to the lilting good humor of Bennet's *Thyrsis, Masterpieces* no. 28, from the elevated spirituality of Palestrina's *Agnus Dei, Masterpieces* no. 24, to the earthy simplicity of street songs.

Some of the guidelines used to match music with word or gesture were:

1. *The proper choice of mode.* Modes with minor thirds were considered proper for tragic, pathetic, deeply serious texts. Modes with major thirds, especially the Ionian, could be used for lighter or brighter moods, and for dances.
2. *The proper choice of figure.* Sustained, slowly moving figures were used for serious texts; lighter, more active figures for less serious or more active feelings. At times, the music matched the words in a

FIGURE 9. *Michelangelo: Engraving of the gate called Flaminia but now called del Popolo. Note the symmetry of the design and the combination of classical elements (arch and column) with Christian motifs (keys and papal tiara). (Courtesy of the Stanford University Libraries.)*

PIVS IIII PONTIF MAX.
PORTAM IN HANCAMPLI-
TVDINEM EXTVLIT VIAM
FLAMINIAM STRAVIT
ANNO III

XXXVI

precise way called *pictorialism,* or *word-painting.* In a French chanson, *La Guerre,* by Jannequin (The Battle), there are marchlike figures and fanfares; Weelke's madrigal *As Vesta was from Latmos Hill descending* has descending figures to describe nymphs and shepherds "running down amain."

To sum up the procedures described above by illustrating their use in a late Renaissance work, the following analysis of Lassus' motet *Tristis* is offered; the text tells of the sadness of soul felt by Jesus during the events leading to the Crucifixion.

1. Listening to the whole piece, we are aware of the continuing *contrapuntal imitation.* Two sections stand out in contrast by their chordal texture, *Nunc videbitis* (Now you will see) and *Ego vadam immolari* (I go to be sacrificed); these are especially expressive accents.

2. Most of the piece remains within its mode, Ionian. But an expressive contrast is created at the words *circumdabit me* (surround me) by changing the third of the mode to minor. Pictorialism is used here, as the figure, with its rounded rise and fall, suggests moving around a point.

3. The piece has seven sections, five contrapuntal and two in chordal style. These begin with the words given below:

   Contrapuntal: *Tristis* (Sad) a slow and melodically quiet subject

   Contrapuntal: *Sustinete* (Tarry), a more rapid subject with more closely spaced entries

   Contrapuntal: *Et vigilate mecum* (And watch with me), a quick, melodically active subject, treated more broadly and intensively than the first two subjects

   (To this point, Lassus has built a steady increase in the pace and intensity of movement.)

   Chords: *Nunc videbitis* (Now you will see), a dramatic slowing down, sharply contrasted to the accumulated momentum of the preceding music.

   Contrapuntal: *Quae circumdabit* (Who surround me) (see *Sustinete* above).

   Contrapuntal: *Vos fugam* (You will take flight), another tightly woven imitative section, again pictorial to represent flight, with voices constantly "Pursuing" each other.

   Chords: *Ego vadam* (I go), in a slightly ornamental chordal style.

4. The last measures of this piece create a strong sense of cadence. As the bass sustains the dominant of the mode, the contrapuntal action above intensifies; the running figures in the upper voices imitate

each other closely. A powerful and totally satisfying sense of arrival is felt as the bass finally moves to the tonic in a broadly scaled authentic cadence. Example 4-5 diagrams this cadential action.

EXAMPLE 4-5. *Diagram of drive to cadence in Lassus:* Tristis

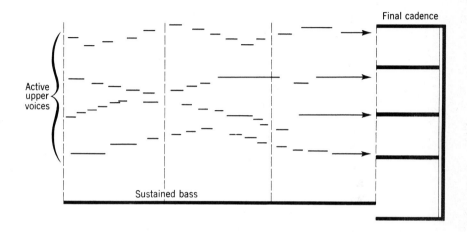

VOCAL FORMS We know Renaissance music chiefly through its vocal repertory—masses, motets, madrigals, chansons. From the Middle Ages through most of the eighteenth century, vocal music enjoyed a superiority over instrumental music in the degree of importance and dignity assigned to it in the minds of musicians and philosophers. This superior rank came about for the following reasons: (1) The human voice was considered the ideal musical instrument, being a *natural* instrument, not a *mechanical* one, and capable of expressing the feelings directly; (2) sacred music, especially plainsong, was the musical counterpart of a sacred text, representing the word of God or interpreting it, therefore representing the *spiritual*, the higher side of man (instrumental music, being mechanical, represented the *physical*, the lower side of man). Thus, for both expressive and moral reasons, vocal music ranked higher in the earlier eras of Western music. Later, beginning in the eighteenth century, as man's view of the world became much more secular and as musical instruments were developed to a very high point of effectiveness, instrumental music pulled even with vocal in rank of importance. The following survey covers some of the important forms of Renaissance vocal music.

SACRED
VOCAL MUSIC

Mass

The Mass is the most important and solemn service of the Roman church, the representation of the sacrifice of Christ. Its musical form became fixed in the fifteenth century with the five standard sections, called the *Ordinary* of the Mass:

1. Kyrie eleison (Lord, have mercy)
2. Gloria (Glory be to God)
3. Credo (I believe in one God)
4. Sanctus (Holy)
5. Agnus Dei (Lamb of God)

There were also a number of optional sections, with texts varied according to the occasion, called the *Proper*.

Masses made use of plainsong or well-known secular melodies as canti firmi; or they were freely composed without preexisting material. One remarkable procedure was to take a preexisting complete piece and elaborate it, adding voices, interspersing new material to create a Mass movement. This technique, prevalent in the later sixteenth century, was called *parody,** a very useful device for shaping a new piece, and one that has been used in twentieth-century jazz. Palestrina's Mass *Veni sponsa Christi* (Come, Bride of Christ), whose Agnus Dei is given in *Masterpieces* no. 24, is a parody Mass, based upon a motet by Palestrina himself; in turn the motet was based upon a plainsong with the same title. The style of Palestrina's Agnus Dei represents the ultimate refinement of Renaissance techniques of composition—a smooth, unbroken flow of triad-based sounds, with occasional suspensions for emphasis; steady movement governed by the tactus; free imitation; light cadences throughout the piece, with a strong cadential point of arrival from dominant to tonic to close the piece.

Motet

The motet was a Latin church piece comparable in length and style to a movement of the Mass. It was sung at services other than that of the Mass itself. Josquin's *Ave Maria* and Lassus' *Tristis* represent this form in its most refined aspect; their style and form have been discussed at length in the preceding part of this chapter.

Chorale

The *chorale*, a product of the Protestant Reformation, was the principal native musical genre in sixteenth-century Germany. Apart from the chorale, and its secular counterpart the *Lied* (song), music in Germany was strongly influenced by Flemish, French, and Italian styles.

---

*Parody here means modification—elaboration, addition—not the distortion implied in the present-day use of the term.

Martin Luther and other early Protestant leaders encouraged their congregations to take part in the musical portion of the church service. Luther helped to compile collections of hymn tunes and chorales with German texts that could be sung by the worshipers. The music for these religious songs was shorter, simpler, and far less pictorial than the motet, which was sung either by professional choir singers or by skilled amateurs of noble birth.

Chorales were set either in chordal style or with some contrapuntal action. Example 4-6 is a late sixteenth-century setting of the well-known chorale tune *Eine feste Burg ist unser Gott* (A mighty fortress is our God). The tune, highlighted in the soprano, is set in a simple chordal texture for performance by the congregation. Note the firmness of the bass; each chord is in root position and, intentionally or not, conveys the impression of solidity expressed in the text.

EXAMPLE 4-6. *Lucas Osiander, Eine feste Burg ist unser Gott (A mighty fortress is our God, a good shield and sword)*

SECURAR VOCAL MUSIC

The Italian Madrigal

Secular vocal music—the Italian and English *madrigals*, the French *chanson*, and the German *Lied*—shared many basic stylistic features with sacred vocal music. The Italian madrigal was the secular counterpart of the motet. The motet (as well as the Mass) conveyed a sense of spirituality colored with restrained passion and delicate sensual beauty, much as religious paintings of the Renaissance do. The madrigal expressed the passions in a more open and intense way, appealing strongly to the senses, but controlled and restrained by Renaissance ideas of refinement and perfection, both in expression and in composition. Marenzio's madrigal *S'io parto* (If I leave), *Masterpieces* no. 27, and Lassus' motet *Tristis* have many features in common—qualities of sound and movement, imitation, treatment of harmony.

The Italian madrigal evolved in the early sixteenth century when Flemish composers came down from the North to adapt the popular Italian vocal form, the *frottola* (see page 82); they upgraded its poetry and incorporated compositional techniques from the motet to create an elegant, sophisticated art form. One of the special features of the

Italian madrigal, as well as of other Renaissance secular vocal music, was a subtle relationship between music and text. Secular music drew its texts from Renaissance poetry, elegant, fanciful, and refined, with many figures of speech and vivid images. Much care was given to the proper setting of these texts to match the nuances of meaning, and often a word or phrase was highlighted by *pictorialism*.

This precise handling of the text-music relationship is present in Marenzio's madrigal *S'io parto*. Some of the features you may note include:

1. Each line of the poetry is set off by a change of texture; for example, the first line of the text is set in slowly moving chords, while the second line takes up an active, quickly moving pattern.
2. Cadences, marking the ends of lines, are much more frequent and clear than in a typical motet; there are eight well-marked cadences throughout the piece.
3. Textural changes occur boldly, often set off by cadences; imitation involves short, rhythmically crisp figures, matching the syllables of the text.
4. By paying attention to the text, the listener can appreciate a number of subtle pictorial touches:
   a. "moro" (I die), a sharp dissonance
   b. "Dolorosa" (Painful), unusual dissonances (slow notes moving stepwise through the chord)
   c. "partir" (leave), a shift to an active, moving rhythm
   d. "dividi" (divide), the only use of short notes, "dividing" longer notes (half notes) by four

*The English
Madrigal* The English madrigal, cultivated during the later years of the reign of Elizabeth I, from about 1590 and afterward when James I became king, was modeled upon the Italian madrigal. The English adapted the techniques of the Italians—part-writing, imitation—to their own highly polished poetry, with its elegant, fanciful imagery, its play with word sounds, and its subtle shifts between duple and triple meters. John Bennet's madrigal, *Thyrsis, Sleepest Thou?*, *Masterpieces* no. 28, is set to a short poem with a pastoral theme; the shepherd, sleeping to forget his sorrow in love, is awakened to April and the cuckoo's cry, but rejects these. Each of these images is set with deft pictorialism. You hear the slow opening chords for Thyrsis' sleep, the active rhythms and rising melodic lines for "hold up thy head," the frank pictorialism of the repeated cuckoo figures, the syncopation on the word "sighed," and the brisk driving cadential figures of the final section on the words "drive him back to London." Within this short poem there is an intriguing mixture of classic Greek and contemporary allusions—Thyrsis and London—as well as the contrast between the

FIGURE 10. *Benedetto Montagna (ca. 1481–1541). The musical contest of Appollo and Pan. This illustrates the combination of Renaissance and classical motifs. Apollo is dressed as a courtier playing a viol, a Renaissance instrument, and Pan is holding the ancient panpipes. This combination of motifs was a favorite theme in madrigals. (Courtesy of the Stanford University Museum of Art.)*

quiet, sentimental country and the busy city. The contrasts of texture and figure in this madrigal are sharply marked; there are frequent cadences, linked throughout the piece with harmonic progressions that have the ring of key-centered harmony heard in later music; many figures are repeated to give a clear sense of inner symmetry in the phrase structure, and, if you listen closely, you can detect shifts between duple and triple meter. All these features are typical of the English madrigal.

The French Chanson Listening to Thomas Crequillon's chanson *Pour ung Plaisir* (For a Delight), *Masterpieces* no. 20, you can hear one of the important features of the French chanson—a lively, very crisp rhythm set by the pattern ♩ ♪♪ at the begining of the piece. This type of rhythm gives rise to well-marked sections, to repetitions of phrases, and to a reduction of contrapuntal complexity in favor of a more chordal texture. These features reflect the spirit of the French language, in which the declamation of the text was clearly and precisely controlled, with particular attention given to the *length* of syllables. While the piece begins with closely spaced imitations of the brief opening figure, it makes very little use of imitation thereafter. In contrast to the typical motet setting of the words, where voices are often singing different parts of the text at the same time, this chanson has the voices together on the text for most of the piece. The text itself echoes a lover's complaint familiar to all times and places, "For a fleeting delight, I now suffer great pain."

POPULAR VOCAL FORMS Popular vocal music of the Renaissance, as well as some of the instrumental music discussed below, can be an easy and satisfying introduction to the music of this age. Many songs were produced that are comparable to the melodies from operettas and musical comedies of the nineteenth and twentieth centuries in their immediate appeal and in the ease with which one or more singers could perform them at sight. The two excerpts given below illustrate the typical style of Renaissance popular music; the texture is chordal, the rhythm is simple and well-marked, the harmony has a strong cadential feeling, the phrases are short. Each country had its own form: in Italy, the *frottola;* in Spain, the *villancico;* in France, the *vaudeville;* in Germany, the *Lied;* in England, the part-song. The texts of these songs covered a great variety of topics, much as theater songs of our age do—amorous, satirical, comments on current topics, pastoral, descriptions of market and hunting scenes, etc. Such pieces are distinguished from the more elaborate forms—the madrigal and chanson—by their sparing use of imitation as well as by the features mentioned above.

Example 4-7 gives the beginning of a frottola published in the early sixteenth century. Note especially the repeated chords that provide a simple note-for-note declamation of the text.

EXAMPLE 4-7. *Frottola (Michael Pesentius)*

Pass - an - do per - una re - zol - la de questa ter - ra, de ques - ta ter - ra

(Passing through this net (of love) there went my love . . .)

Example 4-8 is a setting of a tune popular at the time of Henry VIII of England. The text has the hunt, a favorite pastime of the nobility, as its topic. Note the crisp, regular rhythm, the simple melody with varied repetition of short figures, the balanced phrases, with the first ending on a tonic cadence while the second modulates to the dominant. (The melody is in the middle voice, the tenor.)

EXAMPLE 4-8. *Cornysh: Blow Thy Horn, Hunter*

Blow thy horn hun - ter and blow thy horn on high there

(Melody)

is a doe in yon - der wood in faith she will not die

**INSTRU-
MENTAL
FORMS** Instrumental music of the Renaissance today provides much pleasurable music-making. People are taking up recorders, lutes, viols, and other Renaissance instruments to play dances, variations, fantasias from this era; this music can also sound effective on modern instruments, offering something on every level of skill.

The sound of Renaissance instrumental music has a much wider range of timbres than that of vocal music. Lutes and other plucked instruments, with their crisp, articulated sounds; viols (bowed string instruments), with their gentle, rather subdued tones; many kinds of wind instruments, some soft and rounded in tone (recorders), other piercing and edgy (shawms); a great variety of percussion instruments—these all gave special color to the basic vocabulary of triads. Movement also had its typical instrumental quality—a much more sharply marked accent than was usual in vocal music. The pluck of the lute and the beat of the percussion instruments, the stroke of the bow and the breath attack of wind instruments were all geared to marking beats and accents more pointedly than voices.

INSTRUMENTAL
PIECES BASED
ON VOCAL
MODELS

Many instrumental pieces took vocal works as models. Andrea Gabrieli's reworking of Crequillon's chanson, *Masterpieces* 20 and 21, keeps the basic structure of the vocal piece but adds many running figures to show off the dexterity of the keyboard performer. Gabrieli changed the character of the piece; it was probably played at a slower speed to accommodate the clusters of rapid notes interspersed between the original tones of the vocal chanson. Many French chansons were used as instrumental pieces, and the form was called *canzona alla francese.* When a motet was performed instrumentally, it was called a *ricercar,* meaning "to search." Generally, the ricercar retained the serious, tightly contrapuntal style of the motet, without the instrumental flourishes often found in the canzona.

SECTIONAL
INSTRUMENTAL
FORMS:
DANCE AND
VARIATION

Dancing was one of the chief entertainments in Renaissance life, from the highly refined and delicately nuanced court dances to the robust street and carnival dances. Dances could express a wide range of moods. The *pavane,* a slow dance in duple time, was stately; the *allemande,* a moderately slow dance in duple time, had a restrained, gentle manner; the *galliard,* in quick triple time, was vigorous; and the *courante,* also in quick triple time, had a light and lively character.

Of all forms of Renaissance music, dances had the most precise and clear structure, marked off in well-defined sections. We sense symmetry on a number of levels. For example, in the Lute Dances, *Masterpieces* no. 23, the first period, well-marked by an authentic cadence, has two short phrases, each of which is divided into a pair of sharply contrasted figures. Note that this section makes its cadence on a different tone than the one on which it began; it *modulates.* The second section balances the first, using the same general layout of figures but moving back to the first tone, the home tonic. After this slow duple dance, a quick triple piece provides both balance of form and contrast of mood, and the inner structure of the second dance is as symmetrical as that of the first.

Dances and song tunes were often taken up as themes for *variation,* that is, elaborations and changes based upon the tune. The appeal of a variation composition, then as now, is the fresh quality of texture, movement, and mood given to a familiar melody. The neatly trimmed dance phrases provided a solid, balanced framework for many different kinds of fanciful elaboration. Giles Farnaby's *Variation for Viginals, Masterpieces* no. 29, illustrates some Renaissance methods of variation. The tune can easily be heard in most of the settings, while shorter notes are introduced as the variations proceed. A striking contrast is achieved between the last two settings; first we hear brilliant running figures that eventually veil the tune, while finally the tune reappears above a dense contrapuntal setting to provide a firm, dignified conclusion to the piece.

FREE ELABORATION   During the Renaissance, for the first time in the history of Western music, free instrumental composition came into its own. Composers or performers could choose their own chords, lay out the sections of their pieces according to their own fancy—running figures and arpegios, imitative sections, dancelike phrases—and trim the piece to whatever length they wished. Pieces of this type, called *toccata, intonazione, preambulum,* etc., were signs of the full mastery of the art of composition, since the musician would not rely upon any set forms or preexisting framework of a cantus firmus. They came into being very modestly at first, when the organist had to give church singers the tone upon which they would begin a motet or Mass movement. From a few simple chords and running passages that lasted less than a minute, these free forms grew in scope and power throughout the Renaissance and Baroque eras until they culminated in the monumental preludes, fantasias, and toccatas of J. S. Bach, such as the toccata of his great *Toccata and Fugue in D minor.*

An impressive example of this form is Claudio Merulo's *Toccata, Treasury of Early Music,* no. 29. Two long improvisatory sections frame a short section in the imitative style of the ricercar. As you listen to this piece, note the slow, powerful march of the harmony marked by a number of weighty, drawn-out cadences; observe also how the bass steers the music forward and provides anchorage for the flight of the freely running figures.

In describing the vocal and instrumental music of the Renaissance, we have emphasized their characteristic qualities of sound and movement, the vocal music smooth and blended with a gentle accentuation, the instrumental music varied in timbre, less blended, with a strong and crisp accentuation. But often voices and instruments performed together, either by intention of the composer or due to circumstances. In performing a piece, the most important thing was to have all voices represented; when a vocal performer was not available for a given part, an instrument could sit in; a keyboard player could manage some of the voices or even all of them. The result was a colorful variety of texture and sound for different performances of the same piece.

SUMMARY   Music historians have borrowed the term *Renaissance* from the history of art, literature, and ideas because music paralleled these other aspects of culture both in time and in certain characteristic features. *Humanism* is the term that Renaissance historians apply to the spirit of this age. Specifically it refers to a new interest in the ancient classic culture of Greece and Rome and the application of classic ideas in literature of the sixteenth century. In a broader sense, and this interests us much more, humanism refers to the new attitudes of the Renaissance, which, as Michelet, the French historian put it, led to the "discovery of the world, the discovery of man." Evidences of this spirit of inquiry are found in Leonardo da Vinci's scientific interest, particularly his studies of anatomy, in Copernicus's new theories of astronomy, in the development of the science of perspective by Renaissance painters, and in the penetrating and comprehensive search into human motivations and emotions which Shakespeare's plays embody. Musically, we find analogies to perspective in the creation of a true bass function in harmony. The awakening of the scientific spirit of inquiry might be compared to the development of a balanced, clear, and logical relationship between tones and voices which consonant, triadic harmony, and imitation brought about. Strong personal feelings in drama and poetry are matched boldly by the emphasis on expressive devices and moods, both in the madrigal and the motet.

Historically, the Renaissance saw the first comprehensive effort to break away from the twin authorities of Church and Empire. Political and religious movements had repercussions in the field of fine arts. Much of the music we have examined in this chapter is secular in nature. Both the motivation and the means were present for the Renaissance man to express himself in a personal, warm, and often impassioned style. He no longer was concerned entirely with reframing and renewing hieratic, absolute values; rather his attention turned to his own feelings and the way in which he observed the real world around him, the world of senses and solidity.

In the area of religion, the great, conclusive event was the Reformation, the establishment of new churches, locally controlled, speaking the language of their own country. Not long after, in the middle of the sixteenth century, the Catholic Church took steps to counteract this centrifugal tendency that was manifested on all sides, and in the Counter Reformation, made efforts to reorganize itself and reestablish its supreme authority. The sacred music of Lassus and Palestrina which we have heard was composed in the spirit of the Counter Reformation. Although in many respects it embodies the ideals of Renaissance art in its evenness, balance, smooth flow, and harmonious relationship among all parts, it avoids completely that sense of worldly delight and bold emotional projection which was the guiding spirit in the aesthetics of Renaissance art. To this extent, Roman polyphony is anti-Renaissance; it points to certain mystic qualities found in the art of the seventeenth century.

A great deal of Renaissance music was written to be performed on grand occasions, solemn or festive. There was also music written for performance by musical amateurs in the home, at court, or among friends. Music was one of the graces that had a place in the education of the ideal man of the Renaissance. Dancing, poetry, classics, and music were part of his accomplishments. The satisfactions received from performing madrigals, dance pieces, or other compositions for ensemble can be re-created by the modern amateur. Indeed, you will receive a truer picture of Renaissance music and a deeper personal musical satisfaction if you perform this music rather than listen to it in concert, a purpose for which it may never have been intended.

The points covered in this chapter may be summarized as follows:

1. *Qualities of sound* (texture, harmony): consonance, triads, carefully controlled use of dissonance, occasional striking chromaticism; development of a true bass; fuller sound due to greater number of voices; subtle effects of contrast; wider range
2. *Qualities of movement:* steady, even flow, moderate pace; long, nonsymmetrical phases of movement with much overlap of action between voices in polyphonic pieces; short, symmetrical phases of movement in dances, songs, variation pieces; differences in effect of movement due to elaboration and degree of articulation, especially in keyboard and lute pieces
3. *Effects of arrival:* well-defined cadential procedures with varying degrees of clarity, emphasis, and finality; some codification of chord progression, especially at cadences
4. *Form-building factors:* addition and elaboration upon preexisting material; paraphrase of entire pieces; free ornamentation; imitation; dance forms; some repetition; organization of harmony around tonal center of the mode; cadences to related degrees
5. *Style and expression:* control of expressive values by consistent treatment of consonance-dissonance relationships; use of dissonance for expressive accent; wide range of expressive values subtly

delineated; differentiation of national styles reflecting various language features; pictorialism; concern with the expressive implications of the modes; chromaticism as an expressive nuance

At the beginning of the Renaissance, the trend in music was toward an even, balanced flow. Harmony and sonority were blended, movement was made even and regular, sections overlapped. Passing through this phase, Renaissance music began, in the sixteenth century, to move in an opposite direction. Mixtures of instruments and voices introduced contrasts of sound and sometimes separated the bass from the upper voices. Choruses were divided in some of the greater churches, so that they answered each other back and forth. Cadences became increasingly emphasized, so that they marked the separation of sections more decidedly. Dissonances and chromaticism stood out more boldly. It was as if the "liquid" consistency of the typical Renaissance vocal style were gradually forming an internal "crystal-line" separation, both *vertically* in the opposition of treble and bass and *horizontally* in the sharper marking-off of sections. This trend, already present in the mid-sixteenth century, grew until it led to formation of a new style, the baroque.

DISCUSSION AND REVIEW QUESTIONS

1. Compare medieval harmony with that of the Renaissance.
2. Describe the chief features of Renaissance melody.
3. What is a cantus firmus?
4. List and describe briefly some form-building procedures in Renaissance music.
5. What are the chief forms of sacred music in the Renaissance?
6. What are the chief forms of secular music in the Renaissance?
7. How does Renaissance music reflect the spirit of its age?

CHAPTER FIVE

BAROQUE MUSIC

Baroque music, to most listeners, brings to mind the exuberant concertos of Antonio Vivaldi, the impressive grandeur of George Frideric Handel's oratorios, the rich, complex expressiveness of Johann Sebastian Bach's fugues, sonatas, and cantatas. These works date from the early eighteenth century; they represent the culmination of more than a century of style changes and refinements. Despite their very great differences in texture, form, and expression, these works share some basic features common to all baroque music.

When measured against the typical blend of sound and the unbroken flow of movement in Renaissance music, these works show a separation of elements. The sound is *layered;* the bass and treble clearly work against each other in a *polarized* relationship. Movement is strongly punctuated by cadences to divide the flow into well-marked sections. The vertical and horizontal *fission* that began to appear in Renaissance music has become a consistent feature of the language. Yet the process of separation is held in check by powerful *cohesive* forces: cadences and a sense of key *pull the music together,* rhythmic arrangements *organize* motives into well-defined phrases and periods, and a *consistency* of style and expression is maintained within a given movement.

EARLY As we said in Chapter 4, these aspects already are heard in some
BAROQUE Renaissance music. But the first decisive moves in their direction
(ca. 1600– appear around the year 1600, in a rather spectacular fashion. As you
1620) listen to Claudio Monteverdi's "Tu se' morta" (You are dead), *Mas-*

terpieces no. 31, the first thing you note is the *separation* of the voice from its accompaniment, a *vertical* pulling apart of the texture. When you hear Giovanni Gabrieli's "In ecclesiis" (In the congregation), you are surely impressed by its mosaic-like layout, a chain of short, highly contrasted sections, a *horizontal* separation.

The effect of this process of separation was to highlight individual elements. In the Monteverdi piece, the voice is placed *front and center,* away from the rest of the sound; therefore, it can move freely, projecting the sense of the text with an intense expressive impact, a "personal" message. Often it declaims in an *irregular rhythm* and touches strikingly *dissonant* tones to underline an especially pathetic turn of feeling. In the Gabrieli piece, each phrase has a powerful impact, partly because of its well-turned internal shape, but mostly because of the striking contrasts in *texture, figure,* and *tone color* between phrases. Note especially the *powerful cadences* that close phrases, the *chromaticisms* that project an arresting light-dark effect, the occasional cutting *dissonances,* and the impact that occasional *moments of silence* create against the following sound. Example 5-1 illustrates some of the harmonic and rhythmic features that give this piece a powerful declamatory quality.

EXAMPLE 5-1. *Cadences and chordal color: Gabrieli, "In ecclesiis"*

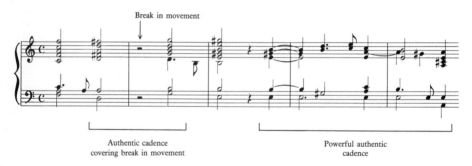

Break in movement

Authentic cadence
covering break in movement

Powerful authentic
cadence

The Gabrieli and Monteverdi pieces represent gateways to the new styles, which will become crystallized in the music of Bach and Handel. This is how the changes came about:

1. The short sections and the bold contrasts of color and texture heard in the Gabrieli piece led to the *concerto* format and to the great choruses, as in Bach's Mass in B minor and Handel's *The Messiah.* This procedure, pitting groups within the entire ensemble or solo-

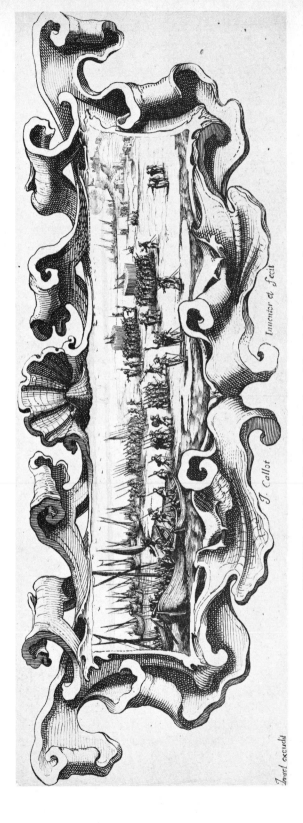

J. Callot

Inuentor et fecit

Israel excudit

FIGURE 11. *J. Callot:* The Exodus of Israel. *A seventeenth-century engraving. Note the intensity of effect created by the grotesque border and the displacement of the groups in the scene itself, requiring the viewer to look from the extreme left to appreciate the symmetry. (Courtesy of Dr. Leon Kolb, San Francisco.)*

ists against each other, was called *concertato*, "striving together." It was already foreshadowed in such works as Josquin's "Ave Maria," with its pairing of upper against lower voices. The concertato style is the basis of the modern art of orchestration.

2. The frequent strong cadences in the Gabrieli piece lead to key-centered harmony. Note in Example 5-1 how the cadences hold the continuity together, despite the breaks in movement that represent the concertato procedure. Note also the striking color effects in the first three measures as the heavy, powerful chords shift chromatically.

3. In the Monteverdi piece, the highlighting of the solo voice represents the principal texture of *all* baroque music—the *separation of treble and bass* to serve specifically different roles in the texture. The treble voice (or voices) takes the principal melodic line; the bass acts as a steady support, *polarized* against the treble. This steady bass was called the *continuo*. In addition to underpinning the texture, the continuo (generally performed by a keyboard player) had the responsibility to fill out the *harmony in the middle register,* to complete the chords indicated by the treble and bass. Numbers indicating intervals above the bass note were added to assist the performer; this procedure was called *figured bass*. Many seventeenth- and eighteenth-century musical scores give only the treble, the bass line, and the figures. Example 5-2 illustrates this type of musical shorthand.

EXAMPLE 5-2. *Figured bass. Bach: Wachet auf (Sleepers, Awake),* cantata

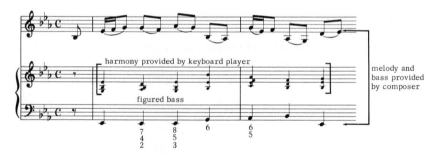

To reinforce the bass line of the keyboard instrument, a violoncello, viola da gamba, or bassoon played along. For late baroque chamber music, one of the preferred layouts was to have *two* treble voices working together against a continuo, as in Example 5-3.

EXAMPLE 5-3. *Handel: Trio sonata in G minor, first movement*

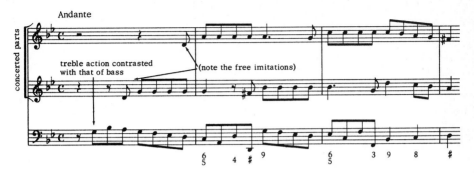

4. An intense quality of expression—powerful statements, pathetic nuances, striking dissonances—highlights the dramatic values in all of baroque music. It eventually leads to a code of expression called the *doctrine of the affections.* This was an outgrowth of the Renaissance notion that each person had a characteristic "humour" (state of being)—melancholic, sanguine, choleric, etc. In the doctrine of the affections, feelings and attitudes were classified (anger, sorrow, joy, love, etc.), and an appropriate musical figure was invented to suggest the feeling. Thus, the affection of Monteverdi's "Tu se' morta" is deepest pathos and tragedy, while that of Gabrieli's "In ecclesiis" has an air of pride and grandeur.

5. The declamatory style of Monteverdi's "Tu se' morta" is called *recitative.* In this new way, around 1600, the setting of a text emphasized the *sense of the words,* so they would not be obscured by complex counterpoints. The new emphasis on the words reflects a shift of focus toward literary and dramatic values. Plays on classic subjects and legends were set to music in this way, and *opera* was born. One of the favorite stories was that of Orpheus, who lost his Eurydice through death and by virtue of his marvelous music-making was able to persuade the gods Zeus and Hades to bring her back to life. The new music-text relationship represented the sense of the text so vividly that the new style was called *stile rappresentativo.* When this freely spun-out music was *alternated with songs* in regular rhythms and well-defined forms, the traditional operatic pairing of *recitative and aria* was established.

   Side by side with the new style, elements of the old carried on, while absorbing many of the later procedures. Dance music, variation, imitation, the older motet style, the *canzona francese*—these all had unbroken lifelines throughout the seventeenth century and into the eighteenth.

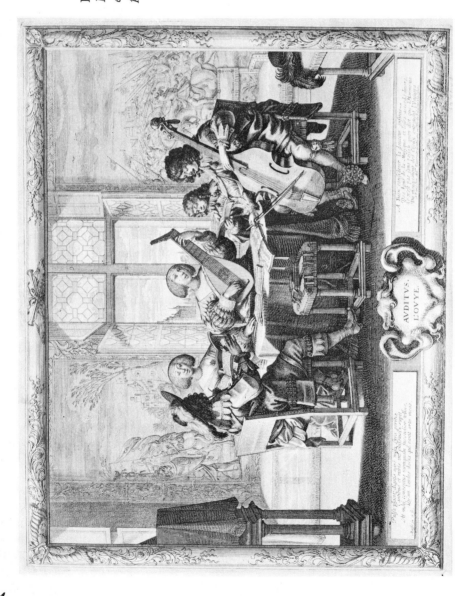

FIGURE 12. *Abraham Bosse: Music Party. A seventeenth-century engraving. (Courtesy of the Metropolitan Museum of Art.)*

The developments in early baroque music may be summarized as follows:

1. The concertato style, combining voices and instruments
2. Sectionalism in structure, with strong contrast effects
3. Further crystallization of harmonic procedures; concentration on cadential progressions; figured bass
4. Polarity of treble and bass; trio-sonata texture
5. Recitative; the beginning of opera
6. Strong, intense expressive qualities; striking use of dissonance

MIDDLE BAROQUE (ca. 1620–1680) Middle baroque music lost much of the excitement and intensity that characterized the innovative and exploratory aspects of early baroque music. Innovation gave way to *codification of procedures* and expansion of forms in the mid-seventeenth century. Early versions of the principal genres of the late baroque begin to appear. Sonatas, suites, cantatas, oratorios, arias, preludes, fugues, the French overture, the concerto, the opera sinfonia—all these began to assume definitive shape during this time. Some of the trends were:

1. *Expansion* of short sections, which eventually became separate movements of concertos, cantatas, sonatas, etc.
2. *Grouping* of dances into suites
3. *Increasingly stronger sense of key,* as a result of concentration of cadential action and emphasis on cadential definition of the tonal center
4. *Exploration of a single affection* throughout a large section or complete movement; evolution of *methods for working over a few important motives* throughout a piece
5. *Simplification of recitative;* clear *differentiation* of recitative and aria

These features can be observed in the middle baroque excerpts from the *Masterpieces* collection. Of special note are: no. 32, the recitative from Giacomo Carissimi's oratorio, *The Judgment of Solomon* (simple recitative); nos. 33 and 34, the sacred cantata by Heinrich Schütz, *Lord, Help,* and the toccata by Girolamo Frescobaldi (systematic development of a few figures, one affection, longer sections, stronger cadential action, clear focus on a ruling tonal center); no. 35, the suite by Johann Jakob Froberger (four dances—allemande, courante, sarabande, gigue); no. 36, the overture to Lully's *Armide* (frequent strong cadences, longer sections well contrasted).

***LATE
BAROQUE
(ca. 1680–
1750)*** Listening to the "Crucifixus" (He was crucified) and the "Et Resurrexit" (And was resurrected) from Johann Sebastian Bach's Mass in B minor, you can sense very strongly the depth and intensity of feeling sustained without a break throughout each piece. The "Crucifixus" relates the most tragic moment in Christendom, the crucifixion of Christ, while the "Et Resurrexit" rejoices in His being risen again. To project these moods, Bach had available all the elements of expression, style, and form which had been steadily defined and codified throughout the seventeenth century, and which formed the musical language of the late Baroque.

The "Crucifixus" blends many elements of form and style, all of them concentrated upon the tragic *affection* which you can sense in:

The *low* center of sound, focused upon the bass line.

The *descending melodic lines* in both voices and instruments that suggest bending down in sorrow.

The *chromatic line* of the bass and later in the voices, again a signal for a tragic affection.

The *rhythm* of the *sarabande*, a slow, grave dance in triple time, maintained throughout the piece in the bass.

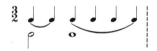

The *four-measure period* which constitutes the bass theme, constantly repeated in the bass (see Example 5-4), maintaining the steady, unbroken mood and providing a pulse, a heartbeat below the *motet-like* entries of the voices in slow notes that cut across the regular rhythm of the bass. The constant repetition of the bass line represents the technique called *ground bass* or *ostinato,* very frequently used in baroque music as a type of *variation,* the variations being assigned to the upper voices.

The *strong impression of key;* all the chord progressions are clustered around the key of the piece, E minor. We hear an authentic cadence every four measures in this key, except for several points where Bach deliberately avoids a cadence to build a broader flow. Note, however, after the entire piece has saturated our ears with the sound of E minor, Bach ends it in a major key—G major—with a very poignant, touching use of chromatic harmonies to reach this new key, as if to suggest the final resignation of the burial rite, and, perhaps, to prepare us for the brilliant sound of the "Et Resurrexit."

The frequent expressive *dissonances,* which the voices introduce against the strong cadencelike action. These are especially affecting at points where the bass completes its cadences.

The *polarity* of texture, upper lines against bass, a typical baroque scoring, creates its own tension, a tug-and-pull of melodic-rhythmic action. It sets the pulse, the heartbeat of the bass against the agony implied in the dissonances and irregular rhythms of the upper voices. (Brahms used this same contrast of bass and treble in the opening of his Symphony No. 1.)

Example 5-4 illustrates the bass lines, the action of the voices, deceptive cadences, the characteristic chromaticism and dissonance that contribute to the mood of this piece, very likely the most powerful expression of tragedy in all baroque music.

EXAMPLE 5-4. *Bach, Mass in B minor, "Crucifixus"*

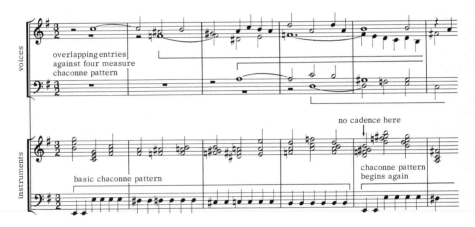

In utmost contrast to the darkness of the "Crucifixus" there follows the jubilation of the "Et Resurrexit." Here are the techniques Bach used to express this joyous affection:

The *sound* is *brilliant;* trumpets and wind instruments impart the mood of victory.

The *movement* is *quick* and *driving.* Bach used here the rhythm of the *polonaise* 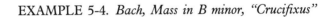, a stately yet vigorous dance in triple time with a powerful lift thanks to its scintillating mixture of longer and shorter notes.

The mood of joy gains excitement through the *interplay* of the entire ensemble, the *tutti,* with solo sections. This is the basic principle of the baroque concerto, borrowed here by Bach to build the feeling of exuberance.

Free imitation is used extensively to build a feeling of climax.

In contrast to the descending lines of the "Crucifixus," the *melodic lines* of the "Et Resurrexit" thrust upward, a signal for new life. The long lines of neatly patterned quick notes that break out frequently (*coloratura*) reinforce the impression of exuberance. Bach holds tightly to just a few striking melodic figures, deploying them in many different ways throughout the piece, to maintain the *unity of affection* yet to achieve within this unity a sense of *progression* and *variety*.

The *key* is *major*. We can sense strong cadences, first in the home key, later in other keys, finally back in the home key. The harmony builds strong drives to all its cadences, creating a compelling feeling of expectation throughout the piece for the completion of each phase of harmonic action.

Harmony also shapes the *form* of the piece. Following the music with a score, you can observe the following layout:

Part I $\begin{cases} a. & D \ major, \text{ measures } 1\text{-}20 \\ b. & A \ major, \text{ measures } 21\text{-}50 \ (51) \end{cases}$

Part II $\begin{cases} c. & B \ minor, \text{ measures } 52\text{-}83 \\ d. & D \ major, \text{ measures } 84 \text{ to end} \end{cases}$

This scheme of keys divides the piece into two large sections, *harmonically*, at measure 50. Part I moves away from the home key to end in A major; Part II begins in B minor and returns to the home key, D major. Above this harmonic substructure, you can hear a *three-part melodic* arrangement. The first two sections, *a* and *b*, form one melodic unit; the *c* section is something of a contrast, thanks to its key; the final D major section restates, in a somewhat condensed form, the melodic material of *a* and *b*, all in the home key. The restatement of the opening material at the end of the piece reflects an important baroque form, the *da capo* form, symbolized by the formula ABA. The melodic sections, each clearly separate, are *fused into an unbroken line of action* by the harmonic movement away from and back to the home key.

The points touched upon in the discussion of the "Crucifixus" and "Et Resurrexit" represent a number of important aspects of late baroque musical style and form. Some of these will now be examined in greater detail.

THE SENSE
OF KEY
In contrast to Renaissance music, which uses cadences only at the ends of phrases, baroque music saturates its harmony with cadences and cadencelike progressions. In doing so, it projects a very strong *sense of key* (see page 43). Within a phrase or period we hear light cadences, while the heavier cadence at the end of a phrase or period creates a very clear and strong effect of harmonic arrival. Riding upon this harmonic movement, we hear intensive play of motives. Each cadential formula serves to hold the music together, while the melodic and rhythmic energy of the motives propels the music forward. This creates a controlled and balanced flight, an interpenetration of forces that enabled baroque music to expand its lines of action to great

lengths. An excellent example of a broadly scaled period built in this manner is the opening of Bach's *Brandenburg* Concerto No. 3 in G major, Example 5-5.

EXAMPLE 5-5. *Bach:* Brandenburg *Concerto No. 3, first movement*

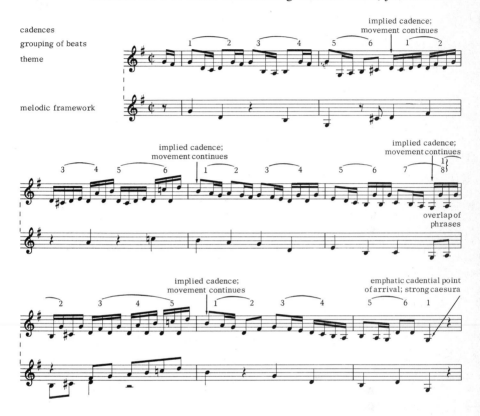

The diagram in Example 5-5 shows (1) *four implied cadences* that build an expectation for the firm cadence at the end of the period; (2) an *irregular phrase structure* cutting across the underlying regular 4-4 meter (to sense this, begin with the underlying beat of the 4-4 meter, then count beats up to each cadence)—the phrases are 6, 6, 8, 5, and 6 beats in length, building a rhythmic tension that resolves at the final downbeat of the period; (3) the *underlying melodic contour* with its broadly scaled fall and rise to a high point, or *apex*, that gives the intensive play of the three- and four-note motives a sense of direction.

Such a period might be compared to the span of a bridge, anchored firmly by its cadential piers and possessed of great internal strength by virtue of its tightly knit construction and its solid materials. The clearness and the emphasis with which the impression of key is given in late baroque music enabled the baroque composer to build a movement in blocks of key *areas.* Each area represented a sharply defined harmonic *position,* established at a specific distance and direction away from the home key. In some cases the music would pause momentarily at a given position or area; at other times it would settle for a while in a new position. Example 5-6 shows the plan for the harmonic areas of the first movement of Handel's Concerto in C major, *Masterpieces,* no. 43.

EXAMPLE 5-6. *Handel: Concerto in C major*

Briefly, then, the late baroque formula for the building of structural units involves (1) active cadentially oriented harmony which projects a strong sense of key, with clear, often emphatic arrival; (2) steady, vigorous beats that crystallize into well-marked larger units, eventually forming periods; (3) intensive play of motives, often sequential, forming large melodic contours; (4) structural units linked through key relationships to form a broad harmonic plan.

IMITATION Baroque music delights in imitation. We hear imitation in most compositions of this era, except for freely composed pieces, such as some *preludes, toccatas,* and *fantasias.* Imitation can be used *systematically* or *incidentally:*

1. *Systematic imitation.* The *fugue* and the *canon* use imitation systematically. The fugue introduces one or more themes or *subjects* in turn in all voices; this is the *exposition,* and it centers upon the home key. *Episodes,* sections that do not present the subject in its entirety, are used to modulate to different keys in which the subject is again presented in new expositions. The harmony eventually returns to the home key for a final exposition. Most of the counterpoint in

fugues is *free;* the character and shape of the subject are retained, but details can be changed to accommodate the harmony. The best way to become acquainted with baroque fugues is to listen to some of the fugues in Bach's *Well-Tempered Clavier.* You will hear many different styles, ranging from the most grave and serious to the lightest, gayest dancelike pieces (see page 113), some with very short subjects, others with very long subjects. Some fugues work their subjects over intensively. Example 5-7, the first fugue in the *Well-Tempered Clavier,* Book I, shows a close-grained counterpoint in a procedure called *stretto,* where voices enter very quickly upon each other.

EXAMPLE 5-7. *Stretto from Bach:* Well-Tempered Clavier, *Book I, Fugue in C major*

In this fugue, the subject is almost always heard, with very little episodic material used. Each beat seems to carry considerable weight, and it is not easy to sense phrases. The effect of this tight, dense action is that of a deliberate, powerful, and thoroughly convincing argument.

The second fugue in the *Well-Tempered Clavier,* Book I, in C minor, is quite a different piece. Its dancelike subject, in the rhythm of a *bourrée,* sets in motion a light, clearly sectioned piece, with a strong sense of inner symmetry, and much episodic material. The subject appears less often than in the first fugue, but its entries therefore have a more striking impact. Example 5-8 gives a diagram of this fugue.

EXAMPLE 5-8. *Diagram of Bach:* Well-Tempered Clavier, *Book I, Fugue in C minor*

Note the disturbance of regular phrase rhythm beginning at measure 17; this intensifies rhythmic action, building up to powerful cadences and a broad effect of arrival. Such interruptions of rhythmic order to prepare for an area of arrival are important aspects of Bach's idea of extended musical structure.

	2		2		2		2		2		2		2		2	
Phrase	1	2	3	4	5	6	7	8	9	10	11	12	13	14	15	16
Material	sub.	sub.			ep.		s.		e.		s.		e.		s.	
Key	C minor		G minor				C minor				Eb major				G minor	

	3		2		2		$2\frac{1}{2}$		2		3		1		$2\frac{1}{2}$		
	17	18	19	20	21	22	23	24	25	2	6	27	2	8	2	9	30	31
		e.		s.		e.		e.			s.		e.			s.	
				C minor							C minor					C minor	

Canon is another form using systematic imitation. In canon, all the voices are taken on a tour of *strict* imitation; all voices sing the same melody in turn, with little or no alteration of the line, and without episodes of nonimitative counterpoint. ("Row, Row Your Boat," a *round,* is a simple canon.) The most celebrated composition that uses canon is Bach's *Goldberg* Variations; the thirty variations of this piece contain nine canons. A successful canon, one that works within the strict conditions of the form and at the same time develops a convincing flow, is a delight for both performer and listener.

2. *Incidental imitation.* Incidental imitation can be used in a composition to introduce a subject in various voices, to set up a give-and-take of figures between voices. It binds the melodic action of the voices firmly without carrying out the imitative procedure as thoroughly as in the fugue and canon. The entry of the voices in Bach's "Et Resurrexit" illustrates this occasional use of imitation. Example 5-4, the "Crucifixus," cites a short section of imitation in the voices against the contrasting figure in the bass.

VARIATION Variation in baroque music, like imitation, could be worked out *systematically* or used *incidentally*. (See page 85.) Systematic variation used a model—a chorale tune, a popular melody, an original theme, or a harmonic progression; a set of short pieces were then composed in which some of the following modifications of the theme could be applied:

1. The melody tones could each be surrounded by groups of short ornamental quick notes.
2. A counterpoint could be added to the melody.

3. The tempo of the melody could be changed.
4. The melody could be broken into short fragments.
5. The harmonic progression of the melody could be used to build a new short piece.

Bach was one of the great masters of systematic variation. You have already heard one example in the "Crucifixus," where he added a rich web of counterpoint above the oft-repeated bass theme. In his *Goldberg* Variations we hear pieces of different styles, including dance types, alternating with canons based upon the harmonic progression of the theme itself. Probably the easiest set of variations to follow is his Passacaglia and Fugue in C minor. The theme, Example 5-9, is a clearly profiled tune, a typical eight-measure dance melody. After Bach announces it simply, as a bass solo, he takes it through a rich and impressive series of contrapuntal settings, and provides a climax to the work with a great fugue whose subject is a variant of the tune. While most sets of variations appeal to the listener through the imaginative changes wrought upon the theme, the Passacaglia and Fugue develops a powerful feeling of accumulation, of drive to the final arrival, a trait often displayed in Bach's music, and nowhere more grippingly than in the latter half of this piece.

EXAMPLE 5-9. *Bach, Passacaglia and Fugue in C minor, theme*

Handel's so-called *Harmonious Blacksmith* is a set of *ornamental* variations. You can easily hear the tune through most of the modifications. This is a tuneful piece, where the mechanical repetitions of the principal theme are given life and interest by the effects of sonority emerging from the harpsichord.

Incidental variation saturates the melodic style of baroque music. More properly, it might be called *melodic ornamentation*. In this procedure, the longer notes that form the backbone of a melody (see Example 5-5) may be broken up into smaller notes that form tight little patterns. This kind of ornamentation could be added whenever the composer (or sometimes the performer) felt that it would enhance the expressive quality of a melody; it could apply to just a few notes or to an entire passage. Example 5-10 illustrates this kind of incidental variation from the "Et Resurrexit." Note the lift given the melody by the *turning* figure in Example 5-10*a*, and the exuberance expressed by the long *running* figure in Example 5-10*b*.

EXAMPLE 5-10. *Incidental variation and melodic ornamentation;
Bach, Mass in B minor, "Et Resurrexit"*

a. Plain melody

Melody with turning figure

Et re - sur - re - - xit, re - sur - re - xit

b. Plain melody

Melody with running figure

Et re - sur - re   xit, re - sur - re - xit

Imitation and variation reflect two important aspects of life and
thought in the Baroque era. Imitation, along with all forms of counterpoint, symbolizes ideas of universal order, where all things have
their own place in the scheme of things and are linked in a systematic
way. We have only to think of Newton, Leibniz, Descartes, Kepler,
Harvey, and Pascal, among many, to realize how thoroughly the
scientific attitude permeated the spirit of the times and guided the
thoughts of men. Variation, on the other hand, suggests the personal
aspect, the realm of feeling, of decoration. We can see a parallel to
musical variation in the highly decorated walls and ceilings of late
baroque churches in Italy, Germany, and Austria.

STYLES AND The feeling for clear and precise order in baroque music is carried
FORMS OF over into its various forms and styles. Baroque music is imbued with a
BAROQUE strong sense of propriety; certain kinds of music belong to certain
MUSIC situations, times, places. On the broadest scale, styles and forms were

classified according to *where* they were used—in the church, in the theater, in the home or salon.

CHURCH Church music was heard and performed in the seventeenth and eight-
MUSIC eenth centuries by more people than music of any other genre. No
matter what their station in life might be—peasants or aristocrats—or
whether they were Catholic or Protestant, some form of church music
was part of their lives, if only in Sunday services. Catholic worshipers
would hear Masses, motets, and other works in Latin, while Protes-
tants would hear cantatas, chorales, and hymns in their native language
and often take part in singing the tunes.

Baroque church music was a great world in its own, encompassing
a wide range of styles, from the simplest to the most elaborate, from
the most severe contrapuntal statements to the freest outpouring of
feelings. The *"Crucifixus"* and the "Et Resurrexit" touch the opposite
poles of church music style. The *"Crucifixus"* is cast in the so-called
stylus gravis (serious or grave style), harking back to the motet techniques of the Renaissance. The "Et Resurrexit" takes up the *stylus
luxurians* (luxuriant or brilliant style), using fanfares, florid runs, and a
dance rhythm. Apart from the traditional use of the Mass and motet,
baroque church music evolved forms of its own—the *chorale,* the
cantata, and the *oratorio.*

Chorale Chorales were simple melodies set to sacred texts. They represented
musically the word of God. As they evolved from their first appearance in the Renaissance (see page 78), they became subjects for many
kinds of musical treatment. They could be sung in unison by the
congregation; they could be harmonized and sung in parts or played on
the organ; they could be elaborated for organ performance with considerable contrapuntal activity in the forms known as the *chorale
prelude,* the *chorale fantasia,* and the *chorale variation;* they were
frequently used as *cantus firmi* in *chorale cantatas,* where the various
movements would use the chorale tune as a theme. Numbers 46 to 48
of *Masterpieces* illustrate how Bach used the chorale melody, *"Christ
lag in Todesbanden"* (Christ lay in the bonds of death). He set it as a
congregational song, as a variation piece for organ, and (from the
cantata of the same name, no. 48) as an extended chorus, where the
chorale melody is accompanied in fugal style by quick motives derived
from the chorale itself.

Cantata Cantata means "sung piece." More specifically, in baroque music, it
referred to a vocal composition, either sacred or secular, with some
form of instrumental accompaniment and laid out in several contrasted
sections. We know the cantata best through Bach's works; he wrote
about 300, of which almost 200 are preserved.

A cantata tells a story or develops an idea. The cantata *Christ lag in Todesbanden* relates Christ's struggle with Death and His eventual victory. Its seven vocal numbers, preceded by a short orchestral *sinfonia,* include two great choral pieces, solos for tenor and bass, a duet for soprano and alto, and a final chorale (see *Masterpieces,* no. 46) that celebrates the victory in a simple style to which the congregation may add its voices. The centerpiece of this cantata, no. 4, *"Es war ein wunderlicher Krieg"* (It was a strange war), vividly depicts the struggle; as the short notes of the speeded-up theme, tossed back and forth in free imitation, "assault" the chorale melody in the alto voice sung in long notes. For the congregation on Easter Sunday, this cantata must have been something of a theater experience, matching in impact any message that a sermon might deliver.

Oratorio The oratorio was the church's answer to opera; both of these great forms evolved in the early seventeenth century in Italy. In the oratorio a sacred story is told in dramatic fashion, with recitatives, arias, duets (perhaps trios), and elaborate choral pieces. In this sense, the oratorio was an extended cantata.

Handel's *Messiah,* familiar to all, and one of the most celebrated works ever composed, not only exemplifies the oratorio but is a treasure house of musical riches and a compendium of baroque techniques of composition. As a rule, we find Handel's music less dense than that of Bach; Handel's counterpoint is more likely to give way to massive effects of sonority and brilliant passage-work; the interwining of contrapuntal lines is more loosely carried out. Handel more than makes up for this by a wonderful sense for the dramatic nuance, by the elegance of his melodic lines, and by the brilliance and power of his sonorities. All these are illustrated in the *Messiah,* and, lest we overlook his contrapuntal skill, one of the most impressive movements of all is the fugue "And with His Stripes."

A special type of oratorio, particularly representative of baroque ideas of expression, was the *passion.* This told the story of the sacrifice of Christ in quasi-dramatic form. For his great *Passion According to St. Matthew,* Bach composed shorter individual numbers than those of the Mass in B minor. Thus, he was able to change the expressive value more quickly, to develop dramatic contrast more vividly, and to carry the story forward more powerfully than if he had written long, broadly developed pieces.

THEATER MUSIC While church music ranked highest in dignity in the seventeenth and eighteenth centuries, touching the lives of most people, the theater and its music were the chief sources of entertainment, both for the upper classes and the lower social ranks, peasants and farmers. Theater music, represented chiefly by *opera,* had both its *serious* and *comic* types.

Serious Opera   The principal types of serious opera, the Italian *opera seria* and the French *tragédie lyrique,* turned to classic antiquity for their stories, to legends and historical tales from Greece and Rome, peopled with gods, heroes, tyrants, and noble lovers; typically, the struggle was between love and duty.

During the Baroque era, Italian opera seria dominated the musical scene. Italian melody was admired and imitated throughout Europe; it was suave, well-turned, ingratiating, easy to listen to. The best singers in Europe were Italian. Putting these two advantages together, it was inevitable that Italian opera developed the principal form of opera, the *aria.* In the aria, a solo vocal number of some extended scope, virtuoso singers could express, with flowing melody and with brilliant running figures, the standard *affective* attitudes of the theater of this time—love, joy, sorrow, anger, despair, triumph, heroism, etc. The most important and extended version of the aria was the *da capo* aria (da capo means "return to the beginning"), laid out as an A B A form. In A the singers expressed one mood; in B, a short contrast was introduced; returning to repeat A, the singers could add elaborations of their own (not written down by the composer), in order to display their virtuosity and musical invention.

Masterpieces, no. 44, an excerpt from Handel's *Rinaldo,* uses the da capo form to express two highly contrasted moods. A is a slow, tragic piece; you can grasp its serious import through the halting, somewhat imbalanced rhythm of the sarabande and the hint of fugal imitation at the beginning. B, in a mood of defiance, has the brisk style of the orchestral introduction. On the return to A, the singer could well add some incidental variations to the melody, consistent with the tragic style.

French opera developed distinctive characteristics in response to the grandeur of Louis XIV's court. Instead of a series of brilliant solo numbers which gave musical heroes opportunities to show off, French opera was a brilliant spectacle. Ballet was of primary importance in the scheme; there was more instrumental music than in Italian opera, because of the superlative orchestral establishment; arias were shorter, often dancelike in style; the dramatic situation was given a greater place in the total scheme.

Although Italian and French serious opera dominated the seventeenth-century musical scene, paradoxically the one piece of serious theater music that has survived from the Baroque is an English work, Henry Purcell's *Dido and Aeneas,* ca. 1689.

Dido and Aeneas has such a poignant and moving dramatic appeal, its music is so wonderfully fresh and colorful, it offers so few problems

FIGURE 13. *Andrea Pozzo: Baroque stage design, from* Fernsehkunst
(*The Art of Perspective*), *1700. Note how the domed ceiling with its
painting creates the illusion of unlimited space* (*continuous expansion*).
(*Courtesy of the Stanford University Libraries.*)

of staging, and it has such a wealth and variety of styles and attitudes that it has commended itself to modern concert or dramatic perform-ance with equal ease. It has been staged effectively by both amateur and professional groups. Since it represents, structurally, the middle baroque style, its individual numbers are relatively short; they make their dramatic point and move on to the next without the intrusion of the personality or prowess of the singer. (The work was composed for a girls' school.) "Dido's Lament," at the end of the opera, is one of the most touchingly sorrowful expressions in the entire history of opera. Like the "Crucifixus" of Bach's B minor Mass, it reveals its basic affective quality in the descending chromatic line of an ostinato bass, above which the perishing Dido sings a melodic line burdened by dissonances and particularly expressive intervals. Example 5-11 shows both the bass line and Dido's song. Compare this with the example from the "Crucifixus" (Example 5-4).

EXAMPLE 5-11. *Purcell:* Dido and Aeneas, *Dido's Lament*

(The dissonances are indicated by the sign +.)

Within the short space of little over an hour, Purcell takes us through a grand sweep of events, from Dido's awakening love, through the plotting of the sorceress to force Aeneas's departure, to the final tragic death of Dido. Note the brilliance of the triumph music, the imaginative tone painting of the sorceress's music, the infectious buoyancy of the sailors' dance.

*Popular Opera:
Opera Buffa,
Opéra Comique*

Popular music, music intended for the middle and lower classes, had existed for centuries before the Baroque era. We have few documents relating to this music before the seventeenth century, but we know that much of it was performed in connection with improvised stage presentations, the most celebrated of which was the *commedia dell'arte*. In this form the traditional characters of broad farce, Harlequin, Punchinello, Columbine, Pantalon, etc., were encountered. The nobility liked to watch episodes of comedy as relief between the acts of their serious operas. As this custom grew, a new form of opera took shape, the comic opera or *opera buffa*.

Aristocratic opera tell us something about the façade of seventeenth- and eighteenth-century history—the magnificent courts, the absolute monarchs, the ideas of grandeur and power. Comic opera deals with the down-to-earth play of situation and often with the overturning of tradition or authority. Comedy thrives on punctured pomposity and outraged dignity. The classic theme of opera buffa shows the servant winning over the master. Giovanni Battista Pergolesi's *La serva padrona* (The maid as mistress) is the most famous early eighteenth-century opera buffa. It created a sensation when it was performed in Paris in 1752. As its title clearly indicates, it represents a triumph for the servant.

Musically, opera buffa also represents a contrast to opera seria. Instead of grandiose arias that developed one affective quality at great length and displayed the arts of the virtuoso singer, we find short, tuneful songs, with emphasis upon a sparkling, witty text. One of the most amusing techniques was *parlando*, a quick patter in an even, steady tempo. Parlando became virtually a trademark of comic opera, surviving many changes of style. (A Gilbert and Sullivan piece would certainly lose much of its appeal without its patter songs.) Comic opera relied upon quick-witted acting and singing, and particularly upon the ability of the performer to etch sharply parodied characterizations or to splash about with broad farce.

An example from Pergolesi's opera illustrates typical style of opera buffa. The duet from *La serva padrona* (The maid as mistress), *"Io conosco,"* has Serpina, the servant girl, trying to persuade Uberto, her master, to agree to do what he will eventually do, that is, take her as his wife. She is teasing and seductive; he is stubborn but intrigued. The music shows some typical late baroque features: steady movement, play of short figures, a firm continuo. But the grand spirit of the baroque is somehow gone; the mood is lighthearted and humorous. Motion is regularly arrested by strong cadences; figures are repeated again and again; the texture is thin, and there is little sense of development or exploration. The motion is often represented by parlando, which narrows and straightens the melodic curve. There is a mixing of figures, rather than a unity of affect. Although Serpina and Uberto do

Troisieme Iournee.
Le Malade imaginaire, Comedie reprsentée
dans le Iardin de Versailles devant la Grotte.

Dcs tertius.
Ægrotus sou Æger imaginarius, Comœdia acta
in hortis Versaliarum ad foris Cryptæ.

FIGURE 14. Engraving of a scene from Molière's Le Malade Imaginaire, in the garden of Versailles in 1676. Note the grand symmetries, both on stage and in the total scene itself, reflecting the notion of classical order that was characteristic of the time of Louis XIV. The music was very likely composed by Lully. (From the Gracely Collection, Stanford University Libraries.)

sing the same melodies frequently, they have their own special moments: Serpina with a soft, flattering figure, Uberto with a grumbling, low-pitched expression of his stubbornness. Here the musical authority of the late baroque style is undermined as well as the social authority of the master who will yield his power to the servant girl.

The French also had their popular theater; comedies, often farcical and satirical, were performed at fairs in the early eighteenth century. These were interspersed with popular songs whose melodies were known to the public but whose texts were newly invented. Eventually this genre became *opéra comique;* exported to Germany, opéra comique furnished the model for German comic opera, *Singspiel.* Several examples of songs from these genres are given in Historical Anthology of Music 291 and 301. The simple, pleasant melodic figures, literally repeated a number of times, show the effort to cultivate a naive "natural" quality in contrast to the complex artificialities of the serious aristocratic musical theater.

Baroque theater music did not survive its age, but its influence upon other genres was profound. Instrumental music borrowed heavily from opera, as did church music. Opera defined and sharpened the portrayal of various affections; the musical styles associated with these were taken up in instrumental music. Many a slow movement is an aria without words; many a quick movement has elements of aria or buffa ensemble. The cantata and oratorio took both recitative and aria from opera. Ballet furnished models for dance movements in sonatas and symphonies as well as characteristic rhythms for themes of other movements.

CHAMBER
MUSIC

Chamber music refers to music performed at home, in a salon, or at court for the pleasure of the participants and perhaps a few listeners. Although it was less impressive than church and theater music, chamber music in the later baroque era had the advantage of flexibility; it was precisely this ability of chamber music to adapt to many situations that enabled it to survive, while the monolithic productions of church and theater disappeared from the musical scene.

The flexibility of chamber music involved a number of factors, including:

1. A wide range of performance skills, from easy teaching pieces to virtuoso concertos; this made some kind of chamber music available to each level of music making.
2. The options with which performances could be arranged, from impromptu spur-of-the-moment get-togethers to formal concerts.
3. Flexibility in scoring; the possibility of substitution—for example,

a flute or oboe for a violin on the treble part, a violoncello for a viola da gamba on the bass, and vice versa.

4. Rapidity and ease of composition; a composer could turn out a complete movement in an hour or so.

5. Ease of circulation; this music could be quickly copied, easily published.

6. Chamber music as a little "theater," that entertained by imitating the grander forms—opera, church music, ballet—and included picturesque touches from the hunt, the military, the pastoral, as well as exotic touches from Spain, Africa, and the Orient.

Dance Music; Nowadays we think of dance music as being outside the mainstream of *the Suite* so-called "concert" and "theater" music, lesser in dignity and more frivolous in feeling. But in the Baroque era, dance music played a vital role. The dance itself was an important form of expression as well as the chief entertainment. When dancers moved through prescribed steps, in patterns of circles, squares, and triangles, they created a "geometry of motion," reflecting the sense of universal order that permeated the thought of these times. Gestures and body attitudes coupled strong hints of feeling with these symmetries of motion, and music reinforced both pattern and feeling, giving a strong lift to the entire experience. You can easily understand why Bach used the characteristic meters, rhythms, and symmetries of dance music in such profoundly moving music as the "Crucifixus" and the "Et Resurrexit"; for him, and for other composers of his time, dance patterns gave a stamp of feeling to a piece and helped to sustain the mood by the orderly arrangement of phrases and periods. In this way, dance patterns took a central place in the doctrine of the affections.

Dance music could be composed in two different ways: (1) it could be trimmed to the steps of the dance itself, with each section no more than eight, twelve, or sixteen measure in length (see *two-reprise* form below), or (2) it could be treated freely, using characteristic tempos and rhythms, but spun out in extended, often irregular phrases and periods. Bach often used this latter procedure; in the following pieces from his *Well-Tempered Clavier*, Book I, you can hear dance rhythms:

Fugue no. 2 in C minor: *bourrée*, a rather quick dance in duple time, with a short upbeat,

Prelude no. 3 in C sharp major: a *corrente* or *passepied*, quick dances in triple time, and

Fugue no. 3 in C sharp major: elements of *gavotte*, a moderately paced dance in duple time with a rhythmic pattern that moves across the bar line ; bourrée; and *polonaise*, a stately dance in triple time,

Fugue no. 15 in G major: *gigue,* a quick dance in triple time,

While dances were used as *topics* for all kinds of pieces, they were also composed separately and gathered into compositions called *suites.* *Masterpieces* no. 35 gives an early example of the standardized order of dances in the baroque suite. Each of these dances represents a different country—the *allemande* from Germany, the *courante* from France, the *sarabande* from Spain, and the *gigue* from England, a sign that dances conveyed local color as well as feeling and pattern.

Baroque dance music, whether for dancing or listening, was laid out in the traditional two-part form. (See pages 61, 84, and 98.) Since each part could be repeated or *reprised,* as AABB, the term *two-reprise* form is used here to designate this plan. From its modest beginnings in some medieval dances, through its growing application in Renaissance and baroque music, the *two-reprise form* eventually, in the later eighteenth century, came to be the master plan for organizing many different kinds of music. In Couperin's *La Galante, Masterpieces* no. 40, we hear a neat, small-scale two-reprise form. The first reprise modulates to the dominant key, representing the *open* part of the form; the second reprise modulates back to the tonic, representing the *closed* part of the form. Note that the beginning of each part uses the same melodic figure, as a kind of *opening rhyme,* while the close of each part also uses similar material, as a *closing rhyme.* These melodic restatements help to bind the form into a tightly knit design. Later, when we explore classic music, we shall see how the two-reprise plan could be expanded to great lengths.

Sonata Sonata means "sound piece," referring to instrumental rather than vocal music. In the Baroque era, the sonata became an important genre of chamber music. It might have as few as two, as many as five or six movements, contrasted in style and tempo. Some sonata movements are clearly borrowed from dance music, other movements might take up the prelude style, the fugue, or the aria. Sonatas, as well as suites, were written for solo instruments, with or without keyboard accompaniment, for small ensembles, and for solo keyboard. They could be performed in the church (*sonata da chiesa*) or as chamber music (*sonata da camera*). In Corelli's Sonata da Chiesa, *Masterpieces* no. 39, you sense an amalgamation of church and chamber styles so often found in baroque music. The first and third movements have the gravity of traditional church music, recalling the tightly bound, flowing style of the motet. The second movement is a sprightly fugue, recalling the style of the canzona, while the last movement brings us into the world of the dance, with its polonaise rhythm and its clearly shaped two-reprise form. In miniature, the last two movements of the

FIGURE 15. *François Boucher:* Dispatch of the Messenger. *A French rococo painting illustrating a wealth of ornamental detail. (Courtesy of the Metropolitan Museum of Art.)*

Corelli sonata embody the same affections as the "Crucifixus" and "Et Resurrexit."

Concerto We have already investigated the concerto style and form when the baroque sense of key was described (see above, pages 98–100). The concerto was a vehicle for *brilliant* instrumental performance in which one or more soloists "stepped out" from the orchestral ensemble to do a solo turn. This results in an interplay between a large group, the *tutti* and one or more *solo* instruments. (The term *concerto grosso* is used to

designate a composition with two or more soloists (the *concertino*
group), while the *solo concerto* features a single solo performer. In both
types, the orchestra is called the *ripieno* or *tutti*.)

The interplay between the orchestra and soloist promotes a vigorous, clean-cut style, an exuberant exercise featuring symmetrical arrangements of short, neatly turned figures. Example 5-12 shows the
bold angular shape typical of baroque concerto themes.

EXAMPLE 5-12. *Concerto themes. Bach:* Brandenburg *Concerto No. 2
in F major, first movement*

Handel: Concerto Grosso in D major

Handel: Concerto Grosso in F major

Bach: Concerto for Violin in E major

In the analysis on page 100 and in Example 5-6 you can see how a
concerto movement is shaped by keys. The tutti-solo arrangement
reinforces the laying out of sections in different keys; an arrival at a
new key can be highlighted by a change of texture from tutti to solo,
or vice versa.

The concerto is usually a three-movement piece. The first movement displays most typically the concertato and virtuoso aspects; the
second movement is frequently patterned after the slow arias of opera;
the last movement may take up again the manner of the first movement, or it may assume the style of a dance, such as a gigue or minuet
for example, ¾ ♩ ♫♫♩|♩ ♩ ♩. In the Baroque period, the con-
certo, more than any other type of composition, provided musicians
the opportunity to exercise themselves boldly and exuberantly, for the
sheer pleasure of making music together.

French
Overture;
Sinfonia

These two forms, originally orchestral introductions to theater or church music, eventually entered the world of chamber and concert music as opening pieces for an evening's musical entertainment. Each of these reflects the national style from which it came. The *French overture* was originally used as a grand introduction for the theater performances at Versailles and Paris during the reign of Louis XIV, 1643–1715. It opened with a stately march that accompanied the entry of the king and the performers into the theater. To enhance the air of ceremony, the march featured dotted rhythms, such as ♩♩♪ ♪ ♪.. ♪ which imitated the roll of drums. Next, a short fugue, followed by a set of dances, concluded the overture. To perform this music, the king provided for the support of a large orchestra, the finest in Europe, directed by Jean Baptiste Lully. *Masterpieces* no. 36, the overture to Lully's *tragédie lyrique, Armide,* illustrates the typically stately and elegant manner of this genre.

The *sinfonia,* from Italy, carried much less musical content than the French overture. It was an attention-getter to prepare audiences in public theaters for the opera to follow. Typically, it began in a brilliant, brisk manner, with fanfares, running figures, bold unisons for the orchestra, now and then a fragment of singing melody. A short aria-like second movement and a dancelike third movement, both generally brief, wound up the form in a perfunctory way unrelated to the mood of the drama to follow. One of the better examples of this genre is reprinted in *Treasury of Early Music,* no. 44, Alessandro Scarlatti's sinfonia to his opera *La Caduta de Decem Viri* (The fall of the ten leaders). You can hear busy figures identical to those of the concerto in the first movement, along with alternations of tutti and solo, all giving an air of general excitement; this is followed by a short middle movement recalling the severe church style; the sinfonia ends with a giguelike piece that gives the impression of being more a fragment than a full movement due to its brevity and lack of distinctive melodic profile. The Italian opera sinfonia was just an *hors d'oeuvre,* rather than a full musical course. From its undistinguished beginning in the later seventeenth century, the sinfonia grew in stature during the eighteenth century as important composers broadened its scope and deepened its expressive message. For a sampling of this genre on the way to its glory as the great classic symphony, you can listen to any one of Mozart's or Haydn's early symphonies or to those of the Mannheim School, which flourished in the mid-eighteenth century just after the time of Bach and Handel.

As we have dealt with baroque music, it has become clear that it could be grouped according to *degrees of dignity* and *national styles,* as well as into church, theater, and chamber music. Degrees of dignity reflected the social order in western Europe at this time, that is, the higher classes (which included great church dignitaries, royalty, and the princely aristocracy), the middle classes (the lower nobility, the trades and professions, and the middle-rank churchmen), and the lower classes (the peasants, workers, farmers, and village churchmen). Church music of gravity, ceremonial music, and operatic music that depicted high, noble passions belonged to the high style; pleasant, entertaining music, inviting a relaxation of protocol, was typical of the middle style; popular songs and pastoral pieces signified the low style. Any well-informed listener would recognize these styles and take them as cues for the affective qualities in the music. The listener would also know which national styles were being used. The ingratiating melodies of the Italian style, with their frequent repetitions of figures and their light texture; the elegant and highly ornamented dances of France; and the complex, somewhat irregular musical language of Germany—these were all known and discussed widely in critical writings of the time.

Before we move on to classic music, a word should be said about baroque instruments and their qualities of sound. The early eighteenth century was a crossover time; older instruments—recorders, viols, harpsichords and clavichords, lutes, etc.—were still much in use, while the newer instruments—the violin family, flutes, oboes, piano, etc.—were also used and coming into greater prominence. Generally speaking, most of the older instruments and the early versions of the types had a softer, less brilliant tone quality than we are accustomed to today. When, for example, you hear a brilliant piece such as the first movement of Bach's *Brandenburg* Concerto No. 2, it is worth knowing that in Bach's time the *tutti* was performed probably by a small orchestra of strings whose tone was darker and softer than those we hear today, and the *solos* were performed by the light-sounding recorder and trumpet, while the oboe at that time had a fuller, broader tone than today's instrument.

We have referred to the sense of order that pervaded music of the Baroque, especially in the later years of this era. If the Renaissance represented human beings' discovery of themselves and the world around them, the seventeenth and eighteenth centuries represented their efforts to put this new-found data into some order, to discover the systems by which both the material and spiritual worlds were organized. This was reflected in the codes and classifications that governed musical technique and expression—the doctrine of the affections; the sense of key; period structure; systematic treatment of motives; imitation and variation; church, theater, and chamber music; high, middle, low styles; Italian, French, and German styles. All this built a monumental musical system that celebrated the great order of things.

Around the middle of the eighteenth century another view began to make itself felt strongly. This was the idea of the *individual,* of the human self—a person's nature, hopes, human rights. Individuals were not simply a part of the scheme of things, accepting their lot; they had the power to shape their own destiny, whatever their station. In philosophy, this view was signaled by Jean-Jacques Rousseau's concept of the "noble savage," embodying the essential virtues of primitive humankind; in politics, the French and American Revolutions challenged traditional authority; in religion, the Masonic order focused upon the virtues of individuals, rather than their station by birth; in science and technology, new discoveries and inventions wiped out old ideas and routines.

In music, the great system of the Baroque began to break up as sentimentality and comedy came more to the fore. You have heard the short melodic fragments, often highly contrasted, the frequent cadences and cesuras, and the easily grasped symmetries that characterize this trend in Pergolesi's *"Io conosco."* The Italian style, imitated by composers of many nations, was the model for this change in expressive attitude, one that found great success among an increasingly larger audience. Eventually, the disintegration of the baroque style, while retaining much of the basic language of that era, opened the way to a new reformation of musical structure, achieved in the *classic* style of the late eighteenth century.

SUMMARY
1. *Sound:* In ensemble music, well-defined levels maintained; in solo music, fairly wide range covering several levels; transparency of sound; retention of one color value; contrast achieved by concertato procedures and by tutti-solo alternations.
2. *Movement; meter and rhythm:* Steady, purposeful, energetic, regular, except in fantasias and recitatives; one quality for a movement or principal section; characteristic rhythmic patterns of dances often used; well-defined duple and triple meters; organization of statement and counterstatement in groups of two; in dance music, clear symmetry of phrases; occasional mixtures of meter between duple and triple, as in the courante.
3. *Arrival:* Clear, often emphatic, strongly directed, rather frequent, but often overridden.
4. *Melody:* Sharply defined motives, treated systematically to form broad melodic arches; motives often arranged sequentially; much use of variation; irregular, declamatory style in recitative.
5. *Texture:* Bass-treble layout; strong sense of polyphonic action, due to active part writing; much use of imitation.
6. *Harmony:* Strong sense of key; circular or "solar" arrangement of degrees within a key, supported by cadences and sequential action; very strong cadential action at the end of major sections; explora-

tory harmony in recitatives with considerable chromaticism; some chromaticism to enrich the key feeling.

7. *Structure:* Fugue, concerto, two-reprise forms, da capo forms, French overture, variation; form expressed through departure from and return to home key; tendency to alternate slow and fast movements; combinations of forms, idioms, types.

8. *Expression:* Doctrine of the affections, establishing a style or manner for each piece, which was then carried out at length; strong characterization of expressive qualities; some pictorialism.

9. *Performance:* In theater, church, and chamber.

*DISCUSSION
AND
REVIEW
QUESTIONS*

1. What changes in musical style took place around 1600?
2. How does baroque music deal with musical expression?
3. How does the sense of key affect musical form in the late Baroque period?
4. How does baroque music use imitation?
5. How does baroque music use variation procedures?
6. What is a cantata?
7. Describe briefly the various kinds of theater music in the Baroque era.
8. Discuss the influence of the dance upon baroque music.
9. Describe briefly some of the principal instrumental forms of the Baroque era.
10. How does baroque music reflect the spirit of its age?

CHAPTER SIX

CLASSIC MUSIC

Today's listener needs no introduction to classic music. Haydn, Mozart, and Beethoven are familiar concert names. Mozart is a best-seller in recordings of classic music. Almost everyone who has played an instrument has had some experience with classic music, from simple minuets to the great concertos and symphonies of the classic masters. Even those whose taste runs to mid-twentieth-century popular music can sense an affinity with classic music, since many of the basic patterns of jazz, rock, and country music stem from dances and songs of this period.

In the time of Haydn and Mozart, more people played and sang music than ever before. This was especially true of the middle classes—businessmen, artisans, civil workers and their families. For them, composers provided easy music—tuneful pieces with light textures, few if any difficult passages, short sections—for entertainment and instruction. At the same time, the grand styles of the symphony, opera, and concerto were being evolved.

The familiar first movement of Mozart's *Jupiter* Symphony is an impressive example of the scope of the grand classic style; in many respects this music is different from any that we have heard thus far. We note a greater brilliance and fullness of sound; a tremendous variety of texture and color; many sharp contrasts of style and dynamics. The marchlike pace builds up into long phases of movement projected on a grand scale; the points of arrival are emphatic and act as long-range harmonic goals, indeed, as areas of arrival following intense action. The shift from one expressive value to another is striking, often surprising. Marches and flourishes, a song, a dance, vigorous contrapuntal wrestlings, and grand climaxes—all find their place within the framework of this piece, a piece that impresses us also by its imposing length. Throughout we sense undercurrents of dramatic force, ready to explode at any time. With all this variety and richness of content, we are constantly aware that the form, long as it is, remains entirely under control, that it seems to pursue its ends with clarity, breadth, and force.

Some of the qualities of classic music represented in this piece by Mozart are:

1. The sound tends to be transparent, even thin, and is set at a rather high level, as a rule. The bass does not have the heaviness of the baroque continuo.
2. Movement is much more regular, more symmetrical than in baroque music. The effect is often that of a clockwork (which eighteenth-century society dearly loved in many forms). The bass does not move as heavily and purposefully as in baroque music. It serves very often to punctuate the music, at points where the symmetry has to be reinforced, i.e., on the strong parts of measures or phrases. Otherwise, it rests, to allow the upper voices freer play of figure and motive.
3. Arrival can be anticipated more easily and is sensed more clearly than in music of preceding eras. Furthermore, the effects of arrival seem to be arranged in a sort of rank, to reinforce the impression of symmetry.
4. Further, you may notice that the texture changes every few moments, sometimes with great contrast; associated with such changes is a diversity of rhythmic patterns in the figures and motives. This is a drastic shift from the baroque system of maintaining a single idea, or affection, throughout a movement.

As you listen to this piece, you can well imagine some kind of dramatic action taking place as moods develop, change, and contrast with each other. We feel a strong flavor of theater here, as in most classic music. Today we recognize changes of mood and conflict-resolution patterns, but eighteenth-century listeners very likely heard much more; they would recognize specific types and styles which they could associate with various affections or picturesque scenes drawn from drama, dance, and ceremony. For today's listeners, a familiarity with these styles and types, these *topics,* can illuminate a view of classic music, enlivening the satisfaction that the scintillating patterns in sound themselves afford.

We have already mentioned topics in discussing baroque music. Dance rhythms were used to suggest various kinds of feeling. (See pages 96–97 and 113–114.) Many a baroque piece begins with a typical dance rhythm and maintains the specific dance style throughout. Classic music dealt differently with its topics. A piece would begin with a dance rhythm or some other characteristic topic, but very soon it would introduce another topic and continue this variegated sequence of contrasted material through the entire movement; as many as fifteen or twenty musical ideas might be presented, dropped, and later recalled. Some of these would be broadly stated themes, others could just be hints lasting a measure or two. The alert listener, then as now, could relish this panoramic line of musical action and the associations—or affects—it suggested.

Topics in classic music covered a wide range, from the serious church style to the most frivolous party dances. The list given below describes those more frequently used.

TOPICS Most of the following have been described in Chapter 5.

DANCES
1. The *minuet,* a rather quick dance in triple time
2. The *sarabande,* a slow dance in triple time
3. The *polonaise,* a moderately quick dance in triple time
4. The *gigue,* a quick dance in triple time
5. The *gavotte,* a moderately slow dance in duple time
6. The *bourrée,* a rather quick dance in duple time
7. The *contredanse,* a dance in duple time
8. The *siciliano,* a rather slow dance in triple time, often used for pastoral effects: $\frac{6}{8}$

Dances from various countries were also used to lend a bit of exotic color—the *fandango* from Spain, the *mazurka,* from Poland, the *tarantella* from Italy, the *Swabian allemande* from Germany, the *schottische* from Scotland.

CAVALIER MUSIC Marching music and fanfare signals were heard everywhere in eighteenth-century Europe, in ceremonies, in battle, and in the hunt. The first movements of sonatas, symphonies, or concertos often imitated these effects associated with aristocratic cavalier life. The march is easily recognized by its quick duple time, often made crisper by dotted rhythms. c . Fanfares, like our bugle calls, build figures from the notes of the major triad, while the hunt signal in various lively rhythms imitates a pair of horns in this well-known pattern:

CHARACTER-   Apart from dances and cavalier music, you can hear many characteris-
ISTIC STYLES tic styles move in and out of the action in a classic piece of broad
              scope. Some of these represent a way of dealing with material; others
              are quite clearly picturesque, referring to some special scene or situa-
              tion.

The Brilliant   This is a legacy from baroque music, affording virtuosos the chance to
Style   display their technique in rapid passages of running notes, scales, and
              arpeggios. (See page 104.)

The Singing   A songlike style with relatively slow melody notes, often accompanied
Style   by patterns of quicker notes. (See Example 6-14.)

The French   (See page 117.)
Overture
Style

Turkish Music   This is an exotic style in quick march time; it imitates the Turkish
              military bands that were part of the retinue of Turkish emissaries to
              European countries. The triangle, cymbal, timpani, and piccolo were
              featured.

Bagpipe and   In this style the bass holds a tone as a *drone*, while the melody is set
Musette   in a simple dance or song manner.
Effects

EXAMPLE 6-1. *Musette: Haydn, Symphony No. 104 in D major,*
finale

The Sensibility   While intimate personal expression was already present in some songs
Style   and arias of baroque music, this attitude took a very important place in
              music of the later eighteenth century. It was cultivated expecially in
              Germany and has been given the name *Empfindsamer* style, meaning
              "sensibility." The leading composer in this trend was Carl Philipp
              Emanuel Bach, the eldest son of Johann Sebastian. Mozart, Haydn,

and Beethoven often spoke in this vein, which had rapid changes in mood and feeling, often unexpected, but almost always melancholy or searching in its effect. Example 6-2 illustrates the "sensibility" style. You hear first a plaintive fragment of melody, interrupted by an impulsive exclamation, then a suspenseful pause followed new melodic fragments suggesting sighs or spasmodic breathing—all these giving the impression of a troubled personal experience.

EXAMPLE 6-2. *Mozart: Fantasia in D minor, K. 397*

Storm and Stress Style The term *Storm and Stress* has been borrowed from literature, from a play by Klinger, *Sturm und Drang*, 1776. It is a very apt description for an agitated, often dissonant and chromatic manner we hear frequently as a contrast to gentler moods within a classic piece. (See page 128.)

Fantasia The fantasia style is very closely related to both the Sensibility and the Storm and Stress. Its chief feature is its break with regularity of process; this could be an abrupt change of mood, unstable harmony, spinning-out of arpeggio figures, irregular rhythms. Example 6-2 above is taken from a fantasia by Mozart; its Sensibility style fits in well with the spirit of the fantasia.

Learned Style This style represents the strongest bond with tradition. It features imitation and free counterpoint, and has a strong link with church music. The *learned* style, also called the *strict* style, stood in opposition to all the other styles described above, which were included in the category called *galant,* a term which referred to music written for the elegant world of the high-born classes. Example 6-3 shows how learned and galant styles could be coordinated in classic music; we hear an alternation of singing style with short passages in closely spaced imitation. Apart from the neatly joined contrasts, you can sense a broad rhythmic action as the two styles alternate.

EXAMPLE 6-3. *Mozart: Quartet in C major, K. 465, finale*

Curiously, in classic music, we often hear a remnant of the traditional motet style—a melody in long notes, proceeding in an even rhythm, as 𝄵 𝅝 | 𝅝 . This was called the *alla breve* style (the *breve* was a long note in eighteenth-century terminology) and, like the learned style, was associated with church music. Alla breve style can be heard at the beginning of the last movement of Mozart's *Jupiter* Symphony; a bit further into the movement the alla breve joins with imitation to recall for the listener, for a short time, the rules and rigors of the past, without, however, burdening the patience with a lengthy contrapuntal discourse.

The most explicit use of topics occurs in vocal music, as in many of the movements of Haydn's oratorios *The Creation* and *The Seasons,* where the titles or the text provide definite clues to the expressive or pictorial subject being treated. In instrumental music, the connection is somewhat looser but still apparent to the knowledgeable listener. Once in a while the imagery is so vivid that some kind of story might be read into the music without violating the spirit of eighteenth-century musical aesthetics. For example, we might read the following allusions into these sections of Haydn's Symphony No. 103 in E♭ major (*Drumroll*):

1. The entire piece has a military flavor, owing to the fanfares of brass and winds heard in each movement.
2. The military mood is set at the very beginning by a roll on the timpani, which was, for the eighteenth century, a regimental instrument.

3. Following the roll on the timpani, the lower instruments play a melody in unison, composed in the manner of a plainsong, punctuated as if with "amens" at each cadence; this melody is repeated by the violins, with a counterpoint added, in the manner of organum (a prayer before the battle?).

4. The actual battle might be visualized in the second movement. Everyone in Europe knew of the battle of Vienna in 1683, when the Turks were repulsed at the gates of the city and the Ottoman advance into Europe was finally halted. One theme serves both parties, Turks and Viennese. The minor version, with its augmented second, is Oriental in flavor, while the major version, with its hint of fanfare, speaks for the imperial Austrian forces. These versions alternate, in the course of which the Turkish champion, represented by the oboe, and the Austrian hero, the *Konzertmeister* violin, have opportunities to declare themselves. A melée follows—the battle itself—signaled by drum tattoos. At the end, the Viennese prevail, since it is their music which we hear last and in C major.

5. The finale is a symphony of victory, a *chasse* (hunt), with fanfares ringing throughout the movement.

Returning now to the first movement of Mozart's *Jupiter*, we can note the following topics in the first half of the movement:

1. March, measures 1–2 and from time to time later
2. Singing style, measures 3–4
3. Learned style, measure 24 *et seq.*
4. Fantasia, measures 30–34
5. Singing style, measure 56 *et seq.*
6. Storm and Stress, measure 81 *et seq.*
7. Gavotte, measure 101 *et seq.*
8. Brilliant style, measure 111 *et seq.*

FORM As you took note of the topics described above, you might well have sensed that the melodic figures which embodied them were laid out in a clearly ordered balanced way, with a symmetrical pairing of statements and counterstatements. This was true no matter how many different topics appeared or how they were similar or contrasted to each other. In fact, the contrasts, since they highlighted each other, promoted the clarity and symmetry of design. In short, classic musical action is organized to promote a clear sense of symmetry; this is done by arranging motives, phrases, and periods so that they complement each other by repetition, variation, or contrast. Compare, for example, the neat back-and-forth of the singing and the learned styles in Example 6-3 with the complex and intricate layout of figures in Example 5-5, illustrating one important difference between the baroque sense of order and that of classic music.

Classic symmetry of form is sensed most clearly in short pieces. For this reason, we turn again to dance music. In addition to furnishing many topics for larger works, dance music provided a basic structural plan for classic form, a sort of genetic code. This was the *two-reprise* plan, a layout with which we have already become familiar in medieval, Renaissance, and baroque music. (See pages 61, 84, 114.) This plan could be trimmed to the briefest, totally symmetrical layouts, as we have seen in *Masterpieces* nos. 12, 22, 29, and 40; it could also be expanded to encompass a movement of the broadest dimensions.

TWO-REPRISE FORM   Examples 6-4 and 6-5 illustrate the short two-reprise form in classic music, closely modeled on dance music. Example 6-4 is totally symmetrical; it has two reprises, each eight measures in length. Note especially that both reprises end solidly in the home key, and that, except for a slight wavering at the beginning of reprise II, the harmony stays in the home key. On the other hand, Example 6-5 makes a decided shift to the dominant at the end of reprise I, and makes its way back home in reprise II, taking four extra measures to do so. Absolute symmetry is *disturbed,* by the change of key; the unfinished harmonic business of reprise I is wrapped up in reprise II, and we have something of a little adventure as the modulations unfold.

EXAMPLE 6-4. *Mozart: Menuetto from* Eine kleine Nachtmusik

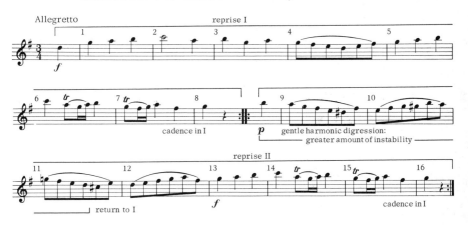

EXAMPLE 6-5. *Haydn: Rondo from Sonata for Clavier in D major*

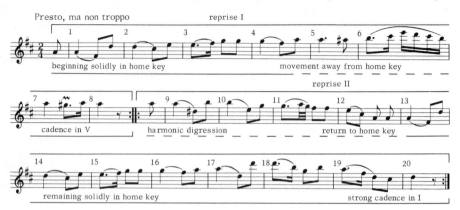

Example 6-6 diagrams the harmonic layout of the two-reprise form; as you listen to the Haydn rondo, pay particular attention to the cadences that end each reprise, since these progressions are critical in shaping the form. The plan that *modulates,* with the key scheme I-V; X-I, is by far the more important in classic music.

EXAMPLE 6-6. *Harmonic plan of two-reprise form*

REPRISE I		REPRISE II	
If the piece is in the major key	I . . . . . . V I	X . . . . . . I X	
If the piece is in the minor key	I III	X I	
Presentation of tonic key	Contrast key: strong cadence	Harmonic digressions	Return to tonic: final cadence

One of the most interesting aspects of two-reprise forms is that in most of them the melodic plan has a somewhat *different* arrangement than the harmonic. In both Examples 6-4 and 6-5, you may have noticed that the melody had a *three-part* layout, that is, ABA; the opening melody, A, returned when the home key was reached again, while somewhat different material, B, began the second reprise. Example 6-7 shows the relationship between the harmonic and melodic levels of the two-reprise form; of these, the harmonic plan is the more basic. (See also page 98.)

EXAMPLE 6-7. *Harmonic and melodic levels of two-reprise form*

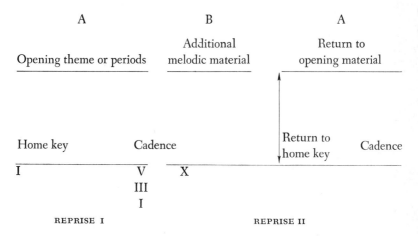

The third movement of Mozart's *Jupiter,* the Menuetto, uses the two-reprise form. First we hear a somewhat stretched-out version of the form (see the following section for a discussion of extensions of form), then a compact version, the Trio, followed by a return (da capo) to the first section. The resulting layout is a *three-part* form— minuet-trio-minuet or ABA, a standard arrangement for dance movements in symphonies, quartets, etc.

As you may imagine, it was not difficult to turn out a routine piece in two-reprise form. Literally hundreds of thousands of such pieces appeared during the later eighteenth century. This was the bread-and-butter music upon which Haydn and Mozart and all the other composers of the time were nourished and raised. Dilettantes and amateurs also tried their hands at writing little dances and minuets. They were taught to compose these pieces along with their lessons at the keyboard. Among the teaching manuals we find such titles as *The Ever-ready Minuet and Polonaise Composer* by Johann Philipp Kirnberger and the *Philharmonic Game* attributed to Haydn. These books provided simple melodic fragments; by throwing dice, the rankest amateur could put together a minuet from certain of these fragments. Serious instruction in musical composition in the eighteenth century also made use of the two-reprise form as a framework within which the virtually limitless combinations, permutations, and arrangements of musical materials could be explored.

FIGURE 16. *Frontispiece of a musical dice game published in Paris around 1790. The publisher's catalog ascribes the authorship to Abbé Maximilian Stadler, friend of Haydn and Mozart. Other such games were supposed to have been composed by Haydn and Mozart themselves. (From a private collection.)*

LARGER
FORMS
The Expanded
Two-reprise
Form

We take delight in the exquisitely turned small forms of classic music, as those of Examples 6-4 and 6-5. We also are deeply impressed and moved by the grander works, with their broad sweep. Formally, the miniature and the monumental would seem worlds apart, yet they both belong to the same family of forms, the two-reprise. Example 6-8 shows how both the small and large versions of the form have the same basic shape; the form is pictured as a bridge in the harmonic sense. Terra firma is represented on both ends by the solid sense of the home key. In the small form, only three pillars are needed; in the large version, additional pillars—strong cadences—are added to provide support for the greater span.

EXAMPLE 6-8. *Diagram of small and large two-reprise plans*

a. Small two-reprise (about 1 minute)

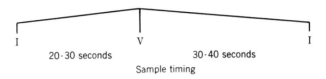

b. Large two-reprise (about 12 minutes)

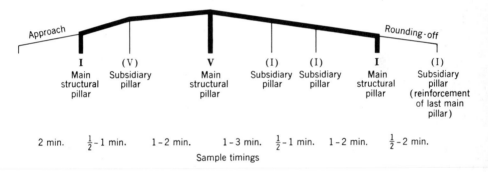

Extended Periods The greater breadth of the larger form comes about in two ways:

1. Each reprise is built with a *group* of periods, rather than a single period.
2. Most of the periods in the larger forms are *expanded* in length.

In the larger forms, you hear many different kinds of melodic material—various topics arranged in motives, phrases, or full periods. Later (Example 6-19), we shall see how this rich, often bewildering melodic content can be sorted out and put into some clear order. But at first, to grasp the unbroken chain of action in a large-scale classic movement, the surest way is to listen for the cadences at the ends of periods and for the powerful effect of harmonic arrival at the points indicated by the *heavy* pillars in Example 6-8*b*; as you listen for these cadences, you link in with the strong goal-directed action that underlies all classic music.

To intensify this goal-directed action, classic music often extends its periods, to create stronger expectations for the delayed cadence and greater satisfaction and fulfillment when the cadences arrive. Examples 6-9 and 6-10 illustrate two ways of extending a period. Example 6-9 interrupts the flow of the singing style just at the cadence point; a *deceptive* cadence breaks in, with a startling change of style to the Storm and Stress. As the new energy introduced plays itself out, we are carried forward to the cadence, eighteen measures later, and it arrives with a grateful return to a simple and beautiful singing melody. In Example 6-10, the harmony *digresses* at the fifth measure, goes "off the track"; circling back, it gathers energy, rides past what would be the normal cadence point of the period, and explodes into a brilliant, rocketlike flight that "zeroes" triumphantly into its cadence. The period has exactly doubled its length, but it has more than doubled its dramatic effect.

EXAMPLE 6-9. *Extended period by deceptive cadence: Beethoven, Violin Concerto in D major, Op. 61, first movement*

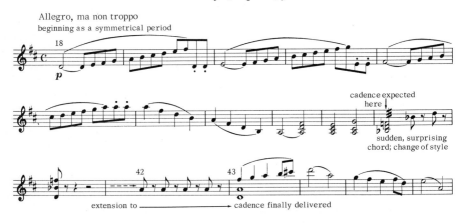

EXAMPLE 6-10. *Extended period by internal harmonic digression: Mozart, Quintet in E♭ major, K. 614, first movement*

Periods can be extended in many ways; Examples 6-9 and 6-10 show two of the most dramatic methods. Additional phrases can be incorporated, the action can run past a cadence point, and cadences themselves can be reinforced by repetition. Returning once again to the first movement of Mozart's *Jupiter* Symphony, you can hear clear cadences at measures 23, 55, 71, 89, 101, 111, and 120 (a score will be helpful here); yet *all* these cadences are somewhat less than conclusive, *except* the last, which "locks up" the harmonic action in this great first reprise. In this sense, the entire first reprise is one gigantic super-period, built of seven extended periods that are skillfully linked together by leaving something unsaid at each cadence point.

Moving along the harmonic path of the two-reprise form, large or small, you can easily grasp how important and basic the sense of key is for classic music. No other style in the history of music makes as clear and emphatic a point of setting forth the key as classic music. The entire cycle of a classic form, large or small, involves presenting a key, departing from it, and returning to end the piece with conviction in the home key, as in the plan I-V, X-I. Thus a sense of key in classic music is very much like the sense of spatial or geographic orientation in the physical world. Home, the *tonic key,* is the point of *departure* and *arrival.*

PLAN OF
MOVEMENTS
IN A CLASSIC
WORK

Classic symphonies, concertos, quartets, sonatas, and other works of comparable size are made up of three or four movements; each of these can be traced to a type of slow or fast movement of a baroque concerto, sinfonia, sonata, overture, or suite. The *Jupiter* Symphony represents the typical layout of movements—fast, slow, dance, fast. Following is a description of a typical three- or four-movement work:

1. The opening movement was serious, broad, brilliant, and searching; it brought all the skills and imagination of the composer into play. Often its basic pace was that of a march; sometimes it assumed the

manner of the eighteenth-century concerto grosso, or a dance, or the singing-allegro. The first movement of the *Jupiter* represents the first movement of the eighteenth-century symphony in the grandest manner.

2. The slow movement appealed to lyric sentiments. Here composers sought for broadly singing, well-rounded, winning melodies. The style was generally that of a song or aria, but occasionally it was a slow dance or march. These movements gained breadth by their slow pace and expansive lyricism, rather than by extensive and searching development. The slow movement of the *Jupiter* Symphony takes up the sarabande as its principal topic, contrasting it later with the singing style and the Storm and Stress.

3. In four-movement cycles, one of the middle movements was generally a dance, a minuet or scherzo. Mozart and Haydn preferred the minuet, as in the *Jupiter* Symphony, but Beethoven quickened the pace to establish the scherzo as the dance movement. We observe, in spite of the dance style and form, much play with motives and part writing, many surprises, contrasts, and unexpected turns of phrase in most of the minuets and scherzos of classic music.

4. As a rule, the last movement was a quick dance, often in hunt style. At other times it matched the first movement in brilliance and scope, particularly in the *Jupiter* Symphony. The last movement often achieved a pitch of excitement toward the very end unequaled by anything previously heard in the entire work. This, of course, was intended as a fitting climax and windup to the whole composition, as at the end of Beethoven's Symphony No. 5.

In compositions intended primarily for purposes of entertainment, such as serenades, divertimenti, and cassations, there was likely to be a greater number of movements. These would be additional minuets, dances, or slow movements. The order of movements given above represents the usual plan; nevertheless, the arrangement is by no means fixed, and many pieces show a different order. In all cases, slow movements were placed to provide a strategic contrast in style and pace with neighboring quick movements. A work might begin with a slow movement, but it would rarely end with one.

The forms, that is, the plans for keys, sections, themes for movements of a classic work, included the *sonata form,* the *rondo,* and the *variation* as the principal types. Of these, the sonata form, as the most extensive embodiment of the I–V; X–I plan, ranked first in importance and in frequency of use. Most first movements and many slow movements and finales use the extended I–V; X–I plan, the sonata form.

SONATA FORM
Sonata form is the broadest embodiment of the two-reprise plan. As you listened to the first movement of the *Jupiter* Symphony, a very broadly scaled version of sonata form, it was clear that the two keys of the first reprise, the I and the V, each occupied a considerable space of time. These sections are designated here as *key areas.*

The following outline lists the important events in the first movement of the *Jupiter* Symphony according to *key areas* and *thematic relationships:*

REPRISE I
Exposition, I–V, *measures 1–120*

Home key area, measures 1–23. The opening theme, with its contrasted march and singing figures, dominates the movement, returning a number of times in varied form as well as being restated at the beginning of the recapitulation.

Shift to second key, measures 24–55. This is a broadly scaled shift, again using the opening theme. Note the impressive preparation for the new melodic idea at measure 56.

Second key area, measures 56–120. A new singing theme (Example 6-11) quickly takes on a dance style, then is interrupted by a powerful Storm and Stress episode, and again we hear a powerful thrust using a figure from the opening theme; this prepares for a new theme that helps wind up the exposition, measure 101. This new tune, a delightful little gavotte melody, Example 6-12, is followed by a brilliant set of flourishes that finally provides an emphatic close.

EXAMPLE 6-11. *Beginning of second key area*

EXAMPLE 6-12. *Closing theme*

Before we move on to the second part of the movement, comprising the development and recapitulation, we should clarify the differences in the view of sonata form given here and the view presented in

many textbooks and dictionaries of music. Sonata form is often described as an order of *themes*—a first theme, generally vigorous in
character, and a second theme, generally singing in style, these two
themes being the organizing features of the exposition; in the development these themes are worked over in various ways, and in the
recapitulation they are again restated. Surrounding the first and second
themes, transitional and accessory material fills out the form. If we
look principally at thematic order, we can see that it applies to many
sonata form movements, but *not* to *all* of them. The harmonic plan is
the more fundamental one; various thematic plans can be superimposed on it, and it is valid and applicable to all. (See page 131 for
diagrams that show the interaction of the harmonic and thematic
layouts.)

REPRISE II; X-I

Development, measures 121-188; *Recapitulation, measures* 189-313

In the exposition, the harmony has led *away* from the home key,
to *settle* on the dominant; we also heard all the melodic material of the
movement laid out in a specific order. In reprise II, the harmonic
direction is *reversed;* the harmony makes its way *back* to the home key,
using melodic material from the exposition in a free way throughout
the development section; the final section, the *recapitulation,* settles
solidly in the home key, using the melodic material of the exposition
in very much its original order.

Mozart, in our example, throws us off balance immediately at the
beginning of the development. Starting on the tone, G, that ended the
exposition, he engages in a bit of harmonic prestidigitation that lands
us, in *four* tones, in a faraway key, measure 123. Blithely, then, the
little tune which closed the exposition takes up again as if all were
calm and placid. Yet, this cheerful latecomer is destined for great
things. Hardly has it come to a cadence when it breaks apart and
begins to struggle with itself in a tight contrapuntal duel that goes on
for many measures and runs through many keys, measures 131-160.
When the air clears, we hear the opening theme, measure 160, but *this
is not the right key!* We are not yet home. Quickly the struggle resumes,
the harmonic wanderings begin again, while the opening motive is
whipped around mercilessly. Finally, there comes a sense of leveling
off; we are being made ready to hear the advent of the home key, and
with a grand gesture it arrives with the opening theme.

The recapitulation closes off the form—thematically, by restating
the melodic material of the exposition, and harmonically, by remaining in the home key. Very often, the composer juggles the melodic
material to offer something of added interest to the alert listener. If
you compare measures 23-36 of the exposition with measures 212-

224 of the recapitulation, you can hear that Mozart, using the same material, has changed the harmony to *minor* to give a more colorful quality to the restatement. To "nail down" the effect of final arrival in the home key, the material originally heard in the *dominant* is now presented in the *tonic.* We can think of the sonata form, both harmonically and melodically, as being one immense musical *rhyme,* in which the melodic material of the recapitulation rhymes with that of the exposition, but has a different harmonic meaning. The following diagram illustrates:

MEANING		SOUND	
Key Area I tonic		A	thematic material
Key Area II dominant		B	thematic material
(III in minor)			
X			
Key Area I tonic		A	thematic material
Adjusted Key Area II tonic		B	thematic material

THE CODA The *coda* is an optional cadential section or area of arrival for the entire movement, reinforcing the cadences at the end of the recapitulation. Sometimes the coda is short; Mozart adds just four measures of fanfare to end this movement with a flourish. At other times the coda may digress harmonically before it drives home the tonic, increasing the expectation for the final arrival. While Mozart and Haydn often add codas, Beethoven almost always does, as a consequence of the tremendous thrust in his music. Checking back to Example 6-8*b*, the rounding-off pictured there represents the coda.

INTRODUC- The first movement of a large classic work sometimes has an intro-
TION duction in slow tempo, which may be modeled upon the French overture (page 117) or upon the first movement of the sonata da chiesa of the Baroque era. One of the most impressive introductions in classic music opens Mozart's *Prague* Symphony. It is an orchestral fantasia in two sharply contrasted sections. First you hear figures drawn from the French overture, interrupted by an extended passage in the Sensibility style, with broken figures, deceptive cadences, and a searching, tentative manner. Then, with a deceptive cadence to the minor mode, the second part moves purposefully and regularly through a range of keys; this section has a strong coloring of the supernatural element, pulsating figures, alternations of loud and soft, and a general mood of apprehension; it prepares, at considerable length, the beginning of the vivacious allegro in the major key.

RONDO The chief purpose of the rondo was to entertain the listener. Therefore, pieces in rondo form were made up of a number of attractive
tunes in dance or song style. This pleasing array of melodies was
arranged so that a principal tune, called a *refrain*, heard at first, would
then be alternated with other tunes, called *episodes*. Example 6-5 is the
refrain of a rondo which has two episodes, neatly contrasted with the
refrain in an A B A C A pattern; each of the sections of this rondo is
laid out as a small two-reprise form.

   When a rondo ended a large-scale work—a symphony, concerto,
or quartet—it took on some of the characteristics of sonata form.
Periods were often extended, and some development of material could
take place. One of the most remarkable rondos in classic music forms
the finale of Haydn's Symphony No. 103 in E♭ major. Virtually all of
its melodic material is derived from two melodic ideas heard at the
beginning—a hunting horn figure and a contredanse tune, which make
good counterpoint with each other. As you listen to this movement,
take note of the way in which Haydn, with his incredible wit and
ingenuity, puts these two figures into different situations—delicately
galant, triumphant, furiously contrapuntal, now and then a touch of
the pathetic—and arranges them into various phrase patterns. Example
6-13 quotes the two figures and shows how the rondo plan is laid out
by keys:

EXAMPLE 6-13. *Haydn: Symphony No. 103 in E♭ major, finale*

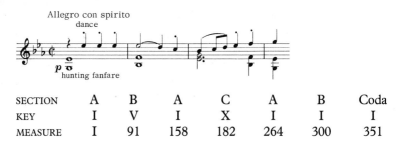

SECTION	A	B	A	C	A	B	Coda
KEY	I	V	I	X	I	I	I
MEASURE	I	91	158	182	264	300	351

VARIATION A set of variations, like the rondo, was an entertainment piece. A
tuneful melody, often in small two-reprise form, provided the framework for a series of short pieces that formed intriguing tableaux with
various kinds of ornamentation or changes of mood.

   Many of us are familiar with the variation set in the first movement of Mozart's Sonata in A major, K. 331. The theme is a graceful
siciliano melody; among the variations we find an elaboration of the
melody and its transformation into a pathetic air, a fanfare, an elaborate slow aria, and a sprightly minuet.

While the variation in Haydn's and Mozart's time was intended for "easy" listening, Beethoven used the form to build works of great scope and power (see page 159).

GENRES During the later eighteenth century a decided swing to the modern concert began to develop; instead of private musicales arranged by wealthy patrons for guests of high station, public concerts were staged in increasing numbers for all who had the price of admission. This shift reflected changes in the social order as well as some remarkable improvements and changes in musical instruments. With development of commerce, thanks largely to the Industrial Revolution, common-born businessmen became wealthy and could afford some of the graces formerly reserved for the aristocracy, among them the cultivation of music. The improvements in string, wind, and brass instruments, and the emergence of the piano as the principal keyboard instrument, were all directed to the production of more brilliant, richer, fuller, and sometimes louder tone than that of baroque instruments. Putting the two together—a larger, perhaps less cultivated audience plus a much louder, fuller, and varied range of sound—a new kind of musical performance arrived, namely the *public concert* in a hall of some considerable size.

Much of the music performed in these concerts has fallen into oblivion; most of it was shallow—*musical descriptions* of battles, hunts, tours, etc., with no more musical content than simple imitation of various effects, or *brilliant acrobatics* to show off the technical skill of the performer, or *routine versions of standard forms,* such as concertos, arias, symphonies. Other works, those of the great classic masters, Haydn, Mozart, and Beethoven, as well as a few from their contemporaries, have survived to become a substantial part of our present-day listening.

THE The classic orchestra was the first to use instruments in the modern ORCHESTRA way—strings as the core, winds and brass as reinforcement, but with considerable exploitation of their individual colors. Generally speaking, the classic orchestra had a light, rather high sound, with violins and principal winds carrying the principal melody. You will hear a great deal of alternation between solo and tutti scoring. The first movement of Mozart's *Jupiter* Symphony exemplifies the fully evolved classic orchestral style, with commanding tutti effects and graceful solo passages for winds and strings. The degree of contrast in effects is much greater than in baroque orchestral music; this reflects the greater range and contrast of topics in a classic movement.

THE
CONCERTO

The classic concerto, along with the symphony, represented the most impressive type of instrumental music in the late eighteenth century. Carrying on the tradition of baroque music (see page 115) the solo or concertino element might be drawn from the orchestra itself. Concertos were written for clarinet, flute, horn, bassoon, cello, oboe, trumpet, and harp. But as classic music expanded its techniques and intensified its expressive qualities, the more brilliant, the more impressive instruments—the violin and particularly the piano—became the leading solo instruments in the classic concerto.

The late piano concertos of Mozart, those he wrote for performance by himself in Vienna, give a panorama of concerto composition that has had implications for concerto procedure over a period of almost two hundred years. In these works we find the lively give-and-take that characterizes the baroque concerto grosso and also the dramatic opposition of forces that distinguishes classic musical expression. Further, in Mozart's piano concertos we meet the brilliant virtuoso soloist, the immediate ancestor of the romantic hero-musician of the nineteenth century, as well as the descendant of generations of composer-performers.

Structurally the concerto is laid out like other works of big scope. Generally there are three movements. The first is a quick piece in sonata form, modified to include an orchestral tutti in the tonic key at the opening before the key area plan begins to unfold. The slow movement is often in the style of an opera aria, in rondo, sonata, or variation form. The finale is again quick and usually has a dancelike quality, with a tune that calls for a rondo form so that it can be heard a number of times.

One of the most delightful of Mozart's concertos is his Piano Concerto in C major, K. 467, whose second movement is familiar to moviegoers as the musical background to the film *Elvira Madigan.* The first movement opens with a jaunty little march tune that quickly becomes embroiled in complex imitations. Throughout the movement this march tune is set off against a wealth of varied melodic material—fanfares, Storm and Stress passages, singing melodies, pathetic turns of phrase—a kaleidoscope of ideas matching the lively interplay between the piano, the strings, and the winds. Note how the piano plays a number of roles—singer, brilliant soloist, and member of the ensemble when the orchestra takes the principal melodic material.

CHAMBER
MUSIC

Around 1750, *chamber music* (music in homes and salons) began to separate into music for orchestra and music for a small number of players. This latter genre is what we understand by the term chamber music. Duets, trios, quartets, quintets, etc., with or without keyboard, for winds, strings, or both—were written in great quantities to satisfy a growing market of amateurs for music they could play at home. Preeminent among all classic chamber music was the string quartet. It became established as a standard genre around 1770 and reached its apex in the great string quartets written by Haydn and Mozart during their mature years and by Beethoven throughout his creative lifetime. These works, a joy to amateur performers as well as standard concert items, represent the ultimate refinement in texture, motive-play, sonority, and elegance of style. Example 6-14 shows how imaginative the treatment of texture became in the hands of a classic master. The singing melody, itself beautifully shaped, is supported by a light accompaniment at first; this accompaniment has a few intriguing turns of figure, giving added life to the texture. The entry of the cello is first held off, but when it comes in, it does so with a striking new figure that cuts across the flow of the upper voices, as if a dancer suddenly leaped on stage to interrupt the gentle action. With this the texture becomes furiously active, with short imitations and a reinforcement of the upper melodic line. The variety of *textures* here is much like the swift, changes of *topic* often heard in classic music.

EXAMPLE 6-14. *Mozart: Quartet in C major, K. 465, first movement*

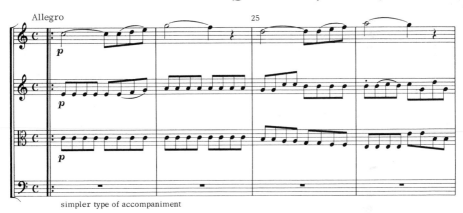

(EXAMPLE 6-14. *continued*)

cadence
of period

part-writing continues the movement

OPERA We know classic music principally through its great instrumental works—the sonatas, quartets, concertos, and symphonies of Haydn, Beethoven, and Mozart. Yet the crowning achievement of this style until Beethoven's time is represented by the operas of Mozart, especially his *The Marriage of Figaro, Don Giovanni, The Magic Flute,* and *Così Fan Tutte.* Opera was the chief musical entertainment in the later eighteenth century, an important professional goal for most composers, and a model for moods, styles, topics in instrumental music.

Mozart's *Don Giovanni* stands out as his richest and most powerful dramatic work. By the time he began to write this opera, he had acquired thorough training in composing Italian opera, both serious and comic; he had absorbed from Gluck ideas of dramatic truth which Gluck had advanced and realized in his so-called *reform* operas, such as *Orfeo, Alceste, Iphigenia in Tauris;* he had developed total command of all techniques of composition. He combined these skills with a remarkably sensitive grasp of human feelings and an incredibly rich invention to create a work that is as alive today as it was when first performed in Prague in 1786.

The plot of *Don Giovanni* is quite simple. Two tragic events frame the action: (1) the midnight seduction of Anna by the Don at the beginning, followed by the duel in which her father is killed, and (2) the great Supper scene toward the end of the opera, when the statue of the Commandant, Anna's father, returns to drag Don Giovanni down to Hell. In between, the action is mainly comedy, with flirtations, escapades, and mistaken identities, shadowed now and then by a return to the somber mood of the beginning. Instead of a plot with many twists, as in Mozart's *The Marriage of Figaro, Don Giovanni* has very little progression of action; the Don remains, until the Supper scene, quite untouched by all the episodic events so delightfully traced out by Mozart and his librettist, Lorenzo da Ponte. On the other hand, each of the characters has a striking psychological image in relation to the

FIGURE 17. *Manuscript of recitative from Act 4, scene 7 of Mozart's*
Marriage of Figaro. *The excerpt is Mozart's own handwriting. (Courtesy of the Memorial Library of Music, Stanford University Libraries.)*

Don—Anna is proud and outraged; her father shows a grave, dignified
anger; Leporello is envious; Masetto is sullen; Zerlina is flirtatious;
Elvira is overwrought; Ottavio represents the gallant virtues of the
gentleman.

For the listener, perhaps the strongest first impression is of the
wide range of moods through which Mozart deftly leads us. The sense
of doom strikes us at the beginning of the overture, as the orchestra, in
a short yet powerful fantasia, evokes images of the supernatural forces
that will eventually bring Don Giovanni to account. The mood then
changes to an effervescent feeling suggesting the Don's galant life-
style. The overture promises a brilliant, fanfare-like ending, but with a
subtle harmonic shift it bypasses the normal effect of arrival and
brings us quietly, yet expectantly to the rise of the curtain.

We see Leporello, the Don's servant, playing the sentry at night, with a humorous, "low-style" foot march as a setting for his grumbling and his envy of his master's station. As Don Giovanni enters, pursued by Anna, the emotional level rises; the music vividly portrays their tug-of-war in a "high-style" march; once again the mood rises, this time to the peak of tragedy as the Commandant, Anna's father, enters, duels with the Don, and is killed; the duel is accompanied by one of the rare bits of specific pictorialism in Mozart, as, in the same mood that opened the overture, the thrusts and parries of the swords are depicted by flashing figures and the death stroke by a sustained dissonant chord. Following the death of the Commandant, Mozart inserts a moment of comedy, one of the most startling changes of mood in all opera; the Don and Leporello converse in *recitativo secco* (dry or simple recitative), and their interchange is loaded with cynical humor (see Example 6-15).

EXAMPLE 6-15. *Recitativo secco: Mozart,* Don Giovanni

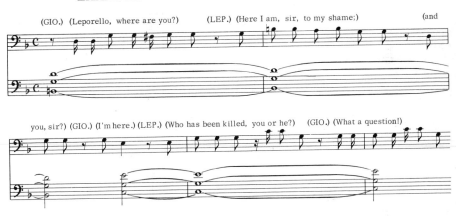

This deep dive into comedy is quickly reversed; Anna, mourning the death of her father, sings one of the most touching recitatives in all opera [in the *recitativo accompagnato* or *obligé* style (accompanied or obligatory recitative)], Example 6-16.

EXAMPLE 6-16. *Recitativo accompagnato or obligé*

The differences between these two kinds of recitative can easily be heard; the *secco* is like conversation, without strong feeling, and is accompanied only by a keyboard instrument; the *accompagnato* has a high charge of feeling, with broken declamation, touches of figure that suggest the meaning of the text, and orchestral participation.

The mood of solemnity returns, and the scene closes as Anna and Ottavio resolve revenge in a brilliant duet. Note the contrasting emotions of the two. Anna begins with wild sorrow in a minor key; Ottavio consoles her, and his music shifts to a major key; the oath is sworn to shifting harmonies, and the duet closes in Anna's key as the two set their high purpose. This final number of the scene uses the dramatic elements of key contrast inherent in the sonata form, as outlined below:

HARMONIC FORM		DRAMATIC FORM
Part I	First key area, minor key	Anna sings; rejects Ottavio in her despair.
	Second key area, related major key	Ottavio offers consolation; contrast to opening mood.
Part II	Shifting harmonies	Both swear revenge; emphasis and accent of accompanied recitative.
	Return to home key	Firm resolution for revenge; Anna's key and the mood of her opening music overcome the contrast of Ottavio's mood and key of consolation.

Viewing the entire first scene, we can see that it has an internal structure which binds the various sections together in a tight and continuous plan of musico-dramatic action. The overture and the final duet, pillars to the form, are in the same key (D), and each uses the sonata form. Indeed, the cadence in D, averted in the overture, is reinforced at the end of the scene as an answer to an important harmonic question. Leporello's music suggests the dance movement of a symphony; the struggle is like the opening key area of a sonata form; the death and recitative have the expressive value of a slow movement.

In the following diagram we can see the drop and rise of expressive intensity throughout this scene:

Overture		Leporello	Struggle	Death; Revenge
Tragic				Tragic
	Galant		Furious action	
		Buffa		

In order to sample more fully the musical content of *Don Giovanni,* considered by many the greatest opera ever written, we shall touch briefly upon some other numbers:

1. When Elvira, who has recently been betrayed by Don Giovanni, appears, in a rage, to find and punish him, she is brought on stage with a rather flamboyant march. She is high-born, but there is a faintly ridiculous touch to her character. She sings a melody which leaps about, and at the end, when she says "gli vo cavare il core" (I'll carve his heart out), she sings a brilliant coloratura melodic arch on the syllable -*vare,* which suggests the twisting and turning of the knife.
2. Perhaps the most delicious comic moment in the opera is the "Catalogue" aria, Act I, in which Leporello tells Elvira, a former love of the Don, that she is but one of the countless conquests made by his master. Leporello covers both quantity and quality, first by ticking off in quick *duple* time the number of conquests in each country and the various social stations of the Don's ladies; then by describing, in a slower *minuet* time, their attributes—blonde, brunette, fat, thin, grand, tiny, young, old. By following the text you can hear how Mozart, in almost every measure, has a musical figure that is apt for what is being said. For example, in the first part, the music suddenly slows down to suggest amazement at his "one thousand and three" conquests in Spain. In the second part, the "grand" and the "tiny" have respectively full and light textures. The aria ends with a musical "leer" as Leporello tells Elvira that she too belongs on the list ("You know all about it").
3. In the champagne aria, "Finch'han del vino," Mozart composed a brilliant piece to suggest the intoxication of a carousal; he drives the music through breathlessly, without a pause, so that Don Giovanni himself is virtually reeling at the end from a lack of respite in singing.
4. Much of this opera is conceived in the buffa manner, but some numbers recall the seria style. The most formalized character of all, Don Ottavio, sings the most formal music. Typical of his music is the aria "Il mio tesoro" (My treasure). An elegant melody, a broad form, with roulades added upon repetitions and at cadential

FIGURE 18. *M. Gauci: Scene from the opera buffa* Il Fanatico per la Musica (*The Musical Fanatic*) *composed by Simon Mayr and performed in London in 1805 and 1806. The music that the singer is playing on his imaginary flute is notated below the picture, and the text reads, "What a beautiful passage! What pleasure it gives me." (Courtesy of the Gracely Collection, Stanford University Libraries.)*

150

points—these demonstrate that Mozart was master of the seria as well as the buffa style; the juxtaposition of this aria with the other elements in the opera, however, give it a dimension of characterization that would be lacking in a pure seria work.

As we studied *Don Giovanni*, it must have been clear that simply to listen to it as a piece of music would be to know only part of it. Beyond the wonderful melodies and exciting passages in the music, there is the visual picture, then the general sense of the words, and finally the subtle nuances in which specific words (in Italian) are shaped and highlighted by the music. This topical content is also present in instrumental music, which often imitated opera in its style; to recognize these topical references is to gain an added delight in listening. Classic music is certainly not to be taken as purely abstract.

CHORAL MUSIC Classic choral music maintained the traditional forms we know already from earlier styles—the Mass, motet, chorale, part-songs, oratorio. It adapted these forms to its own language, coordinating traditional contrapuntal techniques and alla breve style with the popular styles derived from dance music.

In classic choral music, Haydn's oratorio *The Creation* has the same all-embracing scope that Mozart's *Don Giovanni* has in classic opera. It offers something for every listener—broadly scaled, skillfully turned fugues, lyric songs, picturesque word-painting, massive choral pieces, and a wide range of moods.

The three parts of this oratorio tell the story of the creation of the world itself, of plants and animals, and finally of man himself. Haydn, who had written many operas, used his theatrical imagination to its fullest in giving the listener a sense of the vast panorama of creation. Compare, for example, the opening number of Part I with the finale of this first section, nos. 1 and 14. In representing Chaos at first, Haydn wrote one of the most remarkable orchestral pieces of all time, unparalleled in eighteenth-century music for its effects of orchestration, its shifting harmonies, and its juxtaposition of elusive figures. This is a great orchestral fantasia, evoking, like the opening of the overture to Mozart's *Don Giovanni*, a sense of the *dark* side of the supernatural. To celebrate the completion of the first great stage of creation, Haydn wrote one of the most stirring choral pieces we know, the familiar "The Heavens Are Telling," in a simple yet noble style with an air of grandeur about it. The contrast with Chaos is complete: minor versus major key; fragmentary figures versus a beautiful, simple, and thoroughly singable melody; irregular phrase structure versus a comfortable pleasing symmetry; kaleidoscopic, elusive shifts of color versus a bright uncomplicated quality of sound that seems to rejoice in the climate of C major, a key associated at that time with clarity of feeling, joy, and triumph.

Another side of Haydn's art comes to the fore in this work—his word-painting or pictorialism. This is especially to be noted in no. 7, where he describes, with appropriate figures, the creation of the earth itself—oceans, mountains, plains, streams; in no. 16, the eagle, the lark, the dove, and the nightingale appear, each with its signal, while in no. 22, descriptive figures announce the coming of the lion, the tiger, the stag, the steed, cattle, and the worm.

For other examples of classic choral music, touching upon early, fully matured, and very late aspects of the classic style, the following works are suggested:

Mozart: Regina Coeli (Queen of Heaven), K. 108. This motet shows a complete absorption of Italian opera and instrumental style. It is galant throughout; the plan is that of an Italian opera sinfonia or early concert symphony—a fast, brilliant movement, a second movement in the style of a moderately paced minuet, an adagio, and a brilliant contredanse finale. It is distinguished from its model, the sinfonia, by the presence of voices, by the use of a continuo (prescribed for church music), and by a more active and deftly wrought play of figure and motive, which does not, however, disturb the galant symmetry of the phrase structure.

Haydn: Mass in D minor (*Lord Nelson*): "Dona nobis pacem" (Give us peace). This piece is a brilliant concertato piece, brisk, punctuated by trumpet and drum signals; it is very much in the vein of the festive choral music of Bach and Handel. Haydn employs the learned style in fugal expositions, but does not allow himself to be carried away by the counterpoint. The discourse of the fugue is interrupted by declamations; the cadential structure is clear and decisive in its punctuation; and the entire movement embodies the key area structure of the sonata form.

Beethoven: Missa solemnis, Op. 123: "Donas nobis pacem." In contrast to the examples from Mozart and Haydn, which stand firmly in the classic world, Beethoven's music in this case has the impact, the feel, of the grandiose choral style of the nineteenth century. It has a very broad range of sound, with respect to both volume and timbre (disembodied winds, solo timpani); a vast palette of rich combinations gives us expressive values that move from the terror of the last judgment to the final peace which the last downward-bending phrase evokes. There is also a tremendous contrast of material—recitative, march, fanfare, and a principal theme of pastoral quality. The entire piece has a strong declamatory character, so much so that when the orchestra is playing alone, one can imagine that some poetic image related to the text is impelling the music. Formally, we have episodes, as in a fantasia, but the principal material, in the pastoral vein, shows elements of sonata form, especially in the similarity of cadential sections which end the exposition and recapitulation.

SOLO KEYBOARD MUSIC Anyone who has played piano has probably performed some keyboard music of Haydn, Mozart, or Beethoven—a minuet, variation, or sonata. Many classic keyboard pieces were written for the same purpose that they serve today—to furnish music for players of modest skill, at home or in the teacher's studio. Example 2-18 shows a typical easy texture—a tuneful melodic line accompanied by a readily managed left-hand figure which breaks up the chords in tight, repeated patterns known as the *Alberti* bass, after the earlier eighteenth-century composer who is credited with establishing this accompaniment as a typical keyboard style.

Beyond this basic texture, classic keyboard music, either for piano or occasionally for harpsichord or clavichord, made use of many different textures—contrapuntal, brilliant figurations, active give-and-take, full and massive chords. It covered a range of difficulty from simple lesson-type music for beginners to grand concert music for virtuosos. One very revealing aspect of classic keyboard music is that virtually all of it, regardless of the degree of difficulty or whatever its purpose—study, amusement, concert—was *expressive* music, not pure exercises. It drew its content from the familiar topics of the time—songs, dances, marches, pastoral effects, Turkish effects, etc., bringing into the home some reminiscences of the theater, church, and concert hall. We have only to glance through the sonatas of Mozart and Haydn to see how they tell of the great world outside. When you hear the first movement of Mozart's Sonata in D major, K. 284, you can well imagine yourself in the opera house listening to a sinfonia in the Italian style, with its brilliant tutti, its rushing figures, and its general air of excitement.

BEETHOVEN We can readily hear striking differences between the music of Beethoven and that of his immediate predecessors, Haydn and Mozart. The sound is heavier, with greater extremes of loud and soft, high and low; sudden violent contrasts appear, as do mighty crescendos; a sense of greater thrust, of intense struggle, moves much of Beethoven's music. These qualities have led many to regard Beethoven as the herald of the romantic age to come.

But Beethoven held fast to the principles of style and form established during the classic era. He plays with topics, builds extended harmonic drives, lays out his forms by keys, and eventually brings matters into balance with a strong and final sense of arrival in all his music. While making use of classic principles of composition, he often creates problems, raises questions which will be answered as the form of a movement unfolds. The opening theme of his great Symphony No. 3, the *Eroica,* shows this tendency very clearly. The first four measures of the theme make up a simple waltzlike melody, easy to sing and remember since it consists only of notes of the tonic triad. At the fifth measure, this sturdy little tune loses its footing, sinking to a strange chromatic note; eventually, it finds its way back home, but its clarity has disappeared. Throughout the movement this theme will be turned and twisted in many ways, and only in its last appearance, toward the end of the movement, will it find a regular frame, a symmetrical layout proper to its first four measures. Example 6-17 gives the opening theme in its first and last versions.

EXAMPLE 6-17. *Beethoven, Symphony No. 3, Op. 55, first movement*

a. Opening theme, first statement

b. Opening theme, final statement

This treatment of the opening theme represents a huge question-answer relationship, a problem stated and eventually solved; for the listener, attentive to the adventures of the theme, this can help to give a sense of unity to the movement *beyond* the standard relationships usually found in classic music.

The entire symphony burst upon the musical world in 1803 like a thunderstorm. It was much longer, grander in scope, and, to listeners of that time, more violent in feeling than anything they had ever heard. While the four movements of this work use standard eighteenth-century forms—sonata form, march with trio, dance with trio, and variation—they show typical Beethoven modifications.

The first movement is very much expanded over any sonata-form movement previously composed. To appreciate how this greater length is generated, you might listen for two striking procedures:

1. As you count steadily with the quick 3-4 meter, note how often Beethoven throws this meter off balance by accenting the second or third beat: 1 **2** 3 or 1 2 **3,** sometimes destroying entirely the sense of triple time. Example 2-9 quotes the first and one of the most powerful of such rhythmic shifts. The effect is to build a sharp forward thrust in the music.

2. Listen for clear and strong cadences. Beethoven spaces them far apart, building extended periods and great drives to cadences. Typically, the action at the beginning of a period is symmetrical, then an interruption or harmonic digression breaks the symmetry, making room for intense and complex play of harmonic and melodic action.

With a score, you can follow the unfolding of the form, using the précis given below as a guide.

FIRST MOVEMENT
Allegro con brio (691 measures)

Exposition (1–148)	*Relatively short first key area (KA); very long second key area*
KA I (1–37)	*One theme, waltzlike, quick introduction of harmonic instability, imbalance of phrases; different instrumental colors in presentation of theme (measures 3, 15, 37); note drive created by rhythmic imbalance (23–37; see p. 38); shift to second key (45–56), new theme*
KA II (57–148)	*Many motives, frequent harmonic digressions, long periods, much rhythmic imbalance; trailing off after cadence (148–152)*
Development (152–398)	*Two large cycles of action*
Part I (166–233)	*A. Stable section (166–178), theme from measure 45*
	B. Unstable (178–220), several motives combined
	A. Stable (220–236), theme from measure 46
Part II (233–397)	*C. Unstable (236–284), fugato building up to a tremendous cadential drive*
	D. Relatively stable (284–337), a new theme in a distant key, opening theme in several keys, new theme restated
	E. Unstable (338–397), return to home key, extended cadential drive, suspense by understatement just before return

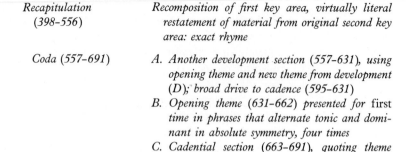

Recapitulation (398-556)	Recomposition of first key area, virtually literal restatement of material from original second key area: exact rhyme
Coda (557-691)	A. Another development section (557-631), using opening theme and new theme from development (D); broad drive to cadence (595-631) B. Opening theme (631-662) presented for first time in phrases that alternate tonic and dominant in absolute symmetry, four times C. Cadential section (663-691), quoting theme from second key area

In this movement much of the expansion takes place at points that the eighteenth-century sonata form was content to pass over rather quickly—in the development section and at the cadential area of the entire movement that completes the recapitulation. Both the development and the coda of this movement are extremely long. In order to support and give point to this length, Beethoven establishes new piers to his structural bridge, new areas of arrival within the form. The diagram below illustrates what happens:

EXAMPLE 6-18. *Diagram of Beethoven: Symphony No. 3, first movement*

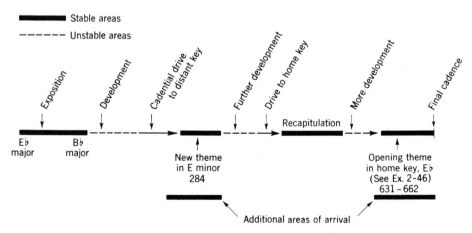

The new theme you hear about midway through the development, in E minor, represents the farthest distance away from the home key; it acts as a station "halfway around the world," and from this point a long and deliberate return to the home key begins; feel the suspense as Beethoven cuts away virtually all of the sound just before the home key, with its opening theme, finally arrives.

The first movement achieves its length by *compressing* events, with a resultant explosion of action. The second movement, in contrast, *stretches out* events, building its great length by a very deliberate unfolding of action. Here we have the slowing down of time; there are instants where everything seems suspended.

In the extremely deliberate motion of the funeral march, activated and yet held in check by the dotted rhythms which signify the tattoo of muffled drums, the filling-out of a two-reprise form takes considerable time. Beethoven adds another dimension to this form: he breaks off the march upon its return and leaps to another plane of action. The notes gradually become quick; the spaces in time are filled in until we have virtually a hurricane of action. Then, suddenly, like the eye of the hurricane, there is an interval of almost dead quiet (measures 154–158), and the storm breaks in with renewed violence, gradually to subside during the restatement of the march. The cycle of action is not yet completed when the march has been repeated; therefore, Beethoven denies the listener the cadence that might have ended the piece at this point and leads, by means of a deceptive cadence, into the final phase. The process of expansion continues until the last measures, where the march theme is broken into fragments, punctuated by intervals of total suspension of action. The tragic implications of this kind of play with musical movement can certainly be felt strongly.

SECOND MOVEMENT

Marcia funebre: Adagio assai (247 measures)

A. (1–68)	*A very slow funeral march in two-reprise form (each part repeated with some changes) followed by a concluding cadential section; minor mode*
B. (69–101)	*A contrasting trio, also in two-reprise form (with neither part repeated), in a lyric style, interrupted by fanfares that provide a rhyme for the two sections*
A.' (105–113)	*Fragmentary return to the march, as if a da capo were to be used to round off the form*
C. (114–173)	*An X or development-like section, beginning with imitative polyphony on a new theme*
A." (174–209)	*Return of the march*

Coda (*209–247*)   *Cadential section for the movement, first digressing harmonically and using a new theme, then returning to a
fragmentary restatement of the march*

In the third movement, the scherzo, Beethoven again goes beyond
the typical classic contrast of slow and fast. This movement embodies
pure energy, a headlong drive now and then carrying hints of a theme.
While based on the two-reprise form of classic dance movements, it
creates a tremendous imbalance between the two reprises, 14 measures
versus 137. Beethoven announces a problem in the first reprise; he
barely touches upon the home key and throws the phrase structure off
balance by groups of six, five, and three measures. The rest of the
scherzo works toward clarification—a triumphant affirmation of the
home key and a "nailing down" of the four-measure phrase structure.
The trio, a delightful horn fanfare, stands in total contrast—a tune in
the home key and a regular phrase structure, especially in the first
reprise.

THIRD MOVEMENT

Scherzo: Allegro vivace (442 measures)

Scherzo (1–166)   *Reprise I (1–28)*
                           Reprise II (29–166)

Trio (167–255)   *Reprise I (167–197)*
                           Reprise II (198–255)

Scherzo da capo and coda (256–442)

In the fourth movement, we might say that Beethoven has returned to the "real" world of musical time and movement, to familiar
ground. The piece is a set of variations built upon a contredanse tune
and its bass, which Beethoven had used before as melodic material in
several compositions. He characterizes the sections of his movement
according to familiar types, as the outline shows. The subject itself is
in a two-reprise form; the following example gives the tune and its
bass:

EXAMPLE 6-19. *Beethoven: Symphony No. 3, finale*

FOURTH MOVEMENT

Allegro molto (473 measures)

Opening flourish (1–11) (*see Example 2-2*)

Home key
{
1. *Decorative variations on the bass (12–75)*
2. *The melody with ornamental garlands (76–107)*
   Transition (107–116)
}

Other keys
{
3. *A fugal passage on the bass subject (117–174)*
4. *A dance, using the melody (175–198)*
   Transition (198–210)
5. *A march, using the bass (211–256)*
6. *A songlike variation, using the melody (257–277)*
}

Home key
{
7. *A fugal passage, on the bass, with the melody chiming in (277–348)*
8. *A slow aria, using the melody (349–380)*
9. *A grand chorale, using the melody (381–396)*
}

Coda (397–473); note return of opening flourish (431–434)

After the chorale, Beethoven abandons the variation procedure. He is making a coda; thus, we hear some free harmonic exploration preparing the final exultant cadential section. The movement concludes with fanfares and rushing passages, incorporating the exciting figure that began the movement with a challenge.

As you can see, Beethoven is not content merely to put together a set of interesting elaborations upon his subject. Instead, he gives the form a broad overall structure by using (1) large key areas: tonic—shifting keys—tonic; (2) an integrated phrase structure, in which cadences are often not clear-cut. Thus two neighboring variations can be linked without a break. As with so much of Beethoven's music, the impression is one of broad gestures, violent drives, and grand ideas; the whole piece is "written large."

Apart from its monumental structure, the *Eroica* is noted for a rather spectacular circumstance concerning its subtitle. Originally composed in honor of Napoleon Bonaparte as a republican hero, the symphony was later given the title *Sinfonia Eroica* when Beethoven learned that Napoleon had had himself proclaimed Emperor of the French; mention of Bonaparte was removed from the title page.

Beethoven's language in the *Eroica* Symphony is classic, though magnified in breadth and intensity. The same is true of his use of the orchestra in this work. He deploys the strings as the principal carriers of the action and uses the four standard winds—flutes, oboes, clarinets, and bassoons—in solos, duets, and ensembles and as reinforcement of the strings; the brass have their moments of solo, but generally provide body and accent to an orchestral tutti.

In his piano music, Beethoven enters a different world, that which we have come to regard as *romantic.* Although the piano had been invented early in the eighteenth century, it remained a gentle, rather light-sounding instrument until late eighteenth-century improvements increased its range and built up its tone quality and force so that it could come into its own as a true concert instrument. Listening to the opening of Beethoven's *Sonata Appassionata,* in F minor, Op. 57, written about the same time as his *Eroica* Symphony, we are immediately drawn into a dark region, uncertain, searching. The opening theme rises from the lowermost range of the piano, breaks off, repeats, hesitates, then explodes into a violent contrast. The action is fragmentary, episodic throughout the entire exposition; we hear three different themes, each in a different key, and each trailing off rather than marching to a decisive cadence. The striking contrasts between the themes represent what will later become a typical layout for romantic sonata form. (See page 183 for a similar arrangement in the Symphony No. 1 in C minor of Brahms.) The entire first movement trails off at the end, as if the sound were fading in the distance, again a typical romantic ending. Listening to this movement, you might well imagine the performer to be an actor, assuming impassioned, even melodramatic postures, and impressing his audience as much by his intense, ever-changing declamation as by the words he is uttering.

The grandeur of the *Eroica* and the fantasy of the *Appassionata* had a profound effect on nineteenth-century composers. We hear echoes of Beethoven's style in the music of Weber, Schubert, Schumann, Berlioz, Brahms, and Wagner, among others. We can even find hints of what later in the twentieth century will become the styles of musical impressionism and expressionism. The pastel colors evoking images of the countryside in the first movement of his Symphony No. 6, the *Pastoral,* have a strong flavor of impressionism, while the serpentine, chromatic subject of his *Great Fugue,* Op. 133, and the intensive, unrelenting exploration and development of this subject throughout the fugue was greatly admired by expressionist composers.

Beethoven inherited Mozart's sense for the dramatic and contrasting relationship; he also learned a tightness of development and motivic interplay from Haydn. He lacked Mozart's spontaneous lyricism; therefore, he did little in the field of opera. He lacked Haydn's spontaneous sense for the play of phrase and effect; therefore, he had to wrestle mightily with stubborn materials. Rarely does a Beethoven phrase or period wind its way comfortably to its end. His imbalances were the grim crises of the romantic age to come, not the inflections and nuances of the eighteenth century. Still, the explosion had not yet come; the centrifugal *forces contained in Beethoven's music are controlled* by a sense of musical *balance*, of *gravitation to a long-range point of arrival.*

There is a strong temptation to draw a parallel between rationalistic thought in the eighteenth century and classicism in music. This is only partly valid as an analogy. Rationalism might be compared to mid-eighteenth-century music, in which a balanced, clear, uncomplicated, and down-to-earth quality was predominant.

Toward the end of the eighteenth century, unsettling forces were at work. The middle-class revolutions in America and France had taken place. Early romanticism had made its first appearance in the *Sturm und Drang* period of German literature and in the writings of Rousseau. German idealism, with affinities to the romantic movement, was being developed by Fichte, Kant, and Hegel. We have seen the analogy to this unsettling influence at work within the harmonic and rhythmic structure of the classic period form. Yet, in no way did this unseat the fundamental premise of classic music, which was the final and complete victory of stability after an engrossing musical experience that involved strong elements of instability.

The last phase of the classic relationship between form and content was reached in Beethoven. Afterward, individual moments of intensity or color in the music began to assume more importance for the composer and the listener than the balanced perfection of the form. This was the way to romanticism.

SUMMARY

1. *Qualities of sound:* much contrast in level, strength, and color; use of crescendo and diminuendo; sharp accents; exploration of higher registers; lighter bass; overall transparency and brilliance; range between two-voiced treble-bass and very full sound.
2. *Qualities of movement:* in a given movement, maintenance of one pace, as a rule; strongly influenced by typical song and dance patterns; characteristic use of syncopation for purposes of intensifying movement; vigorous, accentuated pace, even in slow movements.
3. *Arrival:* extremely important; frequent clear strong points of

arrival; entire sections geared structurally to broad effects of arrival.

4. *Movement and arrival:* clarity of phrase and period structure; symmetrical structure, often broken to extend periods.

5. *Melody:* essentially built on characteristic motives in a statement-counterstatement relationship; frequency of real "tunes"; clarity of phrase and period structure. Many melodies express harmony, built largely on the notes of a chord.

6. *Rhythm:* steady, vigorous, characteristic patterns; often subject to irregularities which are later resolved; dance rhythms dominate; diverse rhythmic patterns; strongly differentiated motives.

7. *Harmony:* strong, clear sense of key; complete saturation by cadential action; characteristic opposition of I and V; periods of broad exploration and instability; cadential drive a basic structural force.

8. *Texture:* basically homophonic, i.e., melody and accompaniment; some polyphony, much give-and-take; polarity of treble and bass; two to four parts, occasionally more; many changes in texture throughout a composition.

9. *Performance:* outdoors and in theater, home, concert hall, and church.

10. Wide range of expressive and stylistic material.

**DISCUSSION
AND
REVIEW
QUESTIONS**

1. What is a musical topic?
2. List some of the principal dance types in classic music.
3. What is musical pictorialism?
4. Discuss the use of two-reprise form in classic music.
5. How may periods be extended, and what is the musical effect of such extensions?
6. Describe the chief harmonic and melodic features of sonata form.
7. In what ways does classic music differ from baroque music?
8. How does Mozart use music for characterization in Don Giovanni?
9. How does classic music use contrast?
10. In what ways did Beethoven use classic methods of composition? In what ways did he go beyond the classic style of the eighteenth century?

CHAPTER SEVEN

ROMANTIC MUSIC

Romantic music is familiar territory for today's listener. And for many, its terrain is the most attractive and picturesque in the entire field of music. It has much to offer that is immediately appealing and moving—the lyricism of Schubert, Chopin, and Mendelssohn, the verve and warmth of Tchaikovsky and Dvořák, the imposing grandeur and introspective profundity of Brahms, the intensity of Schumann, the fantasy of Berlioz and Liszt, the overpowering eloquence of Wagner, the dramatic passion of Verdi—this and much more the nineteenth century has given to music.

It is difficult to define romanticism in music, as in other fields of expression. It has so many facets, each brilliant and each facing in its own direction, that we can often mistake one aspect for the entire structure. Individualism—the characteristic personal language—takes precedence over a common or universal style of expression. Each composer adopts his own distinctive posture and finds special resources which are peculiarly suited to his own genius. In classic music, the sense of structural authority stands above the individual nuance; in romantic music the nuance often asserts itself at the expense of structural balance and clarity. Thus, romanticism in music breaks away from a central authority; it exhibits a centrifugal motion, emphasizing the facets, rather than the form.

Romanticism appears in its fullest flower in such works as the Prelude to Wagner's opera *Tristan und Isolde* (1859), Chopin's Preludes for piano (1839), Schumann's *Carnaval* (1835), Berlioz's *Symphonie Fantastique* (1831), Schubert's song "The Erlking" (1815), and Liszt's Sonata for Piano in B minor (1854). Each of these works has some qualities that mark it especially as being romantic. And of all these compositions, perhaps the most typical of romanticism, and at the same time a unique work in many respects, is the Prelude to Wagner's *Tristan*. For us, it can be a central area of reference from which we can start down the devious paths of musical romanticism.

WAGNER,
PRELUDE
TO TRISTAN
UND ISOLDE

EXPRESSION

As you listen to this piece, you can feel that Wagner is intent on building an all-enveloping mood, a powerful and compelling demand upon the listener to enter into the magic world of the ill-fated lovers, Tristan and Isolde. Wagner prepares us for the feelings and situations in the drama—hate, love, bitterness, yearning, ecstasy, betrayal, and final fulfillment in death—by creating a climate of sound that is intensely rich and restless; the mood at the beginning of the Prelude is sustained, building eventually to an overpowering climax, paralleling the rise and fall of human feeling. In contrast to the expressive aims of earlier music—to stir the feelings by hinting at or suggesting moods—expression in this piece aims at a saturation experience, total and unbroken, to draw in the listener completely.

SOUND

Wagner, the wonder-worker of harmony, draws us into the mood of longing, frustration, and unhappiness with the very first chord. Rich and dark in color, it has an unsettling, dissonant quality that asks for resolution; yet, as we listen, we hear no resolution but a flow of unstable harmonies linked in an ongoing stream, first interrupted by suspenseful silences, then moving continuously forward. Example 7-1 quotes the opening chord and its immediate continuation; this first chord, which has become famous in music, is known as the *Tristan* chord; its special qualities in this piece arise from (1) its use at the *beginning* of the Prelude, (2) the striking way in which it is *scored* (with winds and strings), and (3) its *unexpected continuation* to other dissonant harmonies, instead of being resolved in a traditional way.

EXAMPLE 7-1. *Wagner: Prelude to* Tristan und Isolde

The climate of sound established by this chord is sustained throughout the Prelude and the entire opera, both in the use of unstable harmonies and in the rich, colorful scoring. Example 7-2 illustrates some typical chords in the Wagner vocabulary; as you play these on the piano, sense how dissonance and richness blend to create a compelling and sustained effect.

EXAMPLE 7-2. *Typical chords in the Wagner vocabulary*

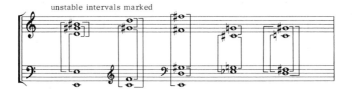

Wagner developed this vocabulary as his personal style evolved by gradually eliminating chords which represented *tonic harmony* and replacing them by chords that represented *dominant harmony,* especially those chords which contained a *tritone* (an augmented fourth or diminished fifth; see pages 40, 42, 43). Each of the chords in Examples 7-1 and 7-2 has one or more tritones. Actually, Wagner represents the end station of a centuries-long trend that began with the unisons, fourths, fifths, and octaves of medieval music, passed through the triadic harmonies of the Renaissance, began to incorporate tritone-containing chords in the Baroque era as dominant harmonies in cadences, and in the classic and early romantic eras increased the use of harmonic dissonances for cadential and expressive force.

MOVEMENT AND ARRIVAL
In listening for *movement* at the beginning of the Prelude, you sense it as being *implied* in the restlessness of the harmonies rather than *spelled out* by a definite pulse or beat. We are aware of a slow tempo and a tentative stop-and-start pace. As the music proceeds, you will finally hear a more definite meter, a slowly swinging triple time as the melodic lines merge and overlap.

As you follow the long spun-out melodic lines, note how their rise and fall in gracefully balanced curves creates wavelike patterns that move gradually upward to an *apex* or *climax,* then drop suddenly to begin again the upward thrust. This rise and fall, matched by the buildup and drop of intensity, is called the *dynamic curve;* it parallels the ebb and flow of human feeling and is one of the principal reasons why Wagner's music has a strong compelling effect. This melodic flow that carries forward in an unbroken line has been described as *endless melody.*

Listening more closely, you can hear that the long melodic lines are built by varied repetitions of short, well-turned motives. While we recognize different motives, we also sense that they have a consistency of pattern among themselves—principally stepwise motion balanced against a striking leap—and that they frequently resemble each other; this promotes the flow of the melody as the motives merge smoothly. Example 7-3 illustrates the consistency of motives in the piece:

EXAMPLE 7-3. *Consistency and similarity of motives from Wagner's Prelude to* Tristan

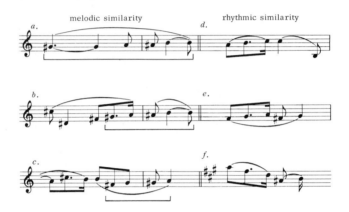

Example 7-4 sketches the first seventeen measures of the Prelude, showing how motives are restated in varied form and how the melody builds to an apex in measure 13.

EXAMPLE 7-4. *Beginning of Prelude to* Tristan

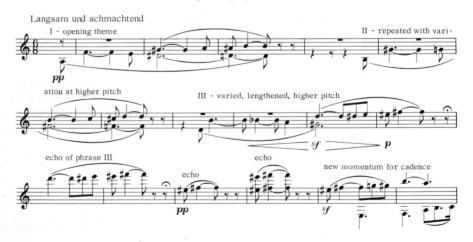

Harmony has its own flow in this piece, as unbroken and "end-less" as the melody. The long chains of unstable harmony lead us to expect a cadence, but we never hear a clear and final-sounding cadence. Yet Wagner is always *aware* of cadential action; his harmonies, strongly dominant in effect, *slide past* the resolution at the last minute, or they resolve to a deceptive cadence, powerful in its effect of punctuation, but leading the ear onward. The final measure of Example 7-4, a deceptive cadence, has a marked effect of arrival; we accept it as a close to what we have heard before; at the same time its surprising harmonic twist opens the way to the ongoing flow.

FORM Listening to the entire Prelude, you can hear that it is built as one huge dynamic curve, reaching a powerful climax near the end, then dropping quickly to the quiet stop-and-start movement with which it began. Within this great arch, certain points can be felt as stations along the way; these are principally broadly declaimed deceptive cadences that echo the gesture at measure 17, in different textures; they also represent the peaks of smaller dynamic curves *within* the form. Example 7-5 diagrams these points; the only authentic cadence among them occurs at measure 24, but the melodic action rides past this point.

EXAMPLE 7-5. *Structural outline of the Prelude to* Tristan

Peaks of the dynamic curve	17,	24,	44,	62,	74,	83	
Cadences	17,	24,	44,		74,		94
Key	A	A	C♯		A		A

Melody helps us to keep our bearings within the form. We hear the half-dozen or more salient motives restated many times, and at the final climax, the opening motive is thundered out by the horns as if to close the melodic circle of the form. Beyond these restatements, we hear entire phrases reiterated in varied form; for example, the phrase of measures 17 to 22 returns at measures 32 to 36, 55 to 58, 58 to 63, and 75 to 78.

As you can see from Example 7-5, the tonal center of the Prelude is A. Yet we never hear a strong confirming cadence in this key; the harmony constantly circles around, as if it were orbiting, but never actually drawn to a landing.

All the special qualities of sound, movement and arrival, the kind of melodic material and its deployment, the unstable harmony, and the broad arch of the form work together to build the intense, compelling

mood that is set in this piece—a deep yearning that longs for fulfillment but will find it only in death.

Often the Prelude to *Tristan* is paired in concert performance with
the final scene of the opera, the *Liebestod* (The Love-Death). These
two "end pieces" join beautifully; the last tone of the Prelude links to
the beginning of the Liebestod as a deceptive cadence. Expressively,
the Prelude projects the longing and sadness of the lovers; the
Liebestod represents their fulfillment in death.

Since the harmony of the Prelude is principally unstable, while
that of the Liebestod has a strong flavor of major harmony, the overall
effect when these are performed in concert is that of a large-scale
cadence. This impression is reinforced by the rhythmic contrast, from
irregular to basically *symmetrical,* as we hear in the first four measures
of the Liebestod. While the Prelude has a complex chain of motivic
layouts, the Love-Death builds its great dynamic curve with two
principal figures—the opening songlike motive and the final cadential
motive, repeated and extended to reach the ultimate climax on the final
phrase "highest joy." After this, the scene and the opera reach a close
with a magic transformation of the opening measures of the Prelude,
extended to reach an intensely poignant plagal cadence that fades
slowly into silence. Example 7-6 quotes these three principal melodic
elements of the Love-Death:

EXAMPLE 7-6. *Wagner,* Tristan, *motives from the Love-Death*

a. Opening melody

b. Cadential figure

c. Transformation of beginning of Prelude into plagal cadence

The music of *Tristan* epitomizes some of the qualities that are typical in romantic music. Now we shall look further into these features as they can be found in other music of this era.

SOUND For the listener, one of the chief differences between romantic music and that of earlier eras can be sensed immediately—a richer, fuller, more varied and colorful quality of sound. This richer effect is produced both by the *instruments* used and by the *harmonic language*. In instrumental music the orchestra and the piano come to the fore during the nineteenth century as the principal media for exploring the broader and more colorful spectrum of sound.

THE ORCHESTRA One of the most familiar and stirring sounds in all music is that of the full orchestra as it was evolved during the romantic era. You have heard it in one of its grandest statements—the opening of Brahms's Symphony No. 1. Compare this in sound to the first measures of Mozart's *Jupiter* Symphony, probably the most impressive orchestral work of the eighteenth-century classic style; strong and full as the Mozart scoring is, it is lighter and much thinner than that of Brahms, with far less concern with richness of tone color. The chart below gives the scoring of these two works; note especially the thicker "middle" of the scoring, as represented by a larger brass section.

EXAMPLE 7-7. *Instrumentation of Mozart,* Jupiter *Symphony (1788), and Brahms, Symphony No. 1 (1876)*

MOZART	BRAHMS
2 flutes	2 flutes
2 oboes	2 oboes
2 bassoons	2 clarinets
2 horns	2 bassoons
2 trumpets	contrabassoon
timpani	4 horns
1st violin	2 trumpets
2nd violin	3 trombones
viola	timpani
violoncello	1st violin
contrabass	2nd violin
	viola
	violoncello
	contrabass

Actually, Brahms was conservative in his orchestration; his scoring represents a rather modest expansion of the classic orchestra. In some scores, the orchestra grew to mammoth size. Even the Prelude to *Tristan,* not one of Wagner's largest scores, calls for winds in threes, tuba, and harp, in addition to strings, brass, and timpani.

Typically, the large forces of the orchestra were deployed (1) to broaden melodic lines so as to give them greater weight and richer tone color, and (2) to fill in the sound, especially in the middle and lower ranges, so as to create a solid "core" of sound. If you look at the score of the first page of Brahms's Symphony No. 1, you can see how he "underlines" the rising and falling lines by *doubling* them, that is, assigning each line to several groups of instruments.

Given the large orchestral forces available in the nineteenth century, it could be expected that composers would take advantage of this resource to build extended *orchestral crescendos.* Although the orchestral crescendo had already created much excitement in the eighteenth century, it was rarely used by Haydn or Mozart; Beethoven made it an integral part of his style, as we have heard in the first movement of his *Eroica* Symphony. Wagner built the entire Prelude to *Tristan* upon the idea of crescendo, both within phrases and up to the final climax.

Along with the more massive sound, we hear many new and striking sounds in the romantic orchestra. New instruments and imaginative treatment of the traditional instruments bring forth a wide and varied palette of color. For example, the *Tristan* chord at the beginning of the Prelude owes much of its poignant effect to its scoring by winds alone—oboes, English horn, clarinets, and bassoons.

Berlioz was the most imaginative and unconventional composer of his time in exploring new orchestral colors. He often assigned leading melodic material to instruments rarely heard, if at all, in orchestral music. Note these passages in his *Symphonie Fantastique;* they are representative of the hundreds of places where he explored striking new orchestral sounds:

1. In the second movement, the hero's dream of a grand ball is told. At the beginning, the misty atmosphere of the dream is set by murmuring strings and an ensemble of harps playing brilliant, skyrocketing arpeggios.
2. Distant thunder is suggested by four timpani at the end of the third movement, In the Country.
3. Also in the third movement, the lonely mountain scene is evoked by the English horn and oboe answering each other as shepherds might do; these passages occur both at the opening and close of the movement.

4. The fifth movement depicts a diabolic orgy. Here Berlioz pulls out all the stops of orchestration; a constant stream of novel and strange effects shapes the picture of this celebration of evil. Perhaps the most striking passage occurs when the doom of sinners is foretold. Berlioz quotes the doomsday tune from plain chant, the "Dies Irae" (Day of wrath). We hear this solemn melody first in the tubas accompanied by large bells, as it might sound in a cathedral; each phrase of this ponderous version is immediately answered by higher instruments, more quickly, and with increasingly grotesque effect as the devils take over.

In this symphony, as in his other orchestral music, Berlioz retains something of the transparency of classic scoring, to project his sense for striking line and color; this aspect of his style probably influenced twentieth-century composers, who turned away from the dense and rich sounds that formed the core of nineteenth-century orchestration. Figure 19 quotes from the fourth movement of the *Symphonie Fantastique.*

THE PIANO The piano, like the orchestra, received its present definitive form in the nineteenth century. Refinements and improvements in the piano gave it a wider range of tonal effects and a more brilliant sound. The most important was the perfection of the sustaining pedal, which allowed a tone to reverberate for a time after being struck. This opened a new world of tone color, of rich pervasive resonances, of delicate atmospheric effects. To illustrate: play the chord C-E-G upward from middle C, holding the right-hand pedal down. Release the keys, while keeping the pedal down; note that the tones continue, and also that there is a faint aura of sound *above* these tones as all the C's, E's, and G's chime in by *sympathetic* resonance. The sustaining pedal increased the amount of sound, enabling composers to create grandiose effects; it also promoted a singing quality of sound by allowing tones to be more easily connected, making it possible to carry broadly sweeping melodies.

Frédéric Chopin was the master of piano texture and color. His Preludes for Piano—short, characteristic pieces—explore a wide range of sounds and figurations. The first Prelude is a typical Chopinesque miniature, with its simple singing melody floating over a finely etched network of sound. In much of his piano music Chopin uses a figure again and again, shaping it so that it has a striking contour and some element of color, a salient tone that adds piquancy to the harmony. Example 7-8 illustrates some of Chopin's figuration:

FIGURE 19. *Excerpt from Berlioz's* Symphonie Fantastique, *March to the Scaffold. Note the massing of instruments in contrasting groups, quick give-and-take, sudden contrast of pianissimo and fortissimo, striking harmonic shifts, brilliance of effect increased by high register of bass instruments. Key to abbreviations of the names of the instruments:*

Fl.: Flute(s)	Tr.: Trumpet(s)
Ob.: Oboe(s)	Tbni.: Trombone(s)
Cl.: Clarinet(s)	Tb.: Tuba(s)
Fg.: Bassoon(s)	Timp.: Timpani
Cor.: Horn(s)	Ptti.: Cymbal(s)
C. à p.: Cornet(s)	

G. C.: Bass drum
Vl.: Violin(s)
Vla.: Viola(s)
Vc.: Violoncello(s)
Cb.: Double-bass(es)

EXAMPLE 7-8

a. Chopin: Prelude in C major

b. Chopin: Prelude in F♯ minor

Robert Schumann, a contemporary of Chopin, and very close to him in stylistic and aesthetic respects, developed a different manner of composing for the piano. As we listen to Schumann's *Carnaval,* we hear much that is similar to Chopin in general mood. But the quality of sound in Schumann's music for piano is heavier, more massive than Chopin's. The center of sound seems lower; the quality of movement appears to be heavier and to involve greater effort. Typically, Schumann uses more notes at a given time than Chopin. Often the performer has to negotiate massive chords which move rather quickly. While Chopin's harmony seems to change at an even, rather slow rate, whether the piece be slow or fast, Schumann's chords change quickly; the harmony boils up, exploring and restless. We hear greater rhythmic imbalance in Schumann than in Chopin. This, together with the restless harmony, gives an impression of instability and constant massive motion.

Chopin's texture and manner point the way to musical impressionism: Liszt, Ravel, and Debussy are his stylistic descendants.

Schumann's texture, both in piano and in orchestral music, was adopted by his protégé Johannes Brahms, and his harmony is a direct forerunner of the harmonic style of *Tristan*. Liszt also learned much from Schumann.

VIRTUOSITY   The search for new, more impressive, richer, and more striking effects led to new, and often greater, demands upon the performers. Greater *virtuosity* was required in all fields of performance. This applied particularly to solo performance. The nineteenth century begins the era of the musical hero, the Paganini, the Liszt, the Rubinstein, the Von Bülow. Both the difficulties of performance and the strangeness of the music itself acted to create a tremendous chasm between the artist and the listener. It was as if the artist were endowed with mysterious magic powers that set him apart from ordinary human beings. Niccoló Paganini, the great violin virtuoso, was considered to be in league with the Devil. Not only the performer, but the composer himself was separated and estranged from his audience, largely because of the elusive or difficult music he wrote in his search for individuality. The demands made by nineteenth-century composers exceed anything that had been required previously.

At the summit of virtuosity stands the Sonata in B minor of Franz Liszt. This work embodies all the varied styles and techniques of piano performance that had been evolved up to this time; it also represents the trend of the later nineteenth century to encompass an entire world of expression and feeling in a monumental composition. Everything in this piece seems to have the air of bigness. Most of the music is phenomenally difficult to play. The range of sound covered is tremendous. The volume of sound moves from the loudest possible sonorities to the merest whispers.

In its effort to encompass a gigantic range of expression, this sonata seems to go far beyond the idiomatic style of the piano at many points. Most of the music is what we would call *pianistic,* yet many passages appear to imitate orchestral sounds. We can imagine bassoons and horns sustaining the first low tones while the string basses and cellos take the slowly descending figure. Certain lyric passages call for flute or oboe; other massed effects suggest a compact sound of brasses. There seems to be some kind of push outward, an effort to exceed the limits of usual or ordinary sound, technique, and expression. Thus, like *Tristan*, the Sonata in B minor is truly a representative work of musical romanticism.

HARMONIC   We have already heard how concentrations of unstable chords created
COLOR   a rich tapestry of color in *Tristan* (see Examples 7-1 and 7-2). Beyond

this special aspect of romantic harmony, simpler chords—triads—can take on an added glow or shade of color, thanks to the resources of scoring evolved during this era. In Example 7-8, the sustaining pedal of the piano spreads a veil of sound over the arpeggiated chords. In Example 7-9, you can sense the weird, ghostly effect created by the low-placed, slowly moving chords; note the hollow quality of the first chord, which lacks a third and sets the mood of unearthly stillness.

EXAMPLE 7-9. *Schubert, "Der Doppelgänger"* (The Phantom Double, *1828*)

By placing chords from *different* keys next to each other, a varicolored effect can be achieved; each hue then contrasts with its neighbor, much as bits of strikingly different colors will highlight each other in a painting. Example 7-10 illustrates this procedure; the passage acts as a curtain or introduction to one of the great melodies in romantic music, the "Going Home" theme.

EXAMPLE 7-10. *Harmonic color: Dvořák, Symphony No. 5 in E minor, "From the New World," Second movement (1893)*

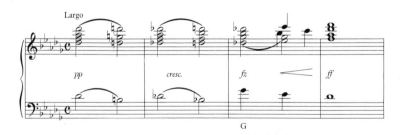

The way in which Dvořák sets the "spots" of harmonic color against each other in the above passage is similar to the color methods used by some painters (Manet, Seurat) of the late nineteenth century—placing dots of different colors next to each other.

MOVEMENT AND ARRIVAL In order to accommodate its more colorful qualities of sound, romantic music typically moves more deliberately, less buoyantly than music of the baroque and classic styles. Even when there is a feeling of quick tempo, it often arises from a rapidly moving pattern of ornamentation, as in Example 7-8, where the underlying pace is rather easy and swinging. When the first movement of Brahms's Symphony No. 1 shifts to a faster tempo, we still have a sense of considerable weight, consistent with the very massive effect of the introduction. To be sure, there are many quick pieces in romantic music, such as the Scherzo from Mendelssohn's *A Midsummer Night's Dream* (1843), but the trend is clearly toward a heavier and slower pace, reflecting the deep and intense moods of this music.

The tentative, uncertain effects of arrival you heard in the Prelude to *Tristan* appear frequently throughout romantic music, matching the emphasis on tone color and deliberate pace. At the end of many compositions the effect of arrival is reduced, to create an effect of trailing off, so that we can imagine the music still reverberating after the sound ceases. For example, Chopin's Prelude No. 1 trails off with a sustained chord; so does his Prelude in A major, that brief, delicate, wistful fragment of a dance. Both the Prelude to *Tristan* and the first movement of Brahms's Symphony No. 1, for all their struggles and intensity, approach their closing moments with a sense of letting go, rather than with the triumphant affirmation of classic music.

Romantic poetry at times showed the same approach to closure. In Shelley's poem *To—*, we are awakened to the lingering fragrance of flowers, the reverberations of tones, the recollection of love, all of which extend beyond the time of the actual experience.

To—

Music, when soft voices die,
Vibrates in the memory—
Odours, when sweet violets sicken,
Live within the sense they quicken.

Rose leaves, when the rose is dead,
Are heaped for the beloved's bed;
And so thy thoughts, when thou art gone,
Love itself shall slumber on.

SHELLEY

While nineteenth-century composers often followed classic models in creating powerful effects of arrival, the less definite treatment of arrival we often hear reflects a characteristic romantic approach both to form and expression—a blurring of lines and a sustaining of mood.

EXPRESSION

INTENSITY

Among the works we have heard so far there is a consistent approach to expression—an intensity of mood—as if the composer were trying to draw us into his world, rather than simply to show it to us. Romantic expression has violent outbursts, restlessness, intense desires and yearnings, ideas of perfect good, utter evil, foreboding, tragedy, and doom.

All these qualities of expression involve personal feelings, personal destinies. Art, music, literature, and philosophy during the nineteenth century are passionately concerned with the individual and his or her fate. They deal with personal reactions, experiences, and emotions. Human beings quest and probe, seeking the solution of the problem of good and evil. Nineteenth-century music draws heavily upon such literary and philosophic concepts. The power of music to convey strong emotional effects was geared to these grand and profound ideas.

In each of Wagner's music dramas, the central issue seems to be a metaphysical conflict. In *Tristan*, love is pitted against honor and tradition; in *Tannhäuser* (1845), sacred love against profane love; in *Parsifal* (1882), the holy against the impious. In the *Ring* cycle (1853-1874), a godlike race struggles against giants and dwarfs; love, honor, and power are set against each other.

Another motive is the search for the *ideal*. Siegfried is the ideal hero; Tristan and Isolde long for an ideal bliss of love; Parsifal seeks the Holy Grail. *Evil*, especially the diabolic, represents the other side of this coin. The Devil figures in many nineteenth-century works—Gounod's *Faust* (1859), Berlioz's *Symphonie Fantastique* (1830), Liszt's *Mephisto* Waltz (1860), Moussorgsky's *St. John's Night on the Bare Mountain* (1867), Weber's *Der Freischütz* (1821). Orchestration and harmony, colorful, rich and varied, are used effectively to suggest these striking, supercharged images and emotional states to the listener.

PROGRAM MUSIC

The color of romantic orchestration and harmony was often used in music that described a scene or a story. This was called *program* music. Among the scenes preferred were those from nature in its various moods. The play of water, the rhythm of the sea waves, the rush of wind and rain, the countryside with its shepherd's and hunter's horns—these and other scenes provided ideas for nineteenth-century program music.

One of the most remarkable descriptive pieces in nineteenth-century music is Mendelssohn's *Hebrides* Overture (1830). This work is an impression of a sea voyage to the western isles of Scotland. Listen to the strange harmonies within the first few measures. How striking is their suggestion of bareness and desolation upon an open sea. The short undulating figure buried within the texture hints at the rolling waves. The sense of bleakness is relieved now and then by brighter moments, as if calm and sun appeared briefly, but the prevailing gray mood is sustained throughout the piece. Mendelssohn here, as in all of his music, shows a remarkable combination of beautifully shaped form based upon classic models and an exquisitely poetic mood that is thoroughly romantic.

The list of romantic works inspired by nature is long. It would include many of Schubert's songs; the third movement of Berlioz's *Symphonie Fantastique*, "In the Country"; the Prelude to Wagner's *Das Rheingold*, which describes the widening flow of the river Rhine by gradually increasing the activity of rolling figures, while keeping the harmony constantly upon one chord, E♭ major; Smetana's *The Moldau* (1879), again the image of a flowing river; Weber, the "Wolf-Glen" scene from *Der Freischütz*. Romantic composers took their cue from Beethoven in using nature as a subject for description. His Symphony No. 6 in F major, the *Pastoral* (1809), departed from the traditional *four-movement* layout of the classic symphony in its *five* impressions of a country scene—pleasant feelings at being in the country, a brook scene, a country dance, a storm, and a song of thanksgiving. As you listen to this work, you can hear how Beethoven adapted his style to the pastoral mood; instead of the powerful thrusts toward important goals, we hear a steady play of smoothly shaped figures placed upon a mellow, sustained curtain of sound, given contour by a gentle rise and fall of melody and dynamics.

Folk cultures represented another rich source for program music. This was a way of expressing the growing awareness of *national* styles in music—Russian, Bohemian, Hungarian, Scandinavian, Spanish, for example.

Russia, with Moussorgsky, Aleksandr Borodin, Nicholas Rimsky-Korsakov, and others, developed a new and highly significant musical language, based upon folk rhythms and Oriental qualities of color. These give a special distinction to Moussorgsky's opera *Boris Godunov* (1874), Borodin's opera *Prince Igor* (1887), and Rimsky-Korsakov's Overture *La Grande Pâque Russe* (Russian Easter, 1888). In all these works you will hear brilliant flashes of color, odd-sounding melodies based on exotic scales, and a violence of rhythm not encountered before in Western music. They represent a deliberate effort to break away from Western European style; they assert the distinction and separateness of a national culture.

One of the most effective ways of bringing the picturesque image of a national or local scene to life was to incorporate dance music. Dvořák's *Slavonic Dances* (1878, 1886), Liszt's *Hungarian Rhapsodies* (1846-1885), Bizet's opera *Carmen* (1873), with its Spanish rhythms, Tchaikowsky's *Capriccio Italien* (1880), Grieg's Norwegian Dances (1870) and his music for Ibsen's play *Peer Gynt* (1876)—make effective use of folk dance styles.

In the later nineteenth century, controversies arose concerning the relative values of program music, music with a pictorial or story association, and *absolute* music, i.e., sonatas, symphonies, concertos, etc., with no specific program. By many, including the critic Edward Hanslick, absolute music was considered to be the higher form of the art. However, the true value of a composition lies in its artistry, program or no program; indeed, there is something of both program and absolute in every composition that stirs the feelings and has beauty of design.

MUSIC AND
LANGUAGE
Romantic music's ties with literature extended beyond the realm of program music. Many composers were writers and critics. Weber, Berlioz, Schumann, Liszt, and Wagner produced excellent musical criticism. Even more striking was the effort on the part of both music and language to capture something of the essence of the opposite art. Composers tried to approximate the declamatory accents of poetry and dramatic speech. Liszt, at the beginning of his B minor Sonata, suggests a profound and impassioned soliloquy; within this piece we hear passages in recitative style, as if a text were declaimed. Indeed, in Wagner's later music dramas, the entire vocal content is cast in the manner called *Sprechgesang*, "speech-song," in which the inflections and rhythms of the German language are delineated in the music.

EXAMPLE 7-11. Sprechgesang (*speech-song*), *Wagner:* Tristan, *Act III*

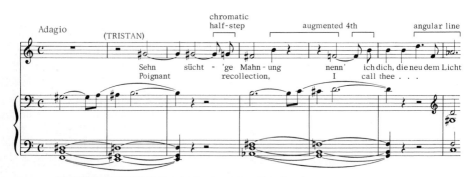

repeated rhythmic pattern in orchestra; irregular pattern in voice

The entire song literature, one of the most distinctive contributions of romantic music, depends upon the close union of words and music. The eloquence, charm, and pathos of poetry is closely matched by the music which romantic composers set to lyric poetry.

While music was striving to become ever more poetic and speech-like in its expression, poets, on the other hand, made efforts to create a musical quality in the sounds of their words. The dark mood of the following excerpt from Edgar Allan Poe's *Ulalume* is measurably enhanced by the vowel sounds he has chosen, framed by alliteration among the consonants and by a singsong rhythm.

> *It was night in the lonesome October*
> *Of my most immemorial year.*
> *It was hard by the dim lake of Auber*
> *In the misty mid-region of Weir.*
> *It was down by the dank tarn of Auber*
> *In the ghoul-haunted woodland of Weir*
>
> POE

In an entirely different mood, John Keats enhances the richness of the scene he is depicting in *The Eve of St. Agnes* by choosing words which have a strongly resonant quality:

> *While he from forth the closet brought a heap*
> *Of candied apple, quince, and plum, and gourd;*
> *With jellies soother than the creamy curd,*
> *And lucent syrops, tinct with cinnamon;*
> *Manna and dates, in argosy transferr'd*
> *From Fez; and spiced dainties, every one,*
> *From silken Samarcand to cedar'd Lebanon.*
>
> KEATS

Before turning to form in romantic music, we can point to some parallels in moods and effects between romantic music and the graphic arts of this era. Eugene Delacroix's famous painting *Liberty Leading the People* has the grand sweep, the heroic motive, and the brilliant color of a Berlioz symphony; Joseph Turner's *The Fighting Téméraire* has the subtle play of color comparable to Chopin's piano textures; Gustave Doré's illustration for the *Wandering Jew,* Fig. 20, depicts a seascape like that suggested by Mendelssohn's *Hebrides* Overture.

FORM

SONATA FORM

With its greater emphasis on color, brilliance, and immediate effect, romantic music modified classic forms and evolved new formal arrangements to accommodate these values. As harmony became richer and less stable, the power of key to define large formal sections dimin-

FIGURE 20. *Gustave Doré: Illustration for* The Wandering Jew. *Nineteenth-century romantic motifs of the wild sea, of terror, and of the supernatural characterize this engraving. (Courtesy of the Stanford University Libraries.)*

ished. *Themes* took on greater responsibility as landmarks in musical form, since they are quickly recognized. This was particularly noticeable in nineteenth-century sonata forms. The chief themes were given striking character and sharply contrasted with each other, much more than in classic sonata form. Generally, the first theme was a bold, vigorous idea; for the second key a more lyric, gentle statement was made. This distinction gave rise to the characterization of the two main themes in a romantic sonata form as "masculine" and "feminine" respectively. More important, the sharp thematic contrast created a marked break in the flow of the music; the exposition, instead of moving steadily and firmly to its conclusion, broke off in the middle, with a marked change in style to introduce the lyric theme, sometimes so different that it seemed to be part of another piece. Then, to bring the exposition to a strong conclusion a new vigorous theme might be introduced. We hear this arrangement in the first movement of Beethoven's *Appassionata* Sonata, Schubert's Symphony No. 7, Tchaikovsky's Symphony No. 6 (1893), Brahms's Symphonies Nos. 1 and 3, Mahler's Symphony No. 2. Example 7-12 quotes the three themes of the exposition of the first movement of Brahms's Symphony No. 1.

EXAMPLE 7-12. *Brahms, Symphony No. 1, first movement*

a. First theme, vigorous

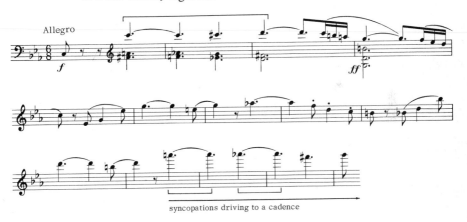

syncopations driving to a cadence

b. Second theme, lyric

c. Closing theme, vigorous

Brahms, in this movement, created a valid compromise between classic and romantic aspects of sonata form; at times he maintained the momentum at critical points and developed strong drives to points of arrival reminiscent of Beethoven's; at other times he allowed the rich and intense immediacy of romantic expression to make itself felt. In order to show the range of treatment that the nineteenth century accorded to sonata form, two additional examples are discussed briefly below:

Tchaikovsky: Symphony No. 6 in B minor (*Pathétique*), Op. 74, first movement. Following a slow introduction, the body of the movement begins in an agitated style, with intensive development of a few short but sharply defined motives. A climax is reached rather quickly, followed by a rapid drop in intensity to reach a moment of complete silence. There ensues, in a slower tempo, the second theme. It is a completely different piece, and it may seem as though we had come to the slow movement of the symphony. The entire second key area is built as a three-part ABA form, A and B each having its own tune. The A tune is one of the most ingratiating melodic inventions in all musical literature. One must pause to take it in, enjoy it, leave it for a gentle contrast, and then welcome it again. The exposition fades away into nothing. The same order of events takes place in the recapitulation, with some variation. Considering the two key areas of the exposition, there are actually two different compositions, linked by a rhetorical pause. Intensity drops, instead of rising as in the classic sonata. Each section is characteristic, inventive, distinctive, indicating that Tchaikovsky is at his best in individual episodes, so familiar in his ballet music. Unity arises from the compatibility of contrasting moods, not from a grand unbroken sweep forward.

Smetana: Overture to *The Bartered Bride* (1866). This is the overture to a comic opera; throughout the nineteenth century we find that music in the lighter vein, such as that of Johann Strauss and Jacques Offenbach, tends to look back to classic models and procedures. Such is the case in this overture, built on the plan and in the spirit of the classic sonata form. It has tremendous verve, stops for nothing, reaches important points of arrival with purposeful drive. The key areas and themes are well marked, the texture has the quick give-and-take of classic scoring, and yet the piece has a distinctly nineteenth-century flavor because of its Slavonic dance rhythms and the colorful harmonies in the second key area, the development, and the coda.

While the greater emphasis on thematic contrast modified the internal structure of the exposition in romantic sonata form, the general outlines of the form remained the same as in the classic era. The development increased in importance, with greater length and complexity, and the recapitulation was the usual restatement of the principal thematic material in the home key. Most nineteenth-century sonata forms required a coda as a final area of arrival; sometimes this involved a change in tempo—a slowing down, as in the first movement of Brahms's Symphony No. 1, or a speeding up, as in the finale of the same work. Thanks to the broadly sweeping melodic style, the tendency to lay out the form in large thematic blocs, and the greater breadth of the development section, romantic sonata forms are typically longer than those of the classic style.

LEITMOTIF; THEMATIC TRANSFOR- MATION
Thematic material played an even more important role in *new* approaches to form evolved in the nineteenth century. A musical idea in the romantic vein is an intense, highly charged fragment of musical expression; it could be used as a point of reference throughout a piece. This technique was used by a number of nineteenth-century composers to help organize their compositions. One procedure was that of the *leitmotif,* developed by Richard Wagner in his later music dramas.

The leitmotif is a short, characteristic musical figure that represents a person, feeling, situation, or object. Whenever one of these comes into view or is referred to in Wagner's music dramas, its leitmotif is announced. While Wagner himself did not use the term leitmotif and did not assign specific meanings to these figures, it is clear that, as he composed, he linked motives and text in a precise way. Ernest Newman, one of the most important writers on Wagner's music, named Example 7-1 the "Grief" motive, linked in the second measure to the motive of Isolde's "Look"; Example 7-3*b* is the "Love Potion," while Example 7-3*f* represents "Deliverance through Death." As you listen to *Tristan,* with some knowledge of the implications of its leitmotifs, you can add this dimension of meaning to the ongoing flow of highly charged musical content and keep your bearings within this immense tide of unbroken movement.

Thematic transformation changes the *character* of a theme while retaining its melodic shape, in contrast to the leitmotif, which *retains* its original expressive quality whenever heard. When a theme becomes transformed, it acts as a kind of "protagonist," a hero that will undergo a number of musical adventures. Liszt's great Sonata in B minor consists of one gigantic movement divided into many contrasting sections; four basic themes are used. Example 7-13 lists the first three themes and a transformation of each:

EXAMPLE 7-13. *Liszt: Sonata in B minor. Thematic transformations*

a. Theme I—brooding, introspective: descending scale

Transformation—brilliant passage-work

b. Theme II—bold, impassioned, electrifying: angular contour

Transformation—lyric, fanciful

c. Theme III—active, percussive: repeated tones

Transformation—songlike

Leitmotif and thematic transformation were generally associated with music of serious import and elevated poetic implications. But in Richard Strauss's *Till Eulenspiegel's Merry Pranks* (1895), the technique served a delightfully comic purpose. The two themes, one a lyric, "once upon a time" sort of statement, and the other a merry scamper for the French horn, are presented at once. Then, following Till's adventures and trickeries, the themes take on a multitude of disguises—roguish, pompous, wistful, grotesque, angry, hectic, etc.—with quick changes of mood recalling the play of figure and topic of eighteenth-century classic music.

Neither the leitmotif nor thematic transformation was new in romantic music. Mozart assigned distinctive material to the Commandant in *Don Giovanni* (the ombra style) and to Papageno (bird music) in *The Magic Flute.* Bach's cantatas change the character of the melody in various movements, as in *Christ lag in Todesbanden* (page 106). Beethoven's *Grosse Fuge* changes the character of its two themes in each of its four main sections. But the prominence of these procedures and the reliance placed upon them to organize musical form was new in romantic music. Both procedures had tremendous influence upon music to follow. Wagner's leitmotif was imitated by Debussy in *Pelléas et Mélisande* (1902), while Liszt's thematic transformation led directly to twelve-tone music.

Other distinctive uses of thematic material in nineteenth-century music include the *idée fixe* and the *remembrance motive.* Berlioz's idée fixe, representing the artist's vision of his beloved in the *Symphonie Fantastique,* is the principal theme of the first movement, then recurs as a lyric episode in each of the next three movements, finally to be transformed into a grotesque witch's dance in the last movement. Berlioz used this theme, Example 7-14, as a signal to bind all five movements together.

EXAMPLE 7-14. *Berlioz:* Symphonie Fantastique, *idée fixe*

Remembrance motives were devices used in opera in much the same manner as the leitmotif, but only to pinpoint important characters or situations, not as the principal melodic technique. Verdi used remembrance motives in *Aida* (1871) to characterize Aida (a slow, lyric, chromatic figure) and Amneris (a rapid, agitated figure), introducing these figures again and again at critical points in the opera.

ONE-MOVE- Both the leitmotif and thematic transformation are linked to a new
MENT FORM approach to form in the nineteenth century, evolved from the eighteenth-century fantasia. A large work, instead of consisting of a number
of movements, could be written as one long movement, divided into
many sections, and unified by using the same thematic material
throughout. Liszt's Sonata in B minor represents this procedure.

To give the entire work some definite contour, Liszt took elements from the sonata form. He set the bold theme against the lyric
theme, with the usual contrast of key areas. In the center of the work,
he built a broad area of development, and the sonata winds up with a
recapitulation of the two principal themes. This we can recognize as
the outline of a sonata form, but, from phrase to phrase and section to
section, we frequently lose that sense of purposeful arrival and clearly
directed movement which gave rise to the classic sonata form. The
episodes are so different from each other, and frequently so loosely
connected, that they would need little to make them independent
pieces.

Liszt turned this particular fact to advantage; the contrast in style
between the first and second sections is so great that they take on the
roles of an opening and a slow movement respectively. The development is still another movement, a grand fantasy, while the recapitulation acts as a broad epilog. Liszt took the cue from Beethoven in this
respect; a number of the later works of Beethoven display multi-
sectional form, such as the "Grosse Fuge" and the finale of the Ninth
Symphony.

In orchestral music, the long single-movement layout was known
as the *symphonic poem* or the *tone poem.* The very name indicates an
expressive link with poetry, with epic or heroic tales told in verse. The
best-known of these works are those of Liszt and Richard Strauss.
Liszt's *Les Préludes,* his most famous symphonic poem, uses two basic
themes in thoughtful, pastoral, agitated, amorous, martial, and triumphant moods. Strauss shaped his tone poem *Till Eulenspiegel* as a huge
rondo.

Before concluding this discussion of large-scale form in romantic
music, we should mention another important trend—the *retrospective*
view, a backward look to forms and styles of earlier times. Until the
end of the eighteenth century, composers and listeners were principally concerned with the music of their own times, producing and
consuming it as if it were a commodity of current interest. In the
nineteenth century, a much stronger awareness of the past developed
in all fields—literature, art, music, and in history itself. Mendelssohn's
revival of Bach's music (1829) and the Cecilian movement (1867),
which did the same for Palestrina, were evidences of this trend. Most
often this self-conscious return to the past was done with an effort to
recapture the grand elevated manner of church music, as in the great

fugues of Brahms's *German Requiem* (1868). A different attitude was taken by Berlioz in the finale of his *Symphonie Fantastique,* which he framed as a baroque form—a fantasia, chorale, and fugue. This form and its religious implications—the diabolic parody of sacred liturgy—are appropriate for the picture Berlioz described: ". . . a Witches' Sabbath . . . a fearful crowd of spectres, sorcerers, monsters . . . strange noises, groans, shouts of laughter, distant cries . . . the melody of the beloved . . . trivial, grotesque . . . the "Dies Irae" (Day of Wrath) . . . the "Ronde du Sabbat" (Rounds of the Witches's Sabbath).

This picture of ancient and timeless evil exulting in its night of revelry opens as a monstrous improvisation, a fantasia of short, weird episodes, marked by violent contrasts. The devilish company is gathering, led by the artist's beloved, who has now become a witch (see page 170). The doomsday chorale, "Dies Irae," is intoned (see page 171). When all have gathered, they join one by one in a great round, a fugue, that builds to an enormous pitch of excitement, interrupted by grotesque episodes in which Berlioz introduces some startling orchestral effects. This is all done with a deftness of touch and a sure command of traditional means—counterpoint, form, scoring—pulled into strange shapes.

Expressively, the large-scale forms discussed above deal with heroic, grandiose attitudes. To convey intimate, delicate sentiments, romantic music turned to short forms, short piano pieces, and songs.

THE SHORT PIECE
Piano

In the short piece for piano a single mood is expressed, or perhaps two contrasting moods; these are fragments of feeling that come into view and disappear. Often we have the impression that the music has been going on before it becomes audible and will continue after the final silence. As you listen to a typical short piece, such as the Prelude in C major by Chopin, you can sense the mood being sustained by a singsong regularity in the phrase structure, as pairs of measures balance each other and the music swings along in an easy flow.

Composers of the nineteenth century put a great deal of their personal style into short piano pieces, unlike those of the classic era, whose short pieces were mostly dances for entertainment. The popular Viennese ring of Schubert's *Moments Musicaux,* the fire and grace of Chopin's Preludes and Etudes, the vigor and passion of Schumann's *Carnaval,* the sentimental elegance of Mendelssohn's *Songs Without Words,* the introspective musings of Brahms's *Intermezzi*—these are some of the characteristic styles that give the short piece in the nineteenth century its special charm.

Formal layouts are simple: (1) a single period—for example, Chopin's Preludes in C major, A minor, A major, E minor, and B minor; (2) small two-reprise forms—Schumann's *Carnaval* has many of these; (3) an A B A form, analogous to the minuet and trio—as in Chopin's Prelude in D♭ major. Figuration ranged from the heavy, low-set, full chords of the solemn march of Chopin's C minor Prelude to the airy, thin-spun flight of the treble figure in his G major Prelude. The short piano piece touched upon virtually every facet of expression—tragic, comic, wistful, pathetic, sentimental, mysterious, etc.—each an intimate, brief, yet eloquent statement.

Song The *song,* even more than the short piano piece, was the final embodiment of romantic lyricism. Here poetry and music, which tried to emulate each other, could find their most effective coordination. The piano, with its new versatility—sonority, figuration, range, and singing quality—could become a true partner to the voice. Some of the finest and most characteristic works of the nineteenth century are the song cycles of Schubert, Schumann, Berlioz, Brahms, Hugo Wolf, Richard Strauss, and Gabriel Fauré. The nineteenth-century song is a personal, intense, relatively brief expression of a mood worked out with great attention to *nuance.*

One of the earliest yet finest songs of the romantic era is Schubert's "The Erlking," composed to a poem by Goethe. It tells the story of a father riding at night through the storm with his child. The child senses that the Erlking (an embodiment of Death) is near and is tempting him to join the Erlking and his daughters; the child cries out again and again in terror while the father attempts to reassure him. At the end the father finds the child dead in his arms.

We are brought immediately into the mood of agitation and fear by the agitated triplet figure in the piano that suggests the stormy wind and the menace it brings. Against this background, each character—narrator, father, child, and Erlking—has a characteristic style. The narrator tells the story with a simple melodic line; the father has strong, sturdy melodic figures; the child cries in terror; while the Erlking has beautiful seductive melodies in the vein of nineteenth-century popular tunes. Note how Schubert manipulates keys to give a different color to each phase of the action; how he changes the triplet accompaniment to a singsong when the Erlking speaks; how a dynamic curve is outlined as each cry of the child reaches a higher pitch. At the end, the steady triplets break off, and the narrator announces in a halting recitative that the child is dead. Only this bare understatement could capture the horror of the moment, and the piano, not the voice, has to end the song abruptly.

To build the drama and tension of the story, Schubert composed this song as though it were a scene from an opera, continuously unfolded without repetition of material. This technique is designated as *through-composed;* the procedure here is different from a traditional method of song composition, in which every stanza is sung to the same music (the *strophic* setting).

In many of his songs, Schubert made use of the *strophic* layout; the song "Thränenregen" (Teardrops) from *Die schöne Müllerin* just misses being a fully strophic song, and by just that much becomes an exquisitely touching work of art. The poem speaks of the reflection of the stars and the moon in the brook for the first three stanzas. Schubert has set this as a sentimental melody, with a few melting chromatic nuances; but the mode is *major*. The fourth stanza breaks the spell. Schubert suddenly places his music in the *minor,* makes a turn back to major, but no! at the very end, the minor, the question, the doubt returns and leaves the final impression. Nothing could better suggest this melancholy, this clouding of intimate romantic mood, than the sudden darkening of the harmony.

Another song from *Die schöne Müllerin,* "Ungeduld" (Impatience), is entirely strophic. The basic form is short; each stanza is but eighteen measures long. But notice how convincingly Schubert suggests impatience by a quick pace and restless piano music. Each phrase of the voice is short; there are no real points of arrival, only momentary rest before the pace is picked up again. Each phrase reaches higher than the previous one, until finally the dynamic curve achieves its peak with its refrain, "You are my heart!" Only at this end do we reach our cadence! This is truly a miniature, yet the fervor and the expanse of feeling it suggests carry far beyond its actual extent in time.

Robert Schumann's songs, together with his piano pieces, represent his most characteristic and successful work. In both genres, Schumann was able to project intimacy and immediate intensity of feeling, a sharply delineated sketch that would appear to be improvised upon the instant. In his song cycle *Dichterliebe* (Poet's Love, 1840) to texts by Heinrich Heine, we meet, again and again, a subtleness of expression coupled with a simplicity of means that speaks feelingly and winningly and is sheer magic in its evocation of mood. The fourth song, "Wenn ich in deine Augen seh' " (When I Look into Your Eyes), is short—only two periods in length with a brief epilog that trails off. The harmony is simple, mostly cadences and a few modest digressions; the texture is uncomplicated, the melody like that of a popular folksong. Yet Schumann has employed these materials in a very special way. He has alternated motion and rest between the voice and the piano; the result is a chamber-music texture, a close conversation, rather than melody and accompaniment. At times motion overlaps; at times it pauses momentarily. Through this distribution of movement, Schumann has added a new dimension to the music, reflecting the dialog of the lover and the unspoken response of his beloved.

Brahms was as much a master of the romantic miniature as he was of the grand symphonic style. In his song "Die Mainacht," (1868, The

May Night), he expresses simply yet subtly the mood of sadness in the poem. With a modest accompaniment and a straightforward syllabic setting of the text, he creates a steady, gentle flow that achieves its expressiveness through harmonic shadings, especially the opposition of minor to major harmony. The restless wandering told in the poem finds its counterpart in the shifting keys, and in a remarkable delay of *any* strong cadence until the final measures of the song, upon the last note of the singer. To sense this, listen to the left hand of the piano, which avoids the tonic until it settles upon it throughout the last four measures.

OPERA

Of all musical genres, opera lent itself best to the expression of the emotional and pictorial values characteristic of romanticism. Terror, tragedy, triumph, transfiguration, ecstasy, magnificent scenes of pageant, the mysterious solemnity of the cloister, the weirdness of the supernatural—these and many other moods could be projected with overwhelming impact by the combination of melodramatic plot, elaborate scenery, and a wide palette of colorful harmonies and textures.

Nineteenth-century opera included French and Italian grand opera, comic opera, national opera, the music drama of Wagner, and later in the century the *verismo,* the opera of realism. We know opera of this era best in its two most important types—the opera of Verdi and the music drama of Wagner.

The mature style of each composer is exemplified in scenes familiar to most opera-lovers—Isolde's Love-Death, the final scene of *Tristan,* which we have already discussed (pages 164 to 169), and the "Ritorna Vincitor" (Return Victorious) from Verdi's *Aida.* Listening to these scenes, you can note some striking differences in style. Verdi's sound is thinner, more transparent, less richly mixed, and higher than Wagner's. Verdi highlights the voice as the carrier of musical interest, while Wagner often uses the voice as part of a complex web of intertwining lines. Verdi's music moves with a strong sense of pulse, based on dancelike rhythms; we have already described the rather heavy, smooth flow of Wagner's music. Verdi's well-marked movement tends to form clearly defined phrases and periods, with strong cadential effects, while Wagner's phases of movement disguise points of arrival.

These qualities of sound, movement, and arrival arise from essentially different expressive aims. Verdi was concerned with the bold projection of specific emotions and the striking impact of dramatic incident, while Wagner built sustained, all-enveloping moods.

The emotional content of *Aida* deals with love, patriotism, jealousy, power, and revenge—emotions that strike us with a strong sense of reality. We have felt them ourselves. The emotional content of

Tristan deals with an obscure hate that is magically turned into love by a mysterious potion. This love reaches a state of blind ecstacy and comes to fulfillment in death. These are emotional experiences far beyond the realm of ordinary human joy and suffering. Verdi's plot is a complex set of interwoven motives and events, all pointing to the final tragedy. Wagner's plot is relatively much simpler and has fewer events. Therefore, Verdi's music is dedicated much of the time to developing *action;* Wagner's music, on the other hand, is devoted principally to developing emotional *moods.*

Aida's scene is made up of five short, highly contrasted sections as her feelings shift between her love for Rhadames, the Egyptian captain, and her sense of duty to her father, the leader of the Ethiopians, the foes of the Egyptians. At the very beginning of the scene, the music underscores the emotional pull from two sides. Aida repeats the phrase she has just been singing with the chorus, "Ritorna vincitor." Listen to the orchestra's chord on her last syllable: the upper instruments play a brilliant major chord, suggesting victory, while the bass adds an unstable tone which undermines the position of the harmony and suggests Aida's misgivings. The following example illustrates this penetrating bit of musico-dramatic insight:

EXAMPLE 7-15. *Verdi:* Aida

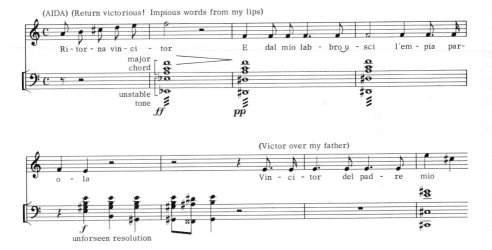

The final section, Aida's prayer to the Gods, is one of Verdi's most beautiful and affecting moments, and shows his ability to use sound in a colorful and expressive manner. The high, shimmering strings, the sustained bright major harmony, and Aida's exquisite melody, set high in the soprano register, provide both a musical and psychological resolution to the conflict projected earlier in the scene.

Aida's "Ritorna vincitor" and Isolde's Love-Death scene show Verdi and Wagner in their typical mature style. The continuously expanding flow of Wagner's music is much more in the spirit of the romantic age than Verdi's well-defined articulations of movement. Verdi becomes romantic in his use of lyricism, in certain uses of chromaticism and harmonic instability, and in his exploration of color values, as in Aida's final song. Wagner shows a debt to classicism in his development of motives, harking back to Beethoven. Wagner's music drama, however, is entirely a creation of the nineteenth century. Verdi's opera is the nineteenth-century version of Italian opera, a genre with a long history and established traditions.

After Wagner and Verdi, the styles they represent continue to live in somewhat altered guise. Richard Strauss used many of the techniques of Wagner, his orchestration, his rich harmony, and the leitmotif, but departed from the grand metaphysical area of expression. Strauss's operas deal with personal issues, often with morbid psychological connotations, as in *Salome* (1905) and *Elektra* (1909).

Giacomo Puccini is the chief heir of the Verdi tradition; also, he is the principal representative of the manner called *verismo*, which sought its subject matter in the realism of nineteenth-century city life. In this respect, Puccini is the counterpart of Zola, De Maupassant, and Flaubert in literature, and of Daumier in art. [*La Bohème* (1896) by Puccini is one of the best-known operas in the entire repertory.] It must be said, however, that Puccini does not use a *realistic* musical technique; rather, his music offers a very sweet, colorful, and ingratiating manner, sentimental instead of brutal.

In the 1820s and 1830s the most spectacular operatic form was French grand opera; this was an elaborate type of production involving vast resources of chorus, ballet, and scenery, as well as the usual apparatus of orchestra and soloists. Grand opera centered upon subjects of historical interest and was directed principally toward the politically élite society of Paris under the rule of Louis Philippe, the "citizen king." Grand opera, whose chief exponent was Giacomo Meyerbeer, adopted in part the Italian musical style of composition, the ingratiating, nicely shaped style of Gioacchino Rossini. But the appeal of such works as Meyerbeer's *The Prophet* (1849) and *The Huguenots* (1836), and Jacques Halévy's *The Jewess* (1835), was in their extremely effective combination of spectacle, popular plot, and assimilable music. Verdi, much later in the century, was to employ the spectacle of grand opera in his *Aida*.

Comic opera also had a vigorous life in the nineteenth century. Many of the tunes from this genre are familiar to us today, such as the Barcarolle from Jacques Offenbach's *Tales of Hoffmann* (1881),

Figaro's "Largo al factotum" and Rosina's "Una voce poco fa" from Rossini's *Barber of Seville* (1816), and the waltzes from Johann Strauss's *Gypsy Baron* (1885) and *Die Fledermaus* (1874), as well as a whole bouquet of tunes from Gilbert and Sullivan's *The Mikado* (1885), *The Pirates of Penzance* (1879), and other amusing and familiar favorites.

One important opera of the nineteenth century, Moussorgsky's *Boris Godunov,* was written in a manner entirely different from Italian, French, or German opera. Moussorgsky's work epitomizes the new Eastern European nationalism that developed in the later nineteenth century. In line with this tendency, Moussorgsky gave a central dramatic position to the chorus, which represents the Russian people. He turned his back on the sophisticated musical language of Western Europe, the language of Wagner or Verdi; instead he used the idioms, sounds, rhythms, and expressive qualities that would suggest the native culture of Russia. Here are two examples which illustrate two important aspects of Moussorgsky's style: (1) his sense for color and immediate impression, as represented in the bell sounds of the coronation scene; (2) his preference for simple, straightforward, down-to-earth music, as represented in an excerpt from Varlaam's song from Act I.

EXAMPLE 7-16. *Moussorgsky:* Boris Godunov

a. Coronation scene

b. Varlaam's song, Act I

Moussorgsky disliked the academic development procedures of Western symphonic and operatic composition. Instead he preferred to create fresh effects, to spin out his material in a somewhat improvisatory manner, ringing the changes upon a few very simple motives. Tone color and rhythmic drive are central points in his style. Thus, Moussorgsky has influenced both the impressionists and the folklore composers of the early twentieth century.

Other characteristic examples of nineteenth-century opera follow:

Verdi: Rigoletto (1851), Act I to the end of the court scene. *Rigoletto* has some interesting points of comparison with Mozart's *Don Giovanni*. In both we have a licentious nobleman, a seduced daughter, an avenging father and a fool. In *Don Giovanni* the father and the fool are separate characters, representing two extremes. In *Rigoletto* they are combined to create one of the most complex characters in all opera. At the end of *Don Giovanni*, the Commandant, as the agent of an authority higher than man, punishes Don Giovanni by dragging him to Hell and thus, in the eighteenth-century view, puts matters to rights. This arrival or cadential effect is reinforced by the final buffalike ensemble. No such balance exists in *Rigoletto*. The avenging father becomes the butt of a grisly joke when he discovers that his attempt to murder the Duke has misfired and that it is his daughter who has become the victim. The opera ends in this mood: there is no resolution, only a fantastic shock that carries far beyond the fall of the curtain. This is a typical romantic treatment of structure—an unanswered question. Evil, not good, triumphs, and Rigoletto, who tried to rise beyond his level, is forced even further down by clever and competent viciousness.

The comparison between the two operas is quite striking in the opening scene. The orchestral introduction has the same ominous tone in each; then the brilliant galanterie which follows in both works presents a similar contrast in the plot motives of the two operas, that is, the gay life as set against the motives of betrayal and revenge. The opening scene of *Rigoletto* is filled with bright tunes—the opening march, the Duke's "Questa o quella" (This Woman or That) cast in a popular Italian song style, the minuet, the perigourdine (a French giguelike dance). Against this background, brilliantly scored, the melodramatic elements of the plot are superimposed and interspersed. The scene builds up to a tremendous climax with a curse and a premonition of horror. The final measures illustrate the kind of immense crescendo (an amplification of the eighteenth-century operatic and orchestral crescendo) with which so many scenes in Italian opera reach their climax and final arrival; the entire scene shows nineteenth-century grand opera at its best, a mélange of spectacle, melodrama, tunefulness—all moving in a powerful theatrical sweep.

Donizetti: Lucia di Lammermoor (1835), the Mad Scene, Act III. This is one of the most famous scenes in Italian opera, a great tour de force for coloratura soprano. Lucy's madness comes on as a result of her murder of Arthur, the man she was tricked into marrying, her true love being Edgar of Ravenswood. The scene is shaped broadly into four sections, the first and third being cast as recitative and arioso, the second and fourth as formal arias. Lucy's derangement is pictured by means of visions, terror, and recollection in shifting moods. Throughout, the extravagant quality is delineated by elaborate coloratura ornamentations of familiar, slowly moving cadential harmonies and sharply etched, ingratiating melodic material. This scene represents early romantic expansion of classic Italian opera procedures.

Bizet: Carmen (1875), Act I through the Habanera. In both its subject matter and its musical idioms, *Carmen* represents a more popular, realistic style than was usual in nineteenth-century opera. Bizet makes much use of local color; the music has a strong Spanish flavor, as in the Habanera (whose tune was not composed by Bizet himself, but by Yradier), the Seguidilla, and the gypsy music. In the opening scene we have a montage of colors, types, and characters; musically, this could be the counterpart of an early impressionistic painting with its brightness and prismatic effects that place separate elements into complementary juxtaposition. The Prelude itself is a set of episodes—toreador march, toreador song, once again the march, and then the music of fate. The opening scene is a colorful square in Seville; there is much movement as characters come and go. Soldiers, children, citizens, cigarette girls, Micaela, Morales, Don José, Zuniga, and finally Carmen—each moves into focus and out again. The music has a decided flavor of the dance, set off by the fanfares and marches of the soldiers. Bizet here sets a mood; relatively little takes place to carry the plot forward. For this we must wait until the end of the scene, when Carmen is arrested by Don José, who in turn finds himself captivated by his prisoner.

CHORAL MUSIC Choral music in the nineteenth century mirrors many of the stylistic elements that characterize the romantic period in general. Grandeur and intimacy are both to be found, the former in such works as Mahler's Symphonies Nos. 2 and 8 and the Requiem of Berlioz, and the latter in many brief part songs by Schumann, Brahms, and others.

Another aspect comes into the picture—revival of the musical past. One of the prime areas of interest was the Renaissance and the style of Palestrina.

Three examples of choral music in the nineteenth-century repertory have been selected to illustrate the antiquarian style, the grandiose style, and the sentimental, intimate part song:

Bruckner: Mass in E minor (1866), Kyrie. The close similarity of the style of this piece to that of Palestrina is immediately sensed. The quasi-imitative entries, the slow, even tempo, the long notes, the conjunct part writing, and the closely spaced, full harmony—all these indicate a conscious effort to capture the spirit of Renaissance music of worship. The principal difference, of course, is in the far richer harmonic palette. We hear many seventh and some ninth chords; dissonance is treated more freely, and the piece is clear in its commitment to *key,* with strong cadences heard often. There is a remarkably close affinity between nineteenth-century chordal texture and its counterpart of the sixteenth century. Both are concerned with sound as a basis for expression; both maintain motion through a continuation of rich sound color.

Berlioz: Requiem: "Dies Irae" (1857). This section of the Requiem, the Mass for the Dead, comprises two sections: the "Dies Irae" (Day of Wrath) itself and the "Tuba Mirum" (Behold, the Trumpet Sounds). In the "Dies Irae," Berlioz recaptures the spirit of the original, the old medieval rhymed sequence, which foretells the Last Judgment. The style recalls that of plainsong and organum; we hear first the principal figure in unison, later elaborated with counterpoint. The archaic effect is enhanced by some elements of modal harmony.

The "Tuba Mirum" is a spectacular pictorialization of the trumpets of the Last Judgment. Berlioz's instructions call for four small bands of brass instruments to be placed at the four corners of the auditorium. They call back and forth to each other with fanfares, sometimes mingling with the full orchestra and chorus. The echoes and reverberations recall the early baroque (Gabrieli's "In Ecclesiis," for example).

Brahms: Liebeslieder Waltzes, Op. 52 (1869). This is a set of eighteen short waltzes, set for two pianos and quartet of four mixed voices (soprano, alto, tenor, and bass). The waltzes are often performed without voices, inasmuch as the pianos contain all the essential musical material; the voices take up the principal melodies and accessory parts. Their main function is to add the personal quality, the singing manner to these very ingratiating miniatures. This is an excellent example of what is called *Gesellschaftsmusik,* music for companionship, full of the quality *Gemütlichkeit,* which may be translated as warm sentimentality. Part songs of a simple popular nature had long been a German tradition; in the nineteenth century the tradition experienced a great upsurge. In these works Brahms's skill in composition is discovered in many deft touches, richness of harmonic color, imaginative figuration, and superb melodies. Further, these works exemplify a characteristic aspect of nineteenth century music, the love of the waltz. We know the waltzes of Johann Strauss, Jr., but perhaps it is not as well known that many composers of the nineteenth century turned to the waltz at some time. Weber, Schubert, Chopin, Liszt, Berlioz, Mahler, Richard Strauss, and many others wrote music that typified the expansive, whirling motion of this dance that so strongly represents the centrifugal spirit of the romantic age.

SUMMARY

Throughout the preceding consideration of romantic music we can sense an implied *centrifugal* tendency. The harmony pulls *away* from the tonic; the rhythm tends to *avoid* strong points of cadential arrival; the texture is fuller, reaching *higher* and *lower,* seeking strange and striking colors; the moods touch upon the *faraway,* the *long ago,* the *supernatural,* the *unattainable.*

All the special characteristics of romantic music, those which set it apart from its predecessors, are gradually exploited more and more as the nineteenth century moves to its close. The process of separation continues, so that by the beginning of the twentieth century a number of special techniques and styles were developed. There are refinements of certain qualities of romanticism, appearing under such names as *expressionism, impressionism, folkloric music,* and *neoromanticism,* which we shall examine in our next chapter.

As a final word on romanticism, we might speculate that it represents a phase of development in the growth of musical self-consciousness. Rationalism and authority might embody a sort of *supra*-consciousness, reflected by the concern with large-scale problems that found their solution in a classic balance. Romanticism represents nineteenth-century *self*-consciousness, the individual regarding himself as the principal focus of interest and importance. We might carry the analogy further and point to the concern with the *sub*-conscious which marks so much of twentieth-century art, philosophy, and psychology. Here, indeed, is the process of separation at work over centuries of thought and expression. Rejecting the answers of the eighteenth century, self-contained but incomplete, romantic artists sought solutions in their own imaginations, feelings, and mystic ethics. Their inability or their unwillingness to reach a convincing resolution eventually engendered disillusionment and a strong counterwave to the expressive ideas so cherished in the nineteenth century. Western humanity, in the romantic age, saw itself moving ever forward, exploring and progressing. As we look back upon this age, we see that it fell short of its hopes, but we can accept romantic expression for what it was, a fascinating, distinctive, colorful tour of the human spirit.

Many of the criteria for listening to romantic music can be adapted from those established for baroque and classic music. The distinctive new features are listed below:

1. *Sound:* New and striking sonorities in the orchestra; exploitation of piano sonorities.
2. *Movement:* A tendency toward a slower, more deliberate pace than in eighteenth-century music; singsong regularity in short pieces, also in sections of some large works; highly irregular movement; continuously intensifying movement.
3. *Arrival:* Weakened, obscured cadences; plagal cadences.
4. *Melody:* Broadly singing style; melody approximating the inflections of speech (*Sprechgesang*); reliance on melody as an organizing element (leitmotif, idée fixe, thematic transformation, "masculine" and "feminine" thematic contrasts in sonata form).
5. *Rhythm:* (see Movement above).
6. *Harmony:* Unstable, tritone-saturated harmonies; exploitation of chord color; elaborate arpeggiation and figuration of chords; rapid modulations (see also Arrival above).
7. *Texture:* Fuller sounds than in eighteenth-century music; exploration of extremely high and low registers.
8. *Form:* Short characteristic pieces; classic forms adapted to romantic style; forms based upon thematic connections; symphonic and tone poem; songs.
9. *Expression:* Intense, immediate emotional impact; heroic, intimate moods; interest in the faraway, long ago, nature, the ideal, the supernatural, the diabolic, the homeland.

**DISCUSSION
AND
REVIEW
QUESTIONS**

1. How does the romantic idea of sound differ from that of classic music? In harmony? In keyboard music? In orchestra?
2. How does romantic music deal with the idea of expression?
3. Discuss romantic uses of melody.
4. What is program music?
5. Discuss romantic methods of relating music and text.
6. How does romantic sonata form differ from that of the classic era?
7. Why did romantic music exploit the short piece?
8. Compare Wagner's and Verdi's operatic styles.
9. Discuss the rise of musical nationalism in the nineteenth century.
10. How does romantic music reflect the spirit of its age?

CHAPTER EIGHT

MUSIC IN THE TWENTIETH CENTURY

Music in the early twentieth century continued the search for new and striking techniques of composition and the development of personal styles which were so characteristic of romantic music. The directions taken by Chopin, Wagner, Liszt, Berlioz, and the nationalist composers led, in the twentieth century, to the establishment of styles of composition widely different from each other. Interest in *tone color* evolved into musical *impressionism; tension,* as embodied in ever-greater saturation of dissonance, led to musical *expressionism,* and the twelve-tone school; *musical nationalism* grew into *folkloric* styles. *Neoromanticism* maintained the colorful, broadly scaled declamation of the later nineteenth century. Efforts to reconcile the new techniques of twentieth-century composition with elements from earlier music characterized the *neoclassic* trend.

Until mid-century, that is, the end of World War II, these styles—impressionism, expressionism, folkloric, and neoclassic—were the leading trends in Western music. Since that time, they have given way to other approaches, although some elements of these early twentieth-century styles have been absorbed in the newer musical techniques. Two important directions have characterized music of the past twenty or thirty years: (1) the use of electronic devices for producing and organizing musical sound; (2) the phenomenal growth of popular music, creating an overpowering presence in today's musical scene. Also, *chance* music, called *aleatory* music, in which the performer plays an important role in putting the music together, has become a significant method of composition. Finally, we should note the influence of music from so-called "exotic" cultures—Indian, Oriental, African—upon Western musical styles. Each of these directions will be explored in this chapter.

It was in the period directly following Richard Wagner that

modern trends of musical composition began to crystallize. From this era, the saturation point of musical romanticism, two very different musical styles evolved. These were *impressionism,* developed principally by the French composers Claude Debussy and Maurice Ravel, and *expressionism,* cultivated by Austrian and German composers, such as Arnold Schönberg, Anton von Webern, and Alban Berg.

IMPRES-SIONISM

EXPRESSIVE VALUES

Impressionism represented a reaction against the philosophic and aesthetic ideas of Richard Wagner. It rejected his grandiose idealism, overdrawn heroic manner, and mysticism. Impressionist composers wished to project vague and evanescent moods; they used many musical devices to evoke such moods. In harmony new, strange, and colorful effects were developed. Impressionist composers were unsympathetic to the Wagnerian conception of artistic expression; yet they found that Wagner's harmonic language contained material that could be used for their own purposes: for example, tone combinations that give an effect of instability, as in the opening of Wagner's *Tristan und Isolde.*

Impressionism seized upon this quality of harmonic color and instability, but used it in an entirely different musical situation. Listen to Ravel's *Ondine.* It begins with a combination of tones quite similar to that which begins *Tristan.* But both the texture and the quality of movement are quite different. Ravel, in contrast to Wagner's profound metaphysical introspection, created a vague, fairylike atmosphere.

EXAMPLE 8-1. (*Note the tones marked by squares*)

a. Wagner: *Tristan und Isolde,* opening

b. Ravel: *Ondine* from *Gaspard de la nuit,** opening

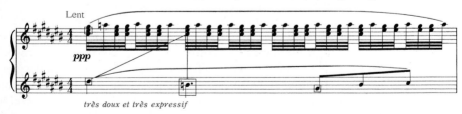

*Permission for reprint granted by Durand et Cie, Paris, France, copyright owners. Elkan-Vogel Co., Inc., Philadelphia, Pa., agents.

Impressionists used many Wagnerian chords solely for the sake of color. Example 8-2 shows a series of these chords. In impressionism, the chord is a resource for sonority effect, not a carrier of a dynamic quality of movement.

EXAMPLE 8-2. *Debussy: Prelude,* Footsteps in the Snow*

It is remarkable that Debussy was able to use such rich harmonic effects in a short piece meant to portray the plaintive and melancholy mood of winter. The harmony actually contributes to the mood; each harmonic effect becomes a separate phase of movement; there is no building up of tension by piling on of momentum. Strong or violent emotional values were avoided; instead a feeling of subtle, subdued restlessness was created that gave the impression of movement being poised in mid-air.

The impressionists were alert to utilize any harmonic resource available. Frequently they turned to the musical systems of the Middle Ages, of folk music, or of exotic countries. Each of these had intriguing qualities, unusual color effects that attracted the impressionists. Here are some examples. The excerpt is given and below it, in each case, the scale upon which the excerpt is based.

EXAMPLE 8-3. *Ravel: Quartet in F, first movement** (1902–1903)

*Permission for reprint granted by Durand et Cie, Paris, France, copyright owners. Elkan-Vogel Co., Inc., Philadelphia, Pa., agents.

Example 8-3 is a graceful, floating melody that takes advantage of the plaintive quality of the Phrygian scale upon which it is based. The Phrygian scale has a half step between the first and second degrees as well as between the fifth and sixth degrees. These half steps, being low in the scale, tend to suggest a resigned, rather than an energetic effect.

EXAMPLE 8-4. *Debussy: Prelude,* Footsteps* (*1910*)

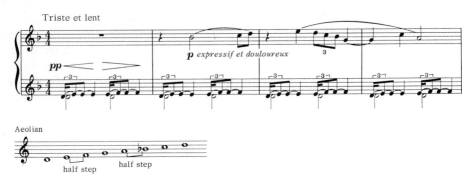

This halting, broken melody also uses a scale which has the half steps placed low. This is the Aeolian scale, with half steps between 2 and 3, 5 and 6. Again the color of the scale sets up the mood.

The pentatonic scale, a gamut of five tones, is used in Example 8-5. Notice that it skips two notes on its way upward. It is a primitive kind of scale and has been used in folk music in many parts of the world, in the Orient, the British Isles, and North America.

EXAMPLE 8-5. *Debussy: Prelude,* The Hills of Anacapri* (*1910*)

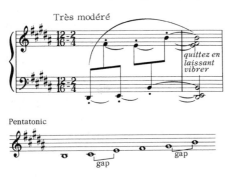

---

*Permission for reprint granted by Durand et Cie, Paris, France, copyright owners. Elkan-Vogel Co., Inc., Philadelphia, Pa., agents.

Debussy employs it here possibly to suggest the echoing reverberation of bells or shepherd's horn through the hills.

When a scale has intervals of different size, like those we have examined, it retains some power to establish points of reference. The special intervals are melodic landmarks. In the *whole-tone* scale, on the other hand, all the intervals are equal to each other, being whole steps. Therefore, this scale cannot establish a point of melodic reference. This vagueness is admirably suited to the aims of musical impressionism; hence, it has been intimately linked with this style, but its actual use has been somewhat less than its reputation would lead us to believe. Sometimes, as in Debussy's Prelude *Sails,* it forms the basis for a large section of a piece; at other times it appears fragmentarily. In *Sails* the whole-tone effect helps create the impression of a slowly swaying passive motion, the easy, indolent mood of a sailboat upon the sea.

EXAMPLE 8-6. *Debussy: Prelude,* Sails* (*1910*)

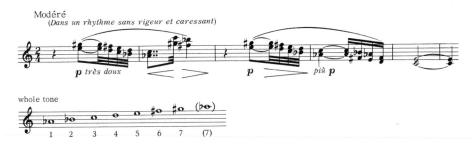

It is interesting to note that Debussy introduced a striking effect of contrast in the middle section of this piece by using the pentatonic scale.

Texture was one of the principal concerns of impressionist composers. Whatever instruments they used, wherever they placed their sounds, they created a transparent, luminous quality of tone with a distinctive color value. Ravel and Debussy were especially fond of exploiting the pedal resources of the piano, which allow tones to reverberate long after the tone has been struck and give the effect of music floating in the air. The excerpt from *The Hills of Anacapri* (Example 8-5) shows how Debussy used this device.

Subject matter in impressionism centered around fantastic, faraway, nostalgic, and pastoral ideas. The music depicted the play of

---

*Permission for reprint granted by Durand et Cie, Paris, France, copyright owners. Elkan-Vogel Co., Inc., Philadelphia, Pa., agents.

water, wind, and sea, the drifting of clouds, or the moods of colorful and exotic scenes. The titles of compositions are strongly evocative, such as *Delphic Dancers, Ondine* (The Water-Nymph), *What the West Wind Saw, The Engulfed Cathedral,* and *Footsteps in the Snow*. At all times, the object was to give a personal impression of some aspect of the external world in a form whose outlines were blurred and whose colors tended toward the pastel.

FORM IN MUSICAL IM-PRESSIONISM Impressionist forms tended to be rather simple. The principal technique of structure was to string out a series of minute and relatively separate effects, much like pointillism in painting; at the same time, a consistency of texture was maintained as well as smooth connection between chords. Small and gentle phases of movement were repeated and varied, but they did not develop any emotional intensity.

Many pieces in this style consisted of a series of episodes, sometimes in ABA form, sometimes in rondo form. The effect of contrast between episodes was created by changes in texture, pace, or harmonic quality. Thus, in *Sails,* Debussy managed to project a striking contrast by using the pentatonic scale for the middle part and the whole-tone scale for the first and last parts.

One form-defining procedure was taken over from the romantic technique of building up to tremendous climaxes. This was the *dynamic curve,* in which a steady increase or decrease in the volume or intensity of sound provided a method for organizing small musical fragments into a larger line; the dynamic curve thus gave some overall shape to a section of considerable extent. The dynamic curve, however, *did not serve an emotional purpose in impressionism,* as it did in romantic music. Rather, it controlled the rise or fall in the intensity of an impression. Its function was pictorial, descriptive. As such, it made an effective framework for *Lever du Jour* (Daybreak), the first number in Ravel's *Daphnis et Chloé* Suite No. 2 (1912). Daybreak, the rising of the sun, and increasing action of the shepherds and shepherdesses—all describe a rising dynamic curve. Ravel begins the piece with the slightest murmur of sound, created by gliding harps and winds and muted, sustained strings, a perfect example of impressionism's pastel tone painting.

After some measures which expand this quality somewhat, a melody takes shape in the lower strings, crystallizing, as it were, out of the amorphous fragments heard at the very beginning. This melody, built principally from one-measure figures, grows by linking its motives together in a general upward direction. The broad dynamic curve of the entire piece is given point and focus by the wide sweep of this melody, which always begins low and rises gradually. Several climaxes are reached, attaining successively higher peaks, and the last, of course, is the highest. In its general contour, this piece resembles the Prelude to *Tristan,* but the details and nuances of style bring about a totally different result. Note in this piece how steady and even the rhythm seems, how stable and placid the general harmonic effect is, and how calmly the bass instruments support the texture. In these respects, Ravel's piece is diametrically opposed to *Tristan.*

Other examples of use of the dynamic curve may be heard in Debussy's *Fêtes* from his Nocturnes for Orchestra (1899), which pictures an approaching and departing group of dancers and merry-makers, and in Ravel's *Bolero* (1927) and *La Valse* (1920), which build up an impression of increasing physical excitement.

HISTORICAL
ANTECE-
DENTS

Impressionism was only in part a reaction against Wagner. Through-out the nineteenth century many pieces written in a pictorial vein to evoke certain moods forecast the impressionism to come. For example Beethoven's Symphony No. 6, the *Pastoral,* is a series of five impressions of various aspects of rural life.

In Mendelssohn's *Hebrides* Overture, constant repetition of a short but graceful motive suggests the play of water, a typical impressionistic subject. Chopin was a valuable source book for the impressionists with his treatment of the piano pedal for sonority and his incredibly imaginative and delicate keyboard figuration. Wagner himself created the impression of water flowing when he spun out rolling motives at the beginning of *Das Rheingold.* These examples are but a few of the pictorial pieces that abound in nineteenth-century music. They serve to show how impressionism grew out of one aspect of romanticism.

IMPRESS-
IONIST
PAINTING
AND
SYMBOLIST
POETRY

Impressionism in music was closely allied with other activities in the creative arts that were taking place in Paris just before the turn of the century. Actually, musical impressionism acquired its name from painting, from the school of Monet, Pissarro, Sisley, and Renoir. These painters achieved the same blurred outlines, the same misty luminous effects that the composers worked out in their music. *Pointillism* was the painter's technique, a method of combining separate tiny bits of color suggesting the prismatic effects of light broken up into its constituent colors. Pointillism created much the same effect in painting that specific small moments of texture and sonority did in music. Both in painting and in music the quality of movement was floating, gentle, disembodied. Whistler's *Nocturne* has the characteristic shadings of impressionist art (see Fig. 21).

Symbolist poets and writers furnished much material for impressionist vocal music. Verlaine, Mallarmé, Maeterlinck, and others culti-

FIGURE 21. *James McNeill Whistler:* Nocturne. *Note the impressionistic play of light and shade in the representation of water, land, and sky.* (*Courtesy of the Metropolitan Museum of Art, Dick Fund, 1917.*)

vated a style characterized by nuance, half-formed ideas, suggestion, and exotic and fantastic atmosphere. This manner of the symbolist writers found a strong response among impressionist composers. The trailing word image could be enhanced by the trailing musical phrase. Frequently symbolist poets tried to develop a purely decorative or musical quality in their texts, a play on sonorities without special reference to meaning. Consider the mellifluous quality of the following excerpt from *Apparition* by Stéphane Mallarmé:

> *La lune s'attristait. Des séraphins en pleurs*
> *Rêvant, l'archet aux doigts, dans le calme des fleurs*
> *Vaporeuses, tiraient de mourantes violes*
> *De blancs sanglots glissant sur l'azur des corolles.*

Debussy's *Prelude to the Afternoon of a Faun* was inspired by

Mallarmé's poem of the same name; his opera *Pelléas et Mélisande* is based upon Maeterlinck's drama; and he wrote songs to poems of Paul Verlaine.

Ravel wrote much that was impressionist in flavor, such as *Gaspard de la Nuit, Daphnis et Chloé,* and *Rapsodie Espagnole,* yet in all his works there was a sense for the long line not entirely compatible with the pointillistic techniques of impressionism. This linear aspect of Ravel's music led him to write works in traditional forms, particularly the sonata form, and to write much music that had no pictorial or special mood values. Frederick Delius in England, Alexander Scriabin in Russia, Charles Loeffler in America, Manuel de Falla in Spain, all wrote music in the impressionist style. Today impressionism has long died out as an active school. Yet much of the harmonic vocabulary of today's music was first defined by the impressionists, and here and there in music written much later, atmospheric touches recall this style.

OPERA IN IMPRESS-IONISM: DEBUSSY'S *PELLÉAS ET MÉLISANDE* (1902) While Debussy renounced the aesthetic doctrines of Wagner and his Germanic predecessors, he nevertheless was influenced in a rather curious way by Wagner when he wrote his opera *Pelléas et Mélisande.* As we listen to this work, we cannot avoid some striking reminders of *Tristan,* some direct and others which seem to be a specific reversal of attitude. Basically, the two stories are similar—there are two lovers and a husband; discovery and the death of the lover follow. Each opera uses a type of declamation suited to the language of its libretto. *Tristan's* vocal lines pick up the extreme highs and lows of the strongly inflected German language; *Pelléas* mirrors the relatively narrow pitch range and the subtle quantitative rhythms of French. Both operas use leitmotifs and build long periods through restatement of these motives upon the dynamic curve. There are similarities in the harmonic language, but as a rule *Tristan* tends to explode into violent expressions of emotion, while *Pelléas* tends to an understatement of feeling, as in the beginning of Act II, when the lovers are alone. Still, we have a true Wagnerian climax in *Pelléas* at the end of Act IV, when Pelléas is killed by Golaud just at the moment of embrace. Throughout *Pelléas,* the techniques of impressionism are used to create and sustain the mysterious, elusive mood that characterizes this work. The interludes that separate the scenes of the opera serve as musical stage settings, bringing to our attention the forest that frames the action of the opera. The very opening measures epitomize Debussy's musical style: the first four measures give us an impression of archaic, remote, and mysterious elements by means of the low-pitched modal harmonies in deliberate, regular motion; the next three measures are built upon a characteristic rich and unstable harmony, carried forward in a rather uncertain wavering motion.

Following are additional examples of impressionism in music:

Delius: On Hearing the First Cuckoo in Spring (1912). A pastoral mood pervades this piece. Among its characteristic features we hear rich, unstable harmonies that seem to melt into each other smoothly and gently; a singsong melody and a regular rhythm; a varied palette of orchestral colors, projecting the gentle, dreamy mood of the piece; a strong element of major and minor harmony, often colored by tones that add piquancy to the basic chord. The dynamic curve is in evidence, but, in line with the expressive quality of the piece, its profile is neither steep nor wide.

De Falla: Nights in the Gardens of Spain: In the Generalife (1915). Many short episodes are joined in this piece, each with its play upon a quality of sound, a melodic figure, and a simple dancelike or songlike rhythm. The contrast is not extreme; there seems to be a deliberate and quiet progression from one episode to another. The orchestration often points up the color of individual instruments, such as the horns. The solo piano is handled in the typical style of the later nineteenth century, as an element of color and figuration. Note the sideslipping of harmonies which suggests the Oriental quality also heard in the flamenco.

Debussy: Sirènes from Nocturnes (1893–1899) for Orchestra. Women's voices in four parts are added here to enrich the color that characterizes Debussy's orchestration. While they are assigned melodic fragments from time to time, the voices are principally concerned with adding their vibrant quality to the sound of the orchestra and with creating brief vocal arabesques that mesh with the decorative figures of the instruments. The harmony has a strong sense of major, often with added tones for color. Movement is gentle and singsong. The entire piece embodies once again the impressionist composer's preoccupation with the play of natural elements, this time the element being the sea.

Debussy: Clair de Lune from the song cycle *Fêtes Galantes* (1892, poem by Paul Verlaine). The elusive imagery of this poem is suggested in the first few lines, paraphrased as follows: "Your soul is a rare landscape, in which charming masqueraders move, playing the lute and dancing, as if they were sad beneath their fantastic disguises." This text is set with an elegant melodic line that scans the syllables rather than reflects the sense of the words. The piano maintains a steady background motion against which it introduces fragments in a pointillistic pattern, although without marked contrast save in harmony. Debussy's harmony (the piece has a strong flavor of Dorian mode) and his figuration represent impressionistic techniques in this work.

**EXPRESS-
IONISM;
TONE-ROW
MUSIC**

EXPRESSIVE
VALUES

Musical expressionism represented the most complete contrast possible to impressionism. Its object was to suggest the innermost world of feeling, not the external world of picture and mood. Expressionism tried to give an idea of the struggles, tensions, and contradictions working within the subconscious. This inner world has strange qualities of meaning; its drives are often perverse and destructive; disparate concepts are linked in an obscure manner. Expressionism deals with strange shapes, odd juxtapositions, disembodied fragments; there is no central core of substance, little contact with familiar realities. There is a striking parallel between the emergence of expressionism and the development of psychological techniques to explore the subconscious. Freud and expressionism are both aspects of man's concern with his inner psychic states. Naturally, the qualities of movement in expressionism would not be clear, direct, and smooth; rather, they are capricious, unpredictable, shifting, angular, irregular, brief, and incomplete.

Arnold Schönberg was the leader in the school of musical expressionism. Probably the most celebrated work of this school is his *Pierrot Lunaire* (1912), a set of twenty-one melodramas for voice and five performers. The poems deal with the nocturnal adventures of Pierrot of the Moon, a fantastic spirit. The imagery is vivid, but the meanings are elusive and dreamlike. Many of the poems have grotesque ideas, but at the same time they invoke an almost painfully nostalgic mood. The voice half sings and half speaks; this technique, developed from Wagner's declamatory recitative style, is called *Sprechstimme*.

Number 5 from *Pierrot Lunaire*, Valse de Chopin, illustrates a typical expressionistic manner:

EXAMPLE 8-7. *Schönberg: Valse de Chopin from* Pierrot Lunaire, *No. 5**

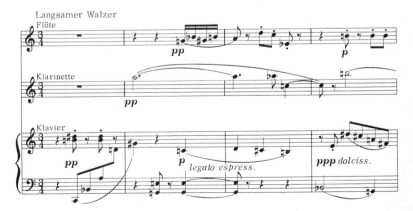

*Copyright 1914 by Universal Edition, Vienna; used by permission of Associated Music Publishers, Inc., New York.

Notice in this example the disembodied texture, the fragmentary bits of melody, the lack of a strong point of reference, and the constant tension. Schönberg here composed a nightmare parody of a waltz. The tiny melodic and rhythmic fragments of this piece could well fit into a romantic waltz if they were set together in a clear relationship of statement and counterstatement and if they were supported by a vigorous rhythmic and harmonic accompaniment.

Although Richard Strauss and Gustav Mahler did not go as far in this direction as later composers did, they dealt with subject matter that showed a strong tendency to portray distorted states of mind and escape from reality. Strauss's *Elektra* deals with matricide and insanity; *Salomé* centers on sadistic lust; *Till Eulenspiegel* upsets the whole world; *Don Juan* allows himself to be killed out of disappointment after surfeit; *Don Quixote* yearns for a lost world and tilts at windmills. Mahler's *Lied von der Erde* (Song of the Earth) combines late Viennese romanticism with some artificial *chinoiserie* in a work whose mood shifts from deep despair at the futility of life to momentary solace in toy scenes. In all this music there is little to suggest regeneration, of good struggling with evil and winning out, perhaps in a better world. The object is to report as strikingly and effectively as possible the nature of the problem, the state of mind; the resolution is not given.

TECHNIQUES   Expressionism was drawn to Wagner's dissonances, to his melodies that gave an effect of distortion through wide jumps and jagged outlines, and to his rhythmic patterns that conveyed a sense of conflict and restlessness. These were all techniques that created a feeling of instability. Expressionism wished to avoid well-defined points of arrival. Through constant use of arbitrary dissonant combinations it avoided giving any sense of tonal center. This was called *atonality.* Melodies that flowed evenly and rhythms that were regular also came under the ban since they can easily create a sense of stability. Yet the most important factor of all in creating expressionism's spidery, grotesque effects was its texture. We no longer hear the substantial central core of sound, the merging of voices that gave body to the texture in music of earlier periods. Rather, there is a use of ornamental melodic voices generally placed at great distances in range from each other. Contrapuntal activity of great intensity is supposed to create musical interest and to compensate for the removal of the musical *terra firma.*

Sometimes the link between expressionism and romantic music appears in a fragmentary way. The last number in *Pierrot* has a nostalgic text, "O alter Duft aus Märchenzeit" (O Ancient Fragrance from Fabled Times). To leave the listener in this mood, Schönberg closed the piece with a cadence on the note E, but the distortion of the lines masks the sense of arrival and retains for the piece something of characteristic expressionist tension. At the same time, the consonant harmonies and the delicate, soft sound have something in common with the indeterminate endings often found in romantic music. Example 8-8 illustrates this effect.

EXAMPLE 8-8. *Schönberg:* O Alter Duft *from* Pierrot Lunaire, *No. 21* *

FORM IN MUSICAL EX-PRESSIONISM With regard to form, expressionist composers faced a difficult problem. They eliminated all the factors that made for clearly perceived stability and for creating a well-defined structural contour. Unpredictable, often contradictory qualities of movement prevented the music from reaching strong points of arrival. Relationships between statement and counterstatement were not easily projected. Large form was not the answer to the problem of structure in expressionism. On the contrary, expressionist music suggested that much was happening in a very short time. Every note and figure seemed an outward symbol of profound inner states of mind and experiences. Hence, a significant musical message could be hinted at in a very short piece. All twenty-one numbers of *Pierrot Lunaire* are short; so are the Six Little Piano Pieces of Schönberg (1911) dating from this period. Laconic manner and compressed form were the most characteristic aspects of expressionist structure. Some works with expressionist qualities, however, retained an expansive late romantic manner and were cast in broad forms, such as Mahler's *Das Lied von der Erde* and Richard Strauss's opera *Elektra.*

Within a given movement we find that the form takes shape by repetition and variation of distinctive melodic figures or by contrasts in texture or manner. The form is no longer outlined by harmonic or rhythmic strong points. For example, consider how Schönberg organized the first nine measures of No. 1 of *Pierrot.*

| A | Measure 1 | Statement of motive |

---

*Copyright by Mrs. Gertrud Schoenberg, Belmont Music Publishers. Used by permission.

A′	Measures 2–6	Counterstatements of first motive
B	Measure 7	New motive, textural contrast
A″	Measure 8	Repetition and variation of first motive
C	Measure 9	New motive, textural contrast

Motive A, a tinkling little arabesque figure that suggests the liquid quality of moonlight, returns throughout the piece as a refrain. We could say, then, that No. 1 of *Pierrot Lunaire* is a rondo.

Expressionist music frequently relied upon a text to give some overall contour to its forms. More than half the works of Schönberg's early period involve a text. The highly charged emotional quality of this style was certainly effective as a setting for words with remote and elusive connotations.

If impressionism borrowed a specific idea of tone quality from Wagner, expressionism developed his melodic, rhythmic, and harmonic techniques. The richness of sound that appealed to impressionism was exactly the value that expressionism eliminated. The diagram below shows the relative historical positions of impressionism and expressionism with reference to Wagner.

EXAMPLE 8-9. *Historical positions of impressionism and expressionism*

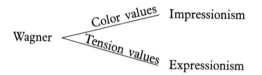

As expressionism developed, certain tendencies became more and more manifest. Habitually a literal repetition of any kind was avoided, since it would create a static effect and break the tension. At the same time, a distinctive melodic figure was used in many varied ways throughout a piece as a means of obtaining some underlying unity. Eventually this led to a systematization known as the *tone-row technique* or the *method of composing with twelve mutually interrelated tones*.

The basic idea of tone-row technique is quite easy to grasp. Suppose we limit ourselves to a row of three notes, for purposes of explanation. In Example 8-10*a* we have the three tones; in *b* we create a pattern or basic figure which reads 1 3 2. In *c* we use the pattern to create melodic figures of various kinds, taking care that no tone is repeated before the others have been heard; in *d* we make a chord of the pattern. Actually, this process has much in common with mathematical combinations and permutations. Provided that the relation-

ships between the notes themselves remain fixed, the row can begin on
any tone, can be played backward or upside down—or can undergo
various combinations of these shifts of position. Change of pitch is
called *transposition,* playing the row backward is called *retrograde
motion,* playing it upside down is called *inversion,* and combining the
last two, upside down and backward, is called *retrograde inversion.*

EXAMPLE 8-10. *Tone-row construction*

a. Three tones. E, G, D

b. Row: E, D, G

c. Melodic line built from row

d. Chords built from row

Now, if we should increase the number of tones in our row to
twelve, to include all the tones of the chromatic scale, we are at the
point of departure for composition in the tone-row technique. Later,
some illustrations of the uses of a twelve-tone row from Schönberg's
Quartet No. 4 will be given. Tone-row technique was codified by
Schönberg in 1924 after he had realized that for many years he had
been moving intuitively in this direction in his own style; his melodies,
textures, and rhythms tended to avoid repetition and to grow through
being varied. The technique was first applied consistently in Schönberg's *Serenade,* Op. 24, composed in 1923.

Each of the three composers who formed the early tone-row
school, Arnold Schönberg, Alban Berg, and Anton von Webern, had

his own personal style. Schönberg retained his romantic connections; works like his String Quartet No. 4 and his Piano Concerto show a strong flavor of Brahms. Berg affected a more spectacular and often more immediately assimilable style. His opera *Wozzeck*, which uses tone-row procedures at various points, suggests the expressionism of Richard Strauss. This work, one of the great musico-dramatic achievements of the twentieth century, is quite comprehensive in its range of style and expression. For example, Berg occasionally uses a simple, affecting melodic style, as in Marie's lullaby "Ei-o-po-peia." Here and there, one hears the sound of a major or minor triad, strategically placed for expressive nuance; also, fragments of marchlike rhythms (Wozzeck is a soldier) crop up now and then. Moreover, Berg's idea of sound leans rather to the rich side than to the spare, open manner of other composers in the expressionistic school. In his *Lyric Suite* for String Quartet, Berg has created atmospheric effects not unlike musical impressionism.

Anton von Webern continued in the terse manner of expressionism, along the lines of the procedure exemplified in *Pierrot Lunaire*. He represents the antiromantic wing of the tone-row school, and his influence is perhaps the strongest among younger tone-row composers, especially his technique of writing very short pieces with very few notes; they have progressively rarefied the musical atmosphere of their compositions until the individual tones have become virtually disengaged from each other in pitch and texture.

For illustration of tone-row techniques of composition, we shall examine some excerpts from Schönberg's Quartet No. 4.

EXAMPLE 8-11. *Schönberg: Quartet No. 4 (1936)**

a. The basic row

b. The opening theme of the first movement, in a vigorous, square-cut style

Allegro molto, energico

*By permission. From Arnold Schönberg's Fourth String Quartet, G. Schirmer, Inc., New York. Copyright 1939.

c. A transitional passage in the first movement, in a capricious, arabesquelike improvisation

retrograde inversion

d. A waltz, from the second movement

row altered yet retaining
some of its original intervals

Tone-row composers have used traditional forms of eighteenth-century music, such as sonata form, rondo, fugue, and variation, in an effort to reconcile themselves with music of the past. These traditional forms were originally based upon clear harmonic orientation and sharply demarcated rhythmic groupings; yet these are the very values the tone-row composers rejected. Whether or not a successful merger of traditional forms and the perpetual variation procedure of tone-row music has been effected is a matter to be decided in each individual case.

HISTORICAL
ANTECE-
DENTS

Expressionism and the tone-row school were the direct descendants of the metaphysical tendencies of the nineteenth century and their attendant chromaticism and dissonance. From the Sensibility and the Storm and Stress down through Beethoven, Liszt, Wagner, and Mahler runs a current of supercharged emotional values. Romantic preoccupation with the dark and sinister aspects of human imagination—witches, unholy talismans, the Devil himself—leads directly to the fantastic world of expressionism.

In retrospect we can see that certain musical techniques point the way from romanticism to expressionism. Prominent among these was an increasing reliance upon thematic values to organize the form of a composition (see Example 7-13). Harmony became involved and complex; it could not give as clear an outline of the form as it did in classic music. Themes became more distinctive and important; they were made points of reference, *leading motives*. In some works, such as Liszt's Sonata in B minor and Strauss's *Till Eulenspiegel*, themes were constantly varied or transformed. Thus the opening theme of Liszt's Sonata has at different times a brooding, a demonic, a plaintive, a masterful, and an apocalyptic quality. This is not far from the perpetual variation of tone-row music.

Beethoven's last string quartets influenced the expressionist composers profoundly. They were impressed by the deeply introspective quality, the tightness of structure, and the rich elaboration of motives that these works exhibited. For example, Beethoven's *Grosse Fuge,* Op. 133, which takes about fifteen or sixteen minutes to play, is built up entirely of two subjects which are developed and varied in an incredibly imaginative way. One of these subjects shows incipient tone-row features.

EXAMPLE 8-12. *Beethoven:* Grosse Fuge, *Op. 133*

Compare the first four notes of this subject with the beginning of Schönberg's row for his Quartet No. 4 (Example 8-11). Note that they are varied inversions of each other.

RELATION-SHIPS WITH ART AND LITERATURE

Musical expressionism was part of a general reaction against late romanticism and impressionism, a reaction that took place as well in literature and art. The term *expressionism* was taken from the German school of painting led by Paul Klee and Vassily Kandinsky. As in music, expressionist painters sought to convey intense and subjective qualities, characterized by strange shapes, odd relationships, and elusive meanings. An analogy between surrealist painting and expressionist music might be drawn considering the ways in which each mode of expression places familiar items into bizarre and unfamiliar contexts, removing them from their ordinary frames of reference.

In literature the dreamlike quality and the hidden meanings of symbolist poetry attracted expressionist composers. Stefan George provided the texts for a number of compositions by Schönberg and his colleagues. We can also see a parallel between expressionism's flow of compact yet obscure associations and the *stream-of-consciousness* technique being developed by James Joyce at that time in his *Ulysses* and other works.

Additional examples of tone-row music follow:

Berg: Violin Concerto (1935). The basic row in this piece has been contrived to give a strong feeling of tonality. Note that the opening notes are arranged according to the tuning of the violin, in fifths, and that the more tense and colorful intervals follow. As first heard, the line is a broadly soaring arch, in the romantic vein; it establishes the rich lyricism and intense pathos which govern the expressive content of this work. The scoring is full and varied, the phrase structure is clear and has a broad sweep, the rhythms often have dancelike values.

Webern: Symphonie, Op. 21 (1928). At the opposite pole from the style of Berg we find the extremely rarefied language of this work, which is actually a relatively short piece for chamber orchestra. In place of the richly declamatory manner of both Schönberg and Berg, we have an emphasis on "stark" design, lined out in the most economical fashion by single tonal points, each of which creates a taut counterstatement to the previous tone through changes in color, register, and duration. Perhaps this is the most idiomatic way in which a row can be used—a pointillistic play among the notes themselves with no direct reference to the rhetoric of earlier styles. The similarity in attitude of this music to certain types of abstract painting and literature is striking.

FOLKLORIC MUSIC

EXPRESSIVE VALUES

At the time that expressionism was coming into full stature, another significant trend was making itself felt strongly in European music. This was the folkloric style. You have heard music from the expressionist school; now listen to the Dance of the Adolescents from Igor Stravinsky's *Le Sacre du Printemps* (1913). There could scarcely be two kinds of music farther apart than expressionism and the folkloric style, as represented by the excerpt from *Le Sacre.* Here is a dance; but it is no dance such as we have encountered before. This is no graceful court dance, nor even a jolly village whirl. It is primitive, tribal, pagan; it suggests a purpose far more serious than the dances which have traditionally provided entertainment in Western culture. The purpose is religious. We are told, in the scenario of the ballet for which *Le Sacre* was composed, that this is a dance of spring. Homage is paid to the earth in the hope of reaping good crops.

Certainly the most salient feature is the emphatic, percussive beat that carries the sound along. All the profound reflections and personal manner of romanticism are cast aside, and the aboriginal values of music, the play of quantities and durations of sound are substituted in the evocation of a raw sense of activity. The beat is in charge.

As a contrast to this expressive quality, we hear, from time to time in *Le Sacre,* a simple folksong manner, often improvisatory in style. Thus, the two aspects of a folk music, dance and song, provide the raw material for a work that is highly stylized, strikingly imaginative, a work that created one of the most celebrated "scandals" in the history of music when it was first presented in Paris in 1913.

TECHNIQUES

Principal among all the technical features of this style is the beat and its treatment. The distinctive rhythmic manner arises from two factors: (1) the ways in which beats are organized, and (2) the ways in which beats are performed.

FIGURE 22. *Vassily Kandinsky:* Composition III. (*From the Collection of the Museum of Modern Art, Mrs. Simon Guggenheim Fund.*)

In earlier styles we heard characteristic ways of treating the beat. Medieval and Renaissance music tended to generate an easy, steady flow of gentle beats. Baroque music also set up such a flow, but with considerably more emphasis. Dance music and music of the classic style organized beats in groups of two, three, four, or six, with regularly spaced periodic accents. Romantic music often displayed irregularities and uncertainties in the flow of beats. But folkloric music, as represented in our excerpt, developed its own distinctive way of organizing rhythmic groups.

In order to demonstrate the effect of handling rhythmic groups in the distinctive folkloric manner, try the following experiment:

1. First, count out a series of four-beat measures, making a stroke at each strong beat, as in Example 8-13.

EXAMPLE 8-13

As you continue, notice that the beats, the accented strong beats, and the general quality of movement remain regular, smooth, and virtually automatic. You lose awareness of the rhythm as an immediate or challenging element.
2. Now try the same flow of beats, but after the first two groups of four, introduce strongly accented beats irregularly, as in Example 8-14.

EXAMPLE 8-14

What a world of difference there is in the whole rhythmic concept! Instead of becoming dormant, the accent develops a life of its own, asserts itself in an electrifying way. The periodicity is broken and the impact of an unanticipated accent gives new energy and momentum to the musical flow.

Example 8-15 from the Dance of the Adolescents of *Le Sacre* illustrates this kind of rhythmic organization.

EXAMPLE 8-15. *Stravinsky:* Le Sacre du Printemps, *Dance of the Adolescents**

In order to secure and emphasize this rhythmic quality, the entire orchestra must participate. The usual custodians of the underlying beat, the percussion, are not sufficient to give the kind of weight, body, and color to the rhythmic strokes of this music. Thus, in Example 8-15 the burden is carried by the strings; they become quasi-percussion instruments, and in the mass that they constitute in the grand symphony orchestra, they carry off the effect brilliantly.

Colorful scoring is closely associated with this rhythmic style. A rhythmic gesture not only involves a stroke; it has arresting, often unique qualities of sonority. As you listen to *Le Sacre,* you hear at every moment strikingly evocative sounds, tone colors splashed on brilliantly and barbarically, yet with subtle insight for the justness of the effect.

In contrast to the rhythmic violence and the flashing colors, the melodic material often has a simple folksong flavor. Melodies tend to be short in phrase; their range is small. They gain length by spinning out; fragments are often repeated with small melodic or rhythmic variations. These melodies tend to focus on a single tone or to move back and forth between a few tones. The melodies frequently use the modal scales described in the section on impressionism. The total effect is rather singsong, as in Example 8-16.

EXAMPLE 8-16. *Stravinsky:* Le Sacre du Printemps, *The Games of the Rival Cities**

---

*Copyright 1921 by Edition Russe de Musique. Copyright assigned to Boosey & Hawkes, Inc. Used by permission.

The harmonic language of this style frequently sounds opaque and crashingly dissonant. Yet if we pull all the pieces apart we find that the harmony is made up of simple, familiar, diatonic units, such as triads, open fifths and fourths, and scales which are put together in layers on top of each other or succeed each other in odd ways to create a dissonant effect. In other words, the harmonic values of folksong represent the starting point for the complex chord structures of the folkloric style. Example 8-15 illustrates the use of two chords from different keys sounded together but kept distinct by well-defined layering. This device is known as *polytonality*. Example 8-17 is an

FIGURE 23. *Gino Severini:* Dynamic Hieroglyphic of the Bal Tabarin. *1912. (From the Collection of the Museum of Modern Art. Acquired through the Lillie P. Bliss Bequest.)*

illustration of *pandiatonism,* a harmonic device in which notes from a diatonic scale are combined in nontraditional ways. Both polytonality and pandiatonism represent efforts to retain some of the stability and orientation value of triads and homogeneous scales while introducing special piquant harmonic effects.

EXAMPLE 8-17. *Stravinsky:* Le Sacre du Printemps, *Rounds of Spring**

FORM IN FOLKLORIC MUSIC
Listening for the definition of form in folkloric music, we discover, as probably the most apparent feature, *contrasts* in texture and mood. The form takes shape in well-demarcated episodes. Within an episode the principal structural unit is a phrase or period whose length is determined by the composer's feeling that a certain effect has been sufficiently exploited. A sense of movement within the phrase is projected by the permutations of rhythm, melody, and texture described above. A natural concomitant of such structure is the dynamic curve, built by the accumulation of intensity, volume of sound, and increase of pace, at times. Arrival is signaled by some sort of climax in the dynamic curve, or by the beginning of a new effect, texture, or harmonic procedure. In this music, statement and counterstatement show a simple, down-to-earth relationship.

This style, with its colorful associations of primitive culture, its dominating dance rhythms, and its episodic forms based on sharp contrast, developed in connection with modern ballet and stage arts. Most of Stravinsky's early music was stage music; his connection with the ballet director Diaghilev is one of the celebrated associations in the history of music and dance.

By way of illustration, let us have a look at the way the first few episodes of *Le Sacre* are fitted together.

The very opening sounds presage the strange and exotic music to come. The improvisation of the bassoon in its highest, most tortured register, the interjected fragments by the clarinets in their lowest, most somber register, the curious pointillism of structure—all these create a world of musical imagery far removed from Western experience. Bit by bit the fragments coalesce, new motives dart in and out; an excitement is growing. The texture, transparent at first, becomes increasingly clouded and heavy. Suddenly the rising dynamic curve breaks off, and the bassoon, alone again, recalls for a moment its speculative thought of the beginning. In schematic terms, the form thus displays an ABA plan. The final A, while it may act for arrival, still has a tentative quality that enables it to serve as a transition to the next large episode, the Dance of the Adolescents. This dance is dominated by the rhythmic figure we first hear plucked by the strings. Around this rhythmic motive, above and below, melodic fragments are superimposed; these figures possess a tremendous rhythmic vitality. When they are combined with the driving rhythmic pulse, the impact is explosive. As we might expect, the overall form of this episode turns out to be a dynamic curve; the dance works itself up to the point of frenzy and rushes directly into the next episode, The Play of Abduction, at which point the tempo becomes headlong. Indeed, this quickening of pace was perhaps the only effective way the music could move ahead from the climax of the previous dance. The remainder of this work should also be evaluated structurally by its gestures, textures, and rhythmic effects, rather than by harmonic or melodic analysis, at least by the layman.

HISTORICAL POSITION OF FOLKLORIC MUSIC As we mentioned above, the first impetus toward the use of folk idioms came from composers in the nineteenth century. The composer who made the sharpest break with Western music was Moussorgsky. His phrase structure, percussive rhythms, and folklike melodic style had much influence on Stravinsky. Another representative of Russian nationalism, Rimsky-Korsakov, taught Stravinsky much in the way of orchestration. It was only when Stravinsky abandoned the folkloric manner for neoclassicism that he turned aside from Rimsky-Korsakov's conception of scoring.

The heyday of the folkloric style was during the second decade of the twentieth century. In addition to Stravinsky, Béla Bartók, who did a monumental study of Eastern European folk music, was the other principal figure in the folkloric trend. In both its techniques and its attitudes, this style has been tremendously influential upon later music. The free play of small, well-defined rhythmic groups is a strikingly characteristic manner among contemporary American composers. Nowhere do we find this better illustrated than in Aaron Copland's *El Salón México*, in which an exuberant offbeat rhythmic manner is combined with brilliant orchestration and a winning melodic content.

The simple song and dance values in folkloric music have been

FIGURE 24. *Thomas Hart Benton:* Homestead. *1934. (From the Collection of the Museum of Modern Art. Gift of Marshall Field.)*

taken up by American, British, Russian, French, and Spanish composers, with or without percussive underpinning. Thus, Virgil Thomson, in his suite taken from music he wrote for the documentary film *The Plow That Broke the Plains* (1936), uses the traditional hymn tune "Old Hundredth" in one movement and the Western song "Montana" in another. Pioneer and rural American life has provided a rich source of material for contemporary American composers, ranging upward from the writer of hillbilly songs to the composer of serious and ambitious symphonies. Folksongs and dances make strong and immediate impressions upon the listener.

Additional examples of folkloric pieces in twentieth-century music follow:

Copland: El Salón México (1937). This is one of the most popular and effective works composed by an American. Its lively shifting dance rhythms, its frank tunefulness, its brilliant and transparent scoring, the harmony that never strays far from the major mode in spite of many incidental dissonances, and its clear structural layout—all contribute to the delight of the listener. This piece exemplifies the picturesque type of folklorism, the kind that deals with local color. In this way, it carries on the tradition of such works as Rimsky-Korsakov's *Capriccio Espagnol* and Tchaikovsky's *Capriccio Italien*.

Bartók: Sonata for Piano (1926). In this work the percussive beat and the irregular rhythm of twentieth-century folklorism are used. The piano is made to act both as a percussion instrument and in its normal capacity as an instrument of figuration. There is a tremendous drive, often built up by the reiteration of a single note or a cluster of tones, especially in the first movement. The repetition of such tones or chords provides the listener with a sense of tonal center. There are very few figures that would qualify as melodies; most of the motives consist of two to eight tones; continuity is built up by varying and contrasting these motives (all of them very sharply characterized) in statements and counterstatements of irregular lengths. The final movement gives us material that has greater tunefulness than any of the preceding movements.

NEORO-MANTICISM

Although the first quarter of the twentieth century saw a reaction against romanticism, we find a direct continuation of romantic modes of expression in many composers. Latter-day romanticism uses the rich textures, the grandly serious manner, and the eloquent declamation of nineteenth-century orchestral music, but carefully adds musical techniques that have been evolved in the twentieth century. The long line and the big design are structural objectives in this style. Jean Sibelius, Sergei Rachmaninov, Howard Hanson, Ernest Bloch, Gustav Holst, Richard Strauss, Gustav Mahler, and Ralph Vaughan Williams have written consistently in a romantic vein.

Bloch's *Schelomo*, Hebrew Rhapsody for Violoncello Solo and Orchestra (1915), illustrates this trend in a very distinctive and personal manner. This piece encompasses a wide range of kaleidoscopic moods, deep introspection, intensely emotional declamation, wild abandon, exaltation, prophetic fervor. The solo cello becomes a hero, just as the soloist in the romantic concerto does. The grandeur of the conception, the fullness and richness of the scoring, and the demands made upon both the soloist and orchestra are in line with nineteenth-century traditions. Structurally, this piece also looks to music of the romantic era; it is in sonata form with well-marked thematic contrasts.

Schelomo cannot be mistaken, however, for a purely romantic composition. We find its harmony, with its biting dissonances, its exotic colors and scales, its strange progressions, often far removed from the world of romantic harmony. Moreover, the debt Bloch owes to the music of impressionism is frequently manifest. The chords that support the solo cello at the beginning of the piece bear witness to Bloch's impressionism; and the frequent use of the celesta in prominent places provides additional testimony.

Following are additional examples of romantic influence in twentieth-century music:

Bartók: Concerto for Violin and Orchestra (1938). This is a broad, eloquent work that treats the violin as a melodic and ornamental instrument par excellence. The beginning of the first movement establishes the romantic mood immediately, as it sets the steady, pulsating accompaniment against the broad sweep of the violin solo. The harmony is clearly set in B minor, represented by its tonic triad at the onset. The violin line has an expansive melody, very much in the vein of the great violin concertos of the nineteenth century, such as those of Brahms and Tchaikovsky.

Britten: Peter Grimes (1945). This opera appears to be modeled to a considerable extent upon the grand opera of the nineteenth century. It has a fairly large cast; the chorus has a very important role; there are arias, concerted numbers, and recitatives. The story itself has a relationship to the topics which romantic composers preferred. Peter Grimes is set against the villagers in a plot that symbolizes the struggle of the individual against the mass, a struggle which he is bound to lose. One number, a recitative at the end of the Prologue, illustrates how Britten used a modern technique, polytonality, to achieve a typically romantic pathos. Peter and his sweetheart Ellen are singing together; he is discouraged, she is reassuring. Britten set Grimes's music in F minor and Ellen's music in E major. The tonic harmonies of these two keys share the third, F minor's third being A♭, which is in pitch equivalent to E major's third G♯. The two lines imitate each other pivoting around the common note. Grimes's version carries an effect of bitterness; Ellen's, of hope. At the end, symbolizing the positive view, Grimes joins Ellen in her E major.

NEOCLASS-ICISM By the middle of the 1920s, preoccupation with romanticism, either for or against, seemed to have passed its most intense phase. Also, by this time, the era of exploration of specific new musical techniques was drawing to a close. Harmonically, any combination of notes seemed to be usable; melodically, there were few restrictions of contour or range; rhythmically, a whole new field had opened up; texturally, a tremendous catalogue of new sounds had been made available. Structurally, however, the new music had raised perplexing new problems. The minutiae of the early twentieth century, which were striking and distinctive gestures in their own right, did not submit easily to being organized into coherent forms. Neoclassicism represents an effort to achieve clarity and the big structural design.

EXPRESSIVE VALUES In the strict sense, neoclassicism refers to the trend that appeared in the middle 1920s to use features of the music of the eighteenth century and earlier periods. Balance and clarity were sought in reaction against the one-sided exaggerations of impressionism, expressionism, and folkloric music. Neoclassicism is characterized by an economy of means; very often a chamber music texture is used. Specific emotional connotations and pictorial values are avoided. There is a sense of purpose, of well-controlled movement directed solidly to a logical point of arrival. We find strong coherence in the melodic lines and the interplay of motives. Neoclassicism is not preoccupied with the easy drift of impressionism, the tortured spasms of expressionism, or the brutal stamp of folkloric music. Hindemith's String Quartet No. 3 (1922) and Stravinsky's Octet (1923) exemplify the neoclassicism of the 1920s.

Neoclassicism might also describe the aims of many composers writing after 1920 to reconcile traditional and contemporary musical values. Serious efforts have been made to codify musical practice in order to establish some areas of common usage. Neoclassicism is an attitude in which a sense for clarity and balance of form governs the use of musical materials.

TECHNIQUES Structural units in neoclassic music are comparable to phrases and periods; harmonic effects of cadence are made, although not with traditional formulas. There is a lively give-and-take with distinctive, easily handled motives and much use of counterpoint. Contrapuntal lines tend to run smoothly, to rise and fall deliberately, and to spin out like the lines of Bach's music. The scoring is economical and transparent; interest has diminished in sound for sound's sake. Example 8-18, from Hindemith's Quartet No. 3, illustrates a typical neoclassic passage. Notice that the cello acts like a basso continuo supporting two solo parts, a typical baroque layout. The interest lies in the steady, controlled, yet free sense of movement that the winding lines create as they work against each other.

EXAMPLE 8-18. *Hindemith: String Quartet No. 3, Op. 22, first movement**

Sehr langsame Viertel (Very slow quarter notes)

In the third movement of this quartet Hindemith coordinated a polarity of texture recalling baroque style with a twentieth-century technique, polytonality, to achieve a very sharply etched contrast between a melody and its accompaniment. The accompaniment, in the lower instruments, strums the chord of A major. The melody, played by the second violin, is very clearly in C major, being anchored on the first and fifth degrees of that key. The contrast is made even more vivid by the rhythmic differences in the two textural elements and by the fact that the accompaniment is plucked while the solo is played with the bow in a very legato style.

Polytonality is often used in neoclassic composition, since it tends to separate the component lines of a texture beyond the degree that pitch itself can accomplish. Bartók frequently uses polytonality, the *Diary of a Fly* from his *Mikrokosmos*, Book VI, being a clear-cut example in which the entire effect is dependent upon simple motives being set against each other in different keys. Milhaud also employs polytonality as a basic technique.

One of the most significant aspects of the neoclassic attitude is the publication of explanatory and didactic works dealing with contemporary techniques. We have already mentioned the systematization of expressionism by means of the tone row. Strikingly enough, this took place just at the time that neoclassicism was making its first appearance in a definite manner. Two other outstanding composers of the present era have concerned themselves with codification: Béla Bartók and Paul Hindemith, both of them neoclassicists. Bartók, in his *Mikrokosmos* (1926–1937), has written a graded series of piano pieces using many contemporary devices for harmony and rhythm. These pieces are

---

*Copyright 1923 by B. Schott's Soehne, Mainz; used by permission of Associated Music Publishers, Inc., New York.

FIGURE 25. *Pablo Picasso:* Pierrot and Harlequin, Seated. *1918–1919. (From the Collection of the Museum of Modern Art, Lillie P. Bliss Collection.)*

intended for the purposes of teaching piano. Hindemith, in his theoretical work *The Craft of Musical Composition* (1937), has made a notable contribution toward a harmonic system in which traditional and contemporary values can be reconciled and evaluated in relation to each other. In his idea of the *two-voice framework* he has proposed a norm for texture; in his idea of *harmonic fluctuation* he has provided a harmonic scheme for organizing basic structural units.

FORM IN NEOCLASSIC MUSIC Neoclassic music uses the forms of earlier periods, the sonata form, the rondo, the concerto grosso, the fugue, the chorale, the variation, the motet, etc. Moreover, some composers have been led to synthesize and coordinate various styles within a given piece, much as classic composers did with the many styles available to them in the eighteenth century. Combining different styles in a composition has its pitfalls; if it is not done with skillful timing, the work may sound stylistically inconsistent, and the composer will be open to the charge of eclecticism. Yet the values to be achieved by a wide range of expression are very rich; they can give contour and strength to the form.

One of the most successful works along these lines of synthesis, and one which has had a tremendously strong popular appeal, is Bartók's *Music for String Instruments, Percussion, and Celesta* (1937).

1. The *first movement* is a fugue, worked out very tightly. The plan of the form is one of the most impressive solutions of the problem in all of modern music. It has no counterpart among the standard forms, yet it is thoroughly logical, and it is typical of Bartók's sense for structure. The diagram below shows the outline of the form:

EXAMPLE 8-19. *Bartók:* Music for Strings, Percussion, and Celesta; *diagram: first movement*

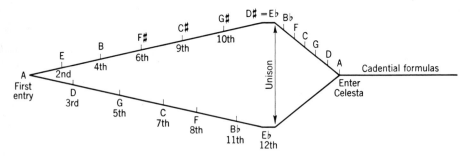

The most remarkable feature of this movement is the effectiveness with which Bartók has succeeded in directing movement forward to strong points of arrival. Notwithstanding the thoroughly dissonant harmony, a sense of progressing tonal centers is present. The entries of the subject explore systematically all the tonal centers of the chromatic scale. When the two streams of harmonic movement reach the point farthest away from the original tonal center, A, they have described a full circle and converge upon the tonal center, D♯-E♭. At this point the polyphonic texture disappears and an intensely powerful unison hammers out the E♭, the tone of arrival and the climax of the form. Reversing the build-up, the music returns to the original tonal center, A, in more relaxed fashion. Upon reaching the tonic, the final area of arrival in the movement, the music undergoes a striking change in texture. A curtain of sound created by the celesta, heard for the first time, and by shimmering strings introduces an element of textural stability not yet heard in the piece. The entries now begin and end on the tonic, giving the effect of being cadential formulas. There is a striking combination of styles in this movement: the neoclassic aspect is represented by the fugal manner and the tightly knit form; the chromaticism of the late nineteenth and early twentieth centuries saturates the harmonic idiom; at the return to A, the curtain of celesta and strings is frankly impressionistic.

Bartók's characteristic use of "wedge" shapes is manifest in this movement. In a wedge plan there is a point of departure that represents stability; this is generally the tonal center. The music progresses by stages away from this center and then returns. The diagram of the form given above shows a typical wedge formation. The subject of the fugue and the cadential formulas at the end of the movement represent this configuration melodically. Notice in Example 8-20*b* that the two lines moving together create a tone row.

EXAMPLE 8-20. *Bartók:* Music for Strings, Percussion, and Celesta, *first movement**

a.

b.

2. The *second movement* represents an electrifying contrast to the first. It is principally a dance, based on short, vigorous motives. The

harmony, in contrast to the complete chromaticism of the first movement, is basically diatonic, with polytonal elaborations. Much is made of the percussive rhythms of folkloric music. The form is a clearly defined sonata form, as is shown in the following outline.

First key area	C	1–19
Transition		20–68
Second key area	G	69–185 (Note the broad cadences
Development		187–372 in G, 180–185)
Recapitulation		373–520
Material of second key area at measure 412		

The key definition in the form is obvious; repetitions and cadences involving the tonal centers leave no doubt about harmonic points of reference. The principal expressive value is the dance quality. As such, then, this movement is quite in the spirit of a Beethoven or a Haydn sonata form. Moreover, the texture and part writing show the active manipulation of motives and the energetic contrasts that characterize classic style.

3. In the *third movement* again we have a tremendous contrast. The sound of the xylophone tapping away by itself at the beginning of this movement is one of the most unexpected and weird effects in all music, particularly as it follows the "down-to-earth" style of the second movement. A bit later the disembodied texture, created by totally different figures in viola, timpani, and xylophone, suggests expressionism, although the improvisatory style of the viola has folkloric associations. The entire movement is concerned with curious effects of sonority, and therefore recalls impressionism. The form, like the first movement, is a "wedge," this time worked out like a palindrome or mirror structure.

A. Improvisation	1–19
B. Lyric melody, first presented, then treated contrapuntally	20–44
C. Bell-like motive, treated percussively in many variations of texture	45–62
B. Return of lyric melody	63–75
A. Return of improvisation	76–83

Bartók, in this movement, has managed to keep the cadential sense very clear. This helps to bind the highly contrasted episodes into a smoothly continuous form. Each succeeding episode seems to come as a point of arrival, a cadential resolution to the movement of the preceding section.

4. The *finale* is a folk dance, an exhilarating summing up of the entire piece. The syncopations and cross-rhythms of folk music permeate the entire piece. The form is episodic, with rondolike refrains; contrasts are sharp; the melodic material is well defined, as dance tunes should be. An interesting and amusing detail of style occurs in measures 262 to 270, where Bartók slips into a typical jazz break by giving a fresh nuance to the syncopations of his refrain theme. Throughout this last movement the sense of tonal center is more clear than in any previous movement. One might say that it is the harmonic area of arrival, then, for the whole composition, a relationship quite proper for a neoclassic concept.

The four movements of this work exhibit relationships between themselves that give the entire composition a special unity. We hear the subject of the opening movement in each of the succeeding movements: briefly and varied in the second movement; restated and developed at length in the B sections of the third movement; altered harmonically in the fourth movement to create a bolder, more diatonic effect, in keeping with the more open and assertive manner of the movement. Further, the four movements of the work show a pairing with respect to form: the first and third, with their qualities of instability, assume the wedge form, while the second and fourth, with their powerful rhythmic drives, are organized respectively as sonata form and rondo. It is only in the last movement that the tonal center A, indicated in the first movement, is vigorously embodied with a strong flavor of the major mode. In this way, the final movement acts as an area of arrival for the entire work.

Some additional examples of neoclassic style in twentieth-century music follow:

Piston: String Quartet No. 3, first movement (1947). Lean, transparent texture in this sonata-form movement accommodates the play of a vigorous figure grouped in irregular meters. (The measure count for the first twelve measures is: 7 7 6 6 5 6 6 6 8 6 5 6.) There is a sense of constant development, clear differentiation of material between the first and second key areas (in F and C, respectively) and a final confirmation of the home key at the end.

Stravinsky: Symphony of Psalms (1930). This work shows a strong influence of baroque style. The first movement is set as a chorale with ornamental accompaniment; the second movement is a double fugue, one subject being assigned to the orchestra, the other to the chorus; the final movement is a choral fantasia in a number of episodes, arranged in something of a mirror order, as in the third movement in Bartók's *Music for String Instruments, Percussion, and Celesta.* The sense of key is very strong in this piece, with much conflict and wavering between major and minor, and especially between the tones E flat and E natural. Stravinsky's harmony, always sonorous, but not always set up in triads, governs his handling of the chorus. In chordal sections we hear a full, often edgy sound, spaced in the traditional distribution of choral music to achieve a balance of texture; occasionally, the chorus is used to declaim in unison or octaves; in the second movement, it engages in the active counterpoint of its fugue. Frequently, chords contain no third, so that the openness of fifths, fourths, and octaves governs the color. In this case, there seems to be a reference to music of the Ars antiqua and Ars nova periods.

Hindemith: Das Marienleben (The Life of Mary) (1948). Out of this cycle of fifteen songs set to poems by Rainer Maria Rilke, we have chosen the ninth, "The Marriage at Cana," to illustrate a modern classicistic treatment of lyric material. This song is the climax of the cycle. The change from water to wine at the feast and its tragic implications are expressed by Hindemith in a monumental variation ricercar, recalling the contrapuntal techniques and structural layouts of the early Baroque era. To suggest the increasing gravity of the sense of the text, Hindemith composes the variations of the subject in augmentation, thus slowing the movement, until at the very end the subject appears in fragments. (See Beethoven, Symphony No. 3, second movement, for a similar effect.) Actually the sound fades to a single sustained tone by the voice, a typically romantic ending quite in keeping with the cryptic and grammatically involuted poetry of Rilke.

Ravel: L'Heure Espagnole (1907). This is a short opera that recalls the opera buffa of the eighteenth century in more ways than one. The story is typically buffa: among the suitors for the favors of Concepción, the wife of Torquemada the watchmaker, the winner is Ramiro, the muleteer, while the well-to-do bachelor Gonsalve and the banker Don Inigo both fail. Ravel has set this piece principally as a series of ensembles and short solo sections. The motive of the clocks gives Ravel the opportunity to compose many sections which have the regular repetitive structure one associates with the ticking and ringing of clocks. The total effect is a curious blend of eighteenth-century sophisticated comedy and tunefulness with Spanish local color and impressionistic techniques of composition.

THE LATER TWENTIETH CENTURY Since 1945 the most important factor in music has been the impact of technology. Long-playing records, tape recorders, electronic means for producing sound, television, portable radios—these have made music available to hundreds of millions more people than could have heard it fifty years ago. Music is everywhere—in the home, in stores, restaurants, theaters, classrooms, automobiles, as well as in the traditional concert hall. You can take it with you wherever you go if you have a cassette or portable radio.

The massive tide of technology has separated, intensified, and broadened two streams of musical activity much more than was the case in past eras, namely, (1) *standardization* and (2) *exploration.* Instant transmission and reproduction of musical sound have created widespread current styles in popular music; while these have changed every few years, nevertheless, at any given time hundreds, if not thousands, of musicians are writing songs that represent a standard popular style. On the other hand, the newer sources of sound, the different ways of using traditional instruments and voices, and the release from the formal performer-audience structure of the concert hall have led postwar composers to experiment with fresh ways of evoking responses from their listeners. In some cases, these newer ways are almost totally different from music of the past; in other cases, some elements of the older procedures have been absorbed into the newer methods.

POSTWAR SERIALISM; TOTAL ORGA- NIZATION In tone-row music, all pitch relationships were organized by the sequence of intervals in a specific tone row. Carrying this principle forward, some postwar composers have serialized other musical values in a piece—note lengths, dynamics, tone color—to approach *total organization* according to a preestablished series. Pierre Boulez's *Structures* for two pianos, 1951-1952, represents this technique. In order to convey the impression of a constantly fluctuating yet strictly ordered continuity of pitches, dynamics, note values, and tone colors, the music has to be written transparently, even sparsely, with a clear separation between successive musical events, a condition that limits broad-scale declamation severely. In his cantata *Le Marteau sans Maître* (The Masterless Hammer, 1954, 1957), Boulez abandoned this rigorous system. He took fragments of poems from a cycle by René Char, a poet of the French Resistance, and set them for alto voice, viola, alto flute, guitar, vibraphone, xylorimba, and percussion. The light and transparent scoring accommodates both the delicate contrast of timbres and the overall compatibility of tone color. Boulez manifests his French heritage by very deft management of declamation—length of words and tones, combinations of sounds, connections between phrases—bringing to mind Debussy's music and the influence of Boulez's teacher, Oliver Messaien. A very striking effect of arrival for the entire work is achieved by the use of the tam-tam, whose deep, gonglike sound has not been heard until the last number; this effect is much like the bell-like sounds of the pianos at the end of Stravinsky's *Les Noces* (The Wedding, 1919). Throughout *Le Marteau* the use of percussion, vibraphone, and xylorimba show the influence of Far Eastern music.

ELECTRONIC MUSIC The ultimate in the composer's control is realized in electronic music. The technology of electronic sound production has revolutionized music in the postwar era, both for composers and listeners as well as for performers. Electronic apparatus can create sound by patterns of oscillation programmed by the composer; it can reproduce sound and modify it in countless ways by means of tape-recording techniques. The areas opened up by these techniques are vast and fantastic. No longer are composers limited by the traditional systems of pitch, time measurement, and tone color. The most subtle variations of all qualities can be projected as easily as any amateur can play a C major scale on the piano. Even more important is the range of effects previously unexperienced in music. Pitches far above and below the orchestral range, mixtures of sound, timbres new to music, stereophonic effects that move the sound around the listening space, all managed with the greatest precision—these are some of the areas being explored in electronic music.

Paradoxically, these ultrasophisticated techniques for manipulating sound have a very direct and physical impact upon the listener. Each sound is striking, novel, focusing the listener's attention upon the most basic aspect of the musical experience, the evocative power of sound. When this takes place, the sense of design tends to become clouded; electronic music does not delineate for the listener the kinds of harmonic, rhythmic, and melodic events that enable us to grasp clearly the overall shape of a Mozart aria or a Chopin prelude.

This does not mean that an electronic piece cannot establish and sustain a powerful expressive message. One of the most moving works of the past twenty-five years is Karlheinz Stockhausen's *Gesang der Jünglinge* (Song of Youth, 1955–1956). The title refers to the hymn from the Scriptures (Daniel 30) sung when three children of Israel were saved by the angel after having been thrown into the fiery furnace by Nebuchadnezzar, King of Babylon. Within the piece the text of the hymn "Praise the Lord" is sung.

Stockhausen used natural sounds, including a chorus of children, and electronically produced sounds, mixing and modifying them. At times, in the midst of the strange ebb and flow of electronic sounds, a boy's voice emerges with a startling sense of presence. In this piece, Stockhausen has shaped his declamation with an effect of impassioned intensity. The screams, moans, hums, and many other effects seem to touch the core of human feeling more immediately than the objective sound symbols of traditional music. This composition is published only as a recording on disc or tape, in several versions; there is no

FIGURE 26. *Class in computer-generated music. (Courtesy of the
Stanford University Music Department.)*

printed score of this work, which means that it was never *intended* to
have a live performance. The only instrument, therefore, appropriate
for this piece is a sound-producing machine.

CHANCE   If serial and electronic music approach the point of total control by the
MUSIC   composer, *chance* music (or *aleatory* music) moves in the opposite
direction—to allot more freedom to the performer than was possible in
traditional Western music.

Every single performance of a chance piece is unique. The performer puts together whatever elements or fragments are provided by
the composer in ways that are fresh and often previously unplanned.
The creative facility of the performer is thus brought into greater play
than in a piece where the notation is fully set down; every performance
is an improvisation, thus linking in with a centuries-old tradition in
the performance of Western music.

The materials provided in chance music exert some control over
what will be heard. Terry Riley's *In C* (1964) consists of a number of
short figures in C major or related to that key, to be played in whatever
order the players wish (the number of players is optional as well). For
the listener, the effect is atmospheric, a climate of C that can be
curiously time-slowing and hypnotic, a result not unlike a Zen experience. Stockhausen's *Zyklus* (1959), for one percussion player manipulating a number of instruments, gives the performer the opportunity to
order the given patterns as he wishes, and in the hands of a skillful

percussionist the piece can create an explosive, breathtaking impact. John Cage's *Radio Music* (1956) calls for eight radios playing simultaneously as the performers move the dials from one station to another, a familiar effect of pandemonium isolated and concentrated for a listening "experience."

The following works from the post–World War II period illustrate various treatments of traditional and newer techniques:

Stravinsky: The Rake's Progress (1953). This opera occupies a unique position, not only in Stravinsky's music, but in the history of Western music. It symbolizes the end of a centuries-long era, as one of the last important repertory compositions in which traditional forms and idioms are used. It is the last of Stravinsky's neoclassic compositions, an opera with a libretto by W. H. Auden; traditional forms of eighteenth-century opera are used—arias, ensembles—with harmony, melody, orchestration, and phrase structure clearly modeled upon Mozart's style. Still, the characteristic elements of Stravinsky's style are clearly heard—subtle distortions of the traditional language.

Penderecki: Lukaspassion (1966), Passacaglia. The passacaglia form here uses a clearly grasped four-note figure. We hear the figure in many forms and textures in a freely deployed serialism. The figure appears in the timpani from time to time to underpin the action; it is also used as the basis of the principal melodic lines, and the notes are sounded simultaneously at times as a cluster of sounds that gives a pungent accent. The entire Passion comes across as a declamation of sounds of all kinds, amplifying and elaborating the straight prose declamation of the evangelist who tells the story of the Passion. Tone clusters, glissandos, complex rhythms superimposed upon each other, and many other effects traditional and novel are handled in the spirit of the recitative and arioso, as in the great Passions of J. S. Bach, with deliberate spacing, development, and control of musical gesture. Penderecki's style is close to the heart of Western music, so that all the fantastic effects, wild dissonances, and complex figures come to a wonderfully clear and bright close on an E major chord, as if the entire work were directed to arrive eventually at such a resolution. Indeed, throughout the work, there is a strong presence of familiar intervals, so that the final chord appears as an ultimate crystallization and ordering of the tensions preceding it.

Crumb: Ancient Voices of Children (1970). This is a chamber music work, a set of songs and pieces based upon poetry by Federico Garcia Lorca, the Spanish poet and playwright. The textures are delicate, using percussion, plucked, standard, and modified instru-

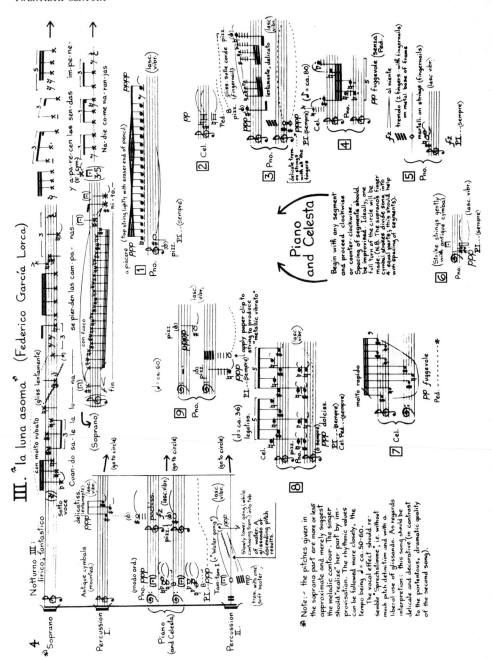

FIGURE 27. *Post–World War II musical notation. Fragments of traditional notation combined with performance instructions. George Crumb,*
Night Music I. (*Copyright 1967 by Belwin-Mills Publishing Corporation. Used with permission.*)

ments to create a rich variety of sounds. Generally, the effect of this music is very theatrical, with a direct impact upon the listener. Crumb draws from folkloric sources—Spanish melodic patterns and rhythms, Oriental timbres. The vocal part ranges from simple melodic declamation to wildly difficult vocalises. There is a sure sense of melody, rhythm, and the mixture of topics; the gestures are spaced and timed carefully to produce the maximum effect. This is a mode evolved in postwar music idiomatic to the new musical resources; the "geometry" of traditional music, with its pairing of matched or complementary statements and counter-statements gives way to a linear rhetoric that either can absorb the listener completely, as in an expressive recitative, or lead to more or less total disengagement.

EXOTIC
MUSIC
Exotic here is applied to music outside the Western tradition—the music of Africa, Asia, Indonesia, and other faraway regions. In the past three or four decades, the music of these cultures has become increasingly familiar to us through radio, recordings, television, and air transport, which has brought troupes of performers to our cities. The influence of exotic music has been felt throughout every aspect of Western music, from the most advanced experimentation to the familiar idioms of popular music. Actually, this is no new trend, but a vast expansion of an interchange that can be traced as far back as the Crusades and the Renaissance, when Arabic and Turkish music was taken up as a colorful touch in dances such as the *moresca,* in *flamenco* music, and in Turkish military effects.

Our listening experience today with exotic music, however, goes far beyond the occasional spicing of a Western idiom. Thanks to appearances of virtuosos on the sitar from India, dance troupes from Africa, musical accompaniments to Japanese films, as well as a wealth of recordings of music from Korea, Indonesia, the Near and Middle East, we can make some contact with the actual musical styles of other cultures. Each of the musical cultures of the world has a long, complex, and rich tradition, and a language comparable to that of Western music in its sophistication; competence in the performance of exotic music requires a lifelong training to master the subtleties of rhythm and pitch that characterize its various styles. Here only some of the most easily recognizable qualities that identify a few of the more familiar exotic styles can be described; the roles played by music in these cultures—in ceremony, dance, song—can be understood only by considerable study and contact.

Japanese Music We probably know Japanese music best through its use in Japanese films which have been widely shown throughout the Western world. In these, the *samisen,* a three-stringed plucked instrument, frequently provides an accompaniment to scenes depicting Japanese life and history. Many of the melodies played on this instrument are based upon a type of pentatonic scale that includes a tritone, an augmented fourth or diminished fifth, among its intervals (for example, D, E, F, A, B). This imparts, especially for Western listeners, a pungent and often quite poignant quality to the melodies, with more than a touch of melancholy. In contrast, the more familiar pentatonic scale (see page 204) has a smoother and sweeter effect for us, since it bypasses the tritone completely. In the hands of a virtuoso, music played on the samisen or on the *koto* (a plucked instrument with seven to thirteen strings) can be very evocative, with very subtle gradations of pitch and time to suggest delicate shades of feeling. This music can have a persuasive "speaking" quality, a manner suggesting the declamation of prose or metric poetry, interspersed with elaborate melodic turns.

African Music   Africa has many musical cultures. Its vast area encompasses hundreds of tribes, each one with its own musical language. Running throughout African music is a characteristic rhythmic feature, an unevenness that combines groups of two and three beats in many different patterns, as

on various levels, sometimes combined with even groupings. This rhythmic style is best handled by percussion instruments—drums, xylophones, rattles, etc.; thus, the complex rhythmic interplay of percussion instruments is, for Western listeners, the most familiar aspect of African music. The melodies are rather simple, with varied repetitions of a few figures, often in the manner of an *ostinato.* We hear

FIGURE 28. *Japanese koto. (Used with the permission of the Asian Art Museum of San Francisco, The Avery Brundage Collection.)*

vertical combinations that resemble Western harmonies—thirds, triads, seventh chords—but the tuning of these differs somewhat from the equal temperament of the Western tradition; particularly noticeable are inflected tones, slightly lower than normal diatonic degrees, that have the effect of "blue" notes in jazz. (See page 247.)

Indonesian The principal impact upon Western listeners made by Indonesian
Music music, from Java and Bali, is a brilliant, kaleidoscopic, pervasive sound of percussion instruments created by the *gamelan,* the Indonesian orchestra. Gongs along with metal and wooden bars provide tones of definite pitch that have a long "decay" period, so that tones are constantly overlapping each other, merging to form vertical sounds that are not truly chords, but layers of sound; many of these combinations are "dissonant" to our ears, but the mixtures of timbres remove any impression of harshness we might associate with dissonance. Together with these instruments of definite pitch, we hear a variety of drums and indefinite-pitch instruments. Voices are used along with the instruments, so that as many as twenty-five or thirty individual lines of musical action may be spinning out at any given time. Improvisation is the procedure by which the music takes shape; the improvised figures are elaborations of a fixed melody, so that the listener senses a consistency in the music based upon the frequent use of characteristic intervals. The scales use different tunings than the tuning of the diatonic Western major-minor system; this gives a special color to every vertical combination and melodic line.

In the gamelan ensemble, each part has its own melodic and rhythmic patterns. While none of these is especially complex, the combination of many instruments and voices creates a dense and highly active aura of sound, anchored by the ponderous strokes of the deep gongs. Indonesian gamelan music has attracted Western composers; its effects were incorporated by Debussy in his String Quartet (1894), by Stravinsky in *Les Noces* (1917), and by Boulez in *Marteau* (1954), as well as by many other composers.

Indian Music Indian music is among the most readily grasped musical styles from far-off lands. It has a clarity of texture and melodic design, a suave sound, and a manner of improvisation not unlike the preludes and fantasias of Western music. The most familiar type of Indian music to our ears is that of the *sitar,* a plucked string instrument similar in structure to the guitar. Sitar music has become known in the West thanks to the many virtuosos on this instrument who have performed in concert, on television, and on recordings. Characteristically, sitar music consists of a single line of very highly elaborated melody supported by a drone and possibly accompanied by a drum. The combination of the crisp pluck and the after-resonance creates a sustained effect, a compelling "monotony." This music moves steadily, with a gentle but marked change in the sense of pulse; series of unequal rhythmic groups liven the movement, coupled with a rounded rise and fall of melody. The melodic basis of sitar music is the *raga*. Indian music has many ragas, which are specific scale patterns containing notes of greater and lesser importance, comparable to the tonics, dominants, and leading tones of our scales. A composition based upon a given raga has a subtle distinction, arising from the prominence of the characteristic tones of the raga. We can clearly discern the successive phases of action in this music, based upon pitch levels, degrees of ornamentation, increase and decrease of intensity, speed of notes, degrees of loudness and softness. For those skilled in the performance of this music, the nuances and the ornamentations represent the goal of their art; a composition may be quite short or it may extend for an hour or more, depending upon the circumstances of place, time, purpose, and mood.

POPULAR MUSIC IN THE TWENTIETH CENTURY

Popular music has existed as long as people have made music. We think of this music as simple, used for singing and dancing, quickly and strongly felt by untrained listeners. Until the beginning of the present century, popular music and so-called "serious" music shared many elements of melody, harmony, rhythm, and texture. Byrd, Bach, Mozart, and Brahms could take the popular dances of their times, and, with various sophisticated touches, turn a galliard, bourrée, minuet, or waltz into a piece that would intrigue the most highly trained connoisseur. But when composers around the beginning of the twentieth century began making drastic and far-reaching changes in the basic idioms of Western music, often altering them beyond recognition, popular and "serious" music parted company, except for deliberate instances of interchange. The gap widened. Now, in the last third of the twentieth century, popular music is the sole heir of the traditional Western music system—functional harmony, basic period and two-reprise forms, consistent metric and rhythmic patterns, melody-bass textures, and simple, balanced melody. It has maintained a strong contact with the "earth," while so-called "serious" music has taken off to explore the musical stratosphere and outer space.

Twentieth-century popular music includes many types and styles—jazz in its many forms, musical comedy, country music, rock 'n' roll—as well as a great deal of mixing of styles. By far the most important of these is jazz.

JAZZ

Jazz has numerous forms; no one definition or description can cover the types of music generally considered to be part of this unique musical language. Several characteristics seem to be consistent:

1. The underlying meter is regular, generally a rather emphatic two-four or four-four measure.

2. Above this there is a great deal of play against the beat, both in terms of syncopation and in slight anticipations or holding back that cannot actually be measured. The latter is what gives jazz its characteristic "pronunciation," causing us to recognize it immediately when we hear it.

3. Reflecting its popular and folkloric origins, jazz tends to build its periods in regular phrases, four measures in length. Marches, songs sung at work, and popular dances of the late nineteenth and early twentieth centuries, such as the cakewalk and ragtime, form one part of the ancestry of jazz. Melodic and rhythmic elements from West Africa also figure in the genealogy of jazz.

4. Melodically, much the same type of pronunciation is found as that which characterizes the rhythm of jazz. Often, tones are slightly inflected; the more prominent of these are known as "blue" notes; these represent a scale (African) that is slightly different from our present-day major and minor scales. When blue notes are sung or played on a variable-pitch instrument (saxophone, clarinet, string, trumpet, or trombone) we get the true "blue" effect. The piano, unfortunately, must play the blue note as a tone in the minor scale, and thus the piano cannot produce the special inflection that gives such an elusive charm to an expertly sung blues.

5. Much jazz is composed on the spot, as it is played. This improvisation is actually the basic rule of the game and is the feature which has led to an impressive body of musical practice in which there are recognized virtuosi who have polished and refined this art in its many facets. This is where jazz differs from other art music of today. It has a common language, spoken by all, but mastered for purposes of expression only by a few. The analogy with the music of the eighteenth century is very close; at that time, dances and marches were also the common idiom, but only a few masters were able to discover fresh and distinctive ways of reaffirming the familiar patterns.

The moods of jazz—exuberant, pathetic, nostalgic, sentimental, driving—are often mixed or traded off in the same piece. These moods are expressed in the earliest jazz, evolved from work songs, marches, spirituals, and dances of the late nineteenth and early twentieth centuries. Early jazz, before World War I, had three styles: *blues, ragtime,* and *New Orleans Dixieland.*

Blues Expressively, the blues touch pathetic moods—sadness, loneliness, stories of disappointment and betrayal, as the most famous blues song, W. C. Handy's "St. Louis Blues," 1914. The slow, steady beat builds into twelve-measure phrases; the harmony uses a progression which had already been used for centuries in some popular dances and songs, as in Stephen Foster's "Old Folks at Home," colored by "blue" notes, i.e., flattened degrees of the major scale. Example 8-21 gives the typical progression of the scale with the "blue" notes marked:

EXAMPLE 8-21. *Blues harmony and scale*

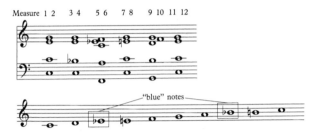

Blue notes, in performance, tend to waver subtly, approached and left with sliding inflection. Together with considerable ornamentation, blue notes give the rather simple melodies of blues a powerful expressive effect. Bessie Smith is generally recognized as the finest blues singer in the history of jazz; fluid and poetic, her style retains much of the primitive poignancy of pre-jazz styles.

Ragtime Ragtime, very popular in the late nineteenth century, and enjoying a refreshing revival at present, has a jaunty, often nostalgic quality. Of all jazz-related styles, ragtime has the most traditional flavor. It is built consistently of symmetrical phrases, regularly punctuated by cadences; it has a very clearly marked melody supported by an emphatically rhythmic bass and "splashy" chords (it is primarily a piano style). It is filled with incidental chromatic touches, lending poignancy to the simple cadential harmony. Its most striking feature, however, is its rhythm. Within its four-measure phrases, the smaller notes, eighths and sixteenths, are grouped to form many syncopated patterns, constantly shifting the accent momentarily, then returning to "nail down" the strong beat. Often the notes will form a series of three-note groups, as:

EXAMPLE 8-22

A number of pianists have recently made a specialty of ragtime, among them Joshua Rifkin and William Bolcom, bringing to life again the music of the most prominent ragtime composer, Scott Joplin.

New Orleans New Orleans jazz could be called the classic type, the first real synthesis of elements to form a model from which later types of jazz evolved. It arose in the first decades of the twentieth century in New Orleans and elsewhere. From work songs, spirituals, blues, and ragtime it acquired its melodic, rhythmic, and harmonic language; its texture, perhaps its most distinctive feature, came from minstrel show ensembles (banjo accompaniment) and local brass bands (cornets, trombones, percussion). New Orleans jazz, also called *Dixieland*, is chamber music. In its way it embodies a traditional texture: (1) *melody* or front line with clarinet, cornet, and trombone, and (2) *rhythm* with banjo, drums, and tuba. Its beat is marked (four to a measure) with a continual flow of melodic action, generally elaborate improvisations upon a simple melody as the instruments trade off solos or weave a free, nonimitative counterpoint. The mood is often exuberant, especially in what is now known as Dixieland. Both harmony and melody are saturated with blue notes or chords, while melody and rhythm have the sliding inflection that gives a special expressive value to single tones and is probably the most single distinctive feature of all jazz. "King" Oliver, "Jelly Roll" Morton, "Kid" Ory, and Louis Armstrong are identified with this style, which presently is enjoying a revival.

Later styles of jazz evolved from the New Orleans style. Chicago jazz has a fuller sound, with a larger instrumentation, leading the way to the big "swing" bands of the thirties (among them Benny Goodman and Glenn Miller) and to the very sophisticated arrangements of "Duke" Ellington. During this time *boogie-woogie* evolved as a speeding up of the blues and incorporation of ragtime syncopations over a driving ostinato bass alternating I, IV, I, V, I chords often complicated by added and blue tones.

As jazz spread throughout the country and overseas, its performers and arrangers became increasingly adept and professional, and the idiom itself took on a sweeter, richer, one could say more "commercial" sound. In turn, this generated a reaction, especially after World War II, with *bop* and *cool* jazz. Dissonant harmonies, sparse textures, clipped declamation, often cryptically understated, gave these latter-day styles of jazz a speculative, elusive quality. "Dizzy" Gillespie, Miles Davis, and Charlie Parker were identified with *bop*, while the principal figure in the cool jazz style was Dave Brubeck, whose training with the French neoclassicist, Darius Milhaud, prepared him to exploit the complex rhythms, pungent harmonies, and chamber-music texture of the *cool* style.

Indeed, during its entire history, jazz has absorbed techniques from many sources; in addition to the popular and folkloric elements from the South and West Africa, jazz has adapted techniques of orchestration from the late romantic symphonic idiom in the big band style, polytonality from neoclassicism, and a pointillistic texture from both impressionism and expressionism in the cool and bop styles, and lately, with the Swingle Singers, a swinging, truly "jazzy" manner of performing late baroque music. Reversing the direction, many modern composers have been fascinated with the early types of jazz, blues and ragtime; Hindemith, Bartók, Krenek, Milhaud, Stravinsky, Honegger, Debussy, Copland, and Ravel—all have borrowed rhythmic patterns, instrumentation, and blue harmonies from jazz.

Milhaud's very entertaining music to the ballet *La Création du Monde* takes off on jazz; throughout the piece we hear the characteristic harmonies and sonorities as well as the steady rhythms that mean jazz to us. We hear, especially, the plaintive tones of the saxophones dominating the orchestral sound. Example 8-23, taken from this work, illustrates blue harmony.

Gershwin's music, such as *Rhapsody in Blue* and the Concerto in F, represents probably the most successful effort to employ jazz idioms in an extended form.

EXAMPLE 8-23. *Milhaud:* La Création du Monde (*1929*)*

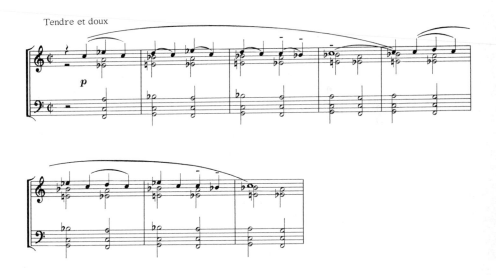

*Copyright 1929 by Editions Max Eschig, Paris; used by permission of Associated Music Publishers, Inc., New York.

ROCK AND COUNTRY MUSIC Twentieth-century popular music expanded its audience enormously with the perfection of radio and disc recordings. These were the principal media until after World War II. In the 1950s, when newer electronic media, television, and tape recordings came into general use, popular music took a sharp turn away from jazz in the traditional or progressive styles. Simpler and more direct styles, basically akin to ballads and folk dances and catering to a youthful audience, came to the fore. These were *rock* and *country* music. While these took some elements of declamation from jazz—melodic slides, syncopated delivery, and some blues harmony—the spirit of improvisation, of play with figures and phrases, was much less evident than in jazz.

Rock has two overpowering elements: (1) a relentless beat, pounded out with great strength by percussion and plucked instruments, and (2) amplified sound, "maxi-sound" produced by electronic means. These two features so dominate the style that possibilities for subtle nuance are sharply reduced, and the music spins out by constant repetition of short figures to create a hypnotic, all-enveloping effect. To be sure, rock has developed many facets of style and expression; individual groups have their own styles, manipulating rhythm, harmony, and texture over the basic beat and within the full sound; exotic elements, especially from Indian music, have been incorporated. In addition to the usual topics—love, hate, joy, betrayal, sadness, etc.—found in popular music, rock songs often deliver a message of social protest, of political awareness of satire, and of counterculture content.

Country music is akin to rock, but its manner of delivery differs. While rock declamation combines shouting with a sliding "croon," country music is immediately recognized by the "twang" of the singer. Country music is closer to a folk art, in that its topics are those of traditional folk music; they tell of the feelings of simple people, rather than demonstrating social and political awareness. The texture of country music ranges from the full sound of ensembles similar to that of rock to a minimum sound—guitar and voice—in simple songs that are modeled on traditional folk airs. While the harmony of country music retains the basic cadential relationships of the eighteenth and nineteenth century, a special flavor is imparted by the use of modal progressions and lowered leading tones, as well as parallel major chords.

Popular music in the twentieth century has been an immensely rich field for musicians of all degrees of proficiency and imagination, from the untrained amateur to the highly trained performer and composer. Each of the styles discussed here—jazz in its various forms, rock, and country—has its own personality, but also has had the flexibility to absorb a great deal of stylistic content from the main trends of concert music.

SUMMARY In retrospect, the twentieth century exhibits three phases: (1) continuation and intensification of tendencies already well developed in romantic music; (2) evaluation and codification of musical procedures; (3) exploration of new sounds and methods of organization. The first period extends to about 1920, the second period to about 1945-1950; the third phase, always present, became greatly expanded after World War II. It is notable that we find tremendous preoccupation with technique throughout the entire twentieth century. The romantic idea of self-expression, which was largely responsible for the development of individual styles, is no longer the basic motivating force in today's stylistic heterogeneity. Very often, the impression is given that a *modus operandi* is being sought, rather than a *modus vivendi.*

Briefly, we shall close with a summary of the principal features of the styles we have discussed:

1. **Impressionism**
   a. *Quality of sound:* Interest in special effects of color, pervasive sonorities, exotic values
   b. *Quality of movement:* Steady, moderate, level, without strong drive
   c. *Expressive values:* Pictorialism, mood projection, prismatic effects, impressions of nature
   d. *Technical resources:* Chromatic chords, modal scales, special effects of sonority, pentatonic and whole-tone scales

2. **Expressionism; Tone-row music**
   a. *Quality of sound:* Hard, edgy, nonblended, frequently without core
   b. *Quality of movement:* Irregular, angular, explosive, highly tense
   c. *Expressive values:* Suggestive of inner states of tension, crises in the subconscious mind; subject matter sometimes turning to night, darkness, nightmares, unreality; parody
   d. *Technical resources:* Atonality, avoidance of traditional harmonic formulas; continuous spinning out; eventually tone-row technique

3. **Folkloric music**
   a. *Quality of sound:* Brilliant, striking colors, often harsh in effect, making strong immediate impact
   b. *Quality of movement:* Percussive, motoric; underlying regular beat grouped into varying measures; alternating at times with singsong lyric style
   c. *Expressive values:* Concern with the play of sounds and colors, based on a direct sensory appeal, but addressing itself to the analytic sense by subtle variations and imbalances; violence and lyricism contrasted

   d. Technical resources: Rhythms and figures based on folk-music patterns; the sounds of folk music; the melodic materials and scales of folk music; modality, polytonality, atonality; pandiatonism; massive effects of orchestration, often to create a percussive quality

4. Neoromanticism

   The sound, movement, expression, and technical resources of neoromanticism resemble very closely those of the late romantic period, particularly the music of Brahms, Mahler, and Bruckner. The harmony makes use of greater dissonance, atonal or polytonal resources at times, and the scoring is more brilliant or exotic now and then. But the fundamental expressive aim is not materially different from that of sixty or seventy years past.

5. Neoclassicism

   a. Qualities of sound: Tendency toward transparency without loss of core; clarity without special search for brilliance; wide range of harmonic usage, from well-defined minor-major sounds to modality, polytonality, and atonality

   b. Qualities of movement: Inclined to be steady, purposeful, with indications of drive to rhythmic and harmonic points of arrival; sense of phrase and period structure quite clear, often with strongly maintained relation of statement and counterstatement

   c. Expressive values: Play of sounds, figures, gestures against each other without special emotional or picturesque connotations; feeling for self-contained, clearly projected design; desire for balance, codification, reconciliation within a large framework

   d. Technical resources: Forms, styles, manners of preceding style periods, handled harmonically with resources developed in the twentieth century; considerable reliance upon contrapuntal procedures; development and working over of motives in the manner of baroque and classic music

6. Total organization

   The organization of all elements—sound, rhythm, dynamics, pitch—by means of a preestablished pattern or series

7. Electronic music

   Development of new types of sound—mixtures, ranges, timbres; precise control of rhythm by programming; impact of sound as a principal expressive effect

8. Chance music

   Improvisation and the appearance of the unexpected as a "here and now" musical experience

9. **Exotic music**

Great variety of percussive and plucked sounds, complex rhythms and rhythmic combinations, relatively simple melodic figures, much improvisation

10. **Jazz**

Blue notes, syncopated and sliding rhythms, much melodic improvisation, "wavering" in melodic declamation, steady beat, regular phrase structure

11. **Rock and country music**

Heavy beat, "maxi-sound"; in country music, also, a simple balladlike style

*DISCUS-
SION AND
REVIEW
QUESTIONS*

1. What were some of the principal influences of Wagner upon musical impressionism?
2. What were some of the principal influences of Wagner upon musical expressionism?
3. What is "pointillism," and how was it employed in musical impressionism?
4. How is a tone row used to organize a piece of music?
5. Describe the principal features of folkloric music.
6. How does neoclassic music reconcile earlier techniques with those of the twentieth century?
7. What effect have recordings had upon musical taste?
8. What new possibilities have electronic techniques opened to musical style and expression?
9. In what ways does exotic music differ from that of the Western tradition?
10. What features do the various types of popular music have in common, and how do they differ from each other?

GENERAL GLOSSARY
OF TERMS

In addition to terms in common use, this glossary defines historical terms and special words employed in this book. (Glossary terms are not included in the Index.)

a cappella: Literally, "for the chapel"; hence without accompaniment. Applied to choral singing without instruments.

accelerando: Becoming faster in tempo.

accidental: A prefixed sign which alters the pitch of a tone. (*See* natural, sharp, flat.)

ad libitum: "At will." Indicates a style of performance in which strict metric regularity is abandoned for a freer quality of movement. Applies also to a voice or part which may be included or omitted at will.

Alberti bass: A simple accompaniment for the left hand of a keyboard instrument, consisting of chord figurations in a narrow range. The Alberti bass was named after Domenico Alberti, an Italian keyboard composer of the mid-eighteenth century. This kind of accompaniment accommodates a simple style of music, especially the singing-allegro much preferred by amateurs in the early classic period and later.

alleluia: A melismatic passage, expressing jubilation and praise.

allemande: A dance of moderate pace, rather heavy quality of movement, duple meter; German in origin.

alto: Voices of upper middle register are called *alto voices.* This applies to singers, violas, horns, clarinets, and other instruments.

anthem: Originally, a sacred choral composition with English words from the scriptures; now applied to sacred or solemn compositions for chorus.

antiphon: A type of plainsong, derived originally from antiphonal or alternating manner of performance (solo versus group).

arco: Literally, "arch" or "bow"; applied, in string performance, to playing with the bow.

aria: A composition for solo singer and accompaniment, generally of considerable length with much melodic elaboration; also applied to instrumental music using the style of the aria. Either an independent piece or part of a larger work.

aria da capo: The standard form for the Italian opera aria of the late Baroque era; it consisted of a principal section, a contrasting middle section, and a return to the principal section, often with elaborations. *Da capo* means "from the head" (beginning) once more.

Ars antiqua: The polyphonic style of the twelfth and thirteenth centuries, characterized by use of the rhythmic modes.

Ars nova: The polyphonic style of the fourteenth century, characterized by the use of duple and triple meter and by complex relationships of rhythm that broke down the system of rhythmic modes.

a tempo: An indication for the performer to resume the original pace after slowing down or speeding up.

atonal: Pertaining to or characterized by harmony that gives no indication of tonal center or avoids procedures that tend to define tonal centers.

augmented triad: A three-note chord consisting of an augmented fifth and a major third above the lowermost note.

authentic cadence: The strongest harmonic effect of arrival. It involves dominant with 5 in bass moving to tonic, and usually 7 moving to 8 or 2 to 1 in uppermost voice.

authentic mode: A mode in which the final occurs as the highest or lowest note of the range or scale.

bagpipe: A style which imitates the effect of the bagpipe, consisting of a drone or sustained tone in the bass, above which the melody plays the characteristic flourishes. Also called musette.

ballad opera: English comic opera of the eighteenth century.

band: A large instrumental ensemble using no strings (except occasionally double-bass).

bass: Usually designates the lowermost voice of an ensemble if the range of that voice lies in the bass (F) clef; applied also to human voices and to the lowermost representatives of instrumental families: cello, string bass, bassoon (and double bassoon), bass trombone, and tuba. Sometimes the very lowest voices are designated as *contrabass.*

basso continuo: See continuo.

beat: A pulse or stroke which, in a series, helps establish the quality of movement, involving pace and accent.

binary form: See two-reprise form.

blues: Originally an important type of early American folksong and folk music, now a jazz style; characterized by certain tones in the melody or harmony that do not correspond to Western diatonic scales, i.e., the *blue* notes, which are obtained by lowering or flatting a given note.

boogie-woogie: A type of fast blues characterized by a driving beat in duple time, over an ostinato bass that moves regularly through tonic, subdominant, and dominant harmonies.

bop: A form of jazz composition developed in the late 1940s; characterized by rather complex harmonies and rhythms, and striking scoring.

bourrée: A popular dance of the Baroque era, in quick duple time, with a short upbeat.

brass instruments: A family of instruments, constructed of metal, producing their tones by lip vibration against a metal mouthpiece. The family includes cornets, trumpets, French horns, trombones, and tubas. The bugle is also a brass instrument.

caccia: Literally "hunt." A canonic piece of the fourteenth century, whose text describes a hunt, a pastoral scene, a market place, or some other aspect of picturesque life. The music often has touches of realistic imitation of the text.

cadence: A pause or stopping point, usually applied to a harmonic progression.

cadential formula: A harmonic phrase which proceeds through the cycle of departure-movement-arrival, as represented by:

1   2

Tonic harmony—subdominant harmony

3   4

Leading-tone harmony—tonic

cadenza: A section in improvisatory style, which allows the performer freedom to elaborate while the accompaniment pauses; in solo music a section resembling a cadenza in style.

canon: A strict or literal imitation by one voice of a preceding voice, at a prescribed interval of pitch and time.

cantata: Literally, a "sung piece." A composition, sacred or secular, for soloists and/or chorus and instruments, containing a number of individual pieces—chorus, solos, recitatives, chorales, sinfonias—at the discretion of the composer.

cantus firmus: Literally, "fixed song." The melody used as a framework upon which a composition was built.

canzona francese: An instrumental paraphrase of the French chanson; the ancestor of many of the instrumental forms of the seventeenth and eighteenth centuries.

cembalo: German and Italian name for the harpsichord.

chaconne: A dance in moderately slow triple time, used characteristically as a pattern for a series of variations. The element might be a melodic line, a harmonic progression, or a recurrent bass line. Similar to the passacaglia.

chance music: Mid-twentieth-century approach to composition in which the composer provides elements to be organized by the performer.

chanson: French secular vocal composition.

chorale: Hymn tune of the German Protestant church; also, composition using a chorale as a cantus firmus.

chorale prelude: An organ piece based upon a chorale tune and performed as a prelude or introduction to the singing of the chorale tune itself by a Lutheran congregation. An important vehicle for variation and elaboration in the baroque music of Germany.

chord: A vertical combination of tones; also refers to figurations made up of familiar combinations, such as triads and seventh chords.

chromatic: Referring to the presence of alterations in the harmony or melody. (*See* natural, sharp, flat, chromatic scale.)

chromatic scale: The scale which uses all twelve chromatic tones, as, for example, from D to C♯.

clavecin: French word for harpsichord.

clavier: Any keyboard instrument.

clef: A sign placed upon a staff to locate the position of tones. Originally these signs were letters: G above middle C, middle C, and F below middle C. The clefs presently in use are treble (G on second line), alto (C on middle line), tenor (C on fourth line), bass (F on fourth line).

coda: Literally, "tailpiece." A section at the end of a movement, intended to provide a satisfactory summing up and conclusion.

commedia dell'arte: Italian improvised comedy of the Renaissance, of which opera buffa was an offshoot. Built on stereotyped plots and characters.

concertante: The principal or solo instruments in an ensemble.

concertato: A style in which the participating voices and instruments "compete" with each other in an active give-and-take; first applied to early seventeenth-century vocal music with instruments.

concertino: The solo group in a concerto grosso.

concerto: An extended composition for solo instrument or instruments and orchestra, usually in three movements.

concerto grosso: A concerto in which the "grosso" signifies the tutti, and the concertino is a small group of soloists.

conjunct interval: A melodic interval that gives the impression of moving by step. The largest conjunct interval is the major second; anything smaller—minor second, microtone—gives a conjunct impression. Anything larger—minor third or more—gives the impression of movement by leap.

consonant: A relative term, generally equated with harmonic stability or euphony: applied to harmonic intervals. Standards of consonance have varied during the history of Western music.

continuo: The bass part in a baroque composition, usually played by a keyboard instrument (or lute) which provides the chords indicated in a figured bass, reinforced by a cello or viola da gamba.

contredanse: A quick dance in duple time, often used in finales.

cool jazz: An outgrowth of bop that carried forward the experimental and inventive trend.

counterpoint: The placing of distinctive musical lines against each other simultaneously.

courante: A moderately quick dance in triple time, employing momentary shifts in accent; French in origin.

crescendo: Increase in strength or loudness of sound.

decelerando: Becoming slower in tempo.

deceptive cadence: A cadence in which the expected chord of resolution is displaced by some other harmony, leaving the ear not quite satisfied, requiring further cadential action.

decrescendo: Decrease in strength or loudness of sound, also *diminuendo.*

detaché: Performed so that the successive tones are separated clearly from each other but not markedly so. (*See* legato, staccato.)

development: Working over of melodic material by (1) breaking it up into its motives, (2) re-forming motives into new phrases, (3) changing the shape of motives, (4) directing the harmony into shifting key patterns. These procedures are usually found in the section following the exposition of a sonata form, but they are constantly used in almost any large composition; specifically, the X section of a sonata form.

diatonic scale: A scale of seven different tones, containing five whole steps and two half steps arranged so that the half steps are placed a fourth or fifth apart. The effect of a diatonic scale is one of evenness and balance.

diminished triad: A three-note chord consisting of a diminished fifth and a minor third above the lowermost note.

diminuendo: See decrescendo.

diminution: Presentation of a subject in shortened note values.

disjunct interval: A melodic interval larger than a second.

dissonant: A relative term, generally equated with harmonic instability, or sometimes with *disagreeable* or *unpleasant* sound; applied to harmonic intervals. Standards of dissonance have varied during the history of Western music. (*See also* consonant.)

divertimento: See serenade.

Dixieland jazz: See New Orleans jazz.

doctrine of the affections: An aesthetic theory of the seventeenth and eighteenth centuries in which certain musical figures were considered apt for various expressive and rhetorical purposes; one affection was maintained throughout a given movement.

dominant: The fifth degree of a scale or key; the triad, seventh, or ninth chord built upon the dominant degree.

duet, duo: A composition for two performers.

duplum: A part above the tenor in Ars antiqua music.

dynamic curve: A means of organizing a large section of music by constant growth in tension, generally leading to a significant climax, or, conversely, by constant decrease to a point of minimum action.

dynamics: The strength of sound. Dynamics signs include:

pp	pianissimo	very soft
p	piano	soft
mp	mezzo piano	moderately soft
mf	mezzo forte	moderately loud
f	forte	loud
ff	fortissimo	very loud
sf	sforzando	sudden, short, strong accent

echo: Repetition of a figure, with a sharp drop in strength of sound.

electronic music: Music produced by means of electronic sound media, which permit a greater range of sound control and experimentation than is possible with traditional instruments.

Empfindsamkeit: See Sensibility.

endless melody: A term applied to Wagner's style in which motives are linked together so that a clear sense of punctuation is avoided, thus creating a very broad phase of melodic movement.

enharmonic: refers to the notation of a tone in two possible ways, for example, as G♯ or A♭. At the piano, enharmonic tones have the same pitch.

episode: In rondo form, a section contrasting with the principal theme or refrain.

estampie: An important dance and song form of later medieval times. It is built structurally in a series of repeated phrases or sections.

étude: Literally, a "study." A short piece, developing one particular type of figuration, designed for pedagogical purposes. In the nineteenth century études were sometimes written for concert performance.

exotic music: Music outside the Western tradition, such as Asiatic, African, North American Indian, etc.

exposition: In sonata form, Part I, comprising key areas I and II.

expressionism: An early twentieth-century school of composition concerned with expression of strongly subjective feelings, often reflecting subconscious imagery; characterized by freely treated dissonances, angular melodic lines, irregular rhythms, and sparse texture.

fandango: A Spanish dance in moderately quick triple time.

fanfare: A flourish upon the notes of the major triad, usually performed by brass instruments, with occasional accompaniment of drums. Frequently imitated by other instruments in music of the classic style.

fantasia: A work of improvisatory character, usually for keyboard (harpsichord, organ); brilliant virtuoso passages, harmonic explorations, irregular qualities of movement.

fauxbourdon: A technique of early fifteenth-century music in which the upper voices move parallel to the lowermost voice at intervals of thirds and sixths; an early stage of the triad system of harmony.

feet: Metric units applied to poetry and taken over in medieval times by music.

figured bass: A bass line in which the chords to be provided above were indicated by numbers that specified certain intervals.

final: The tonic of a mode.

finale: Last movement of a sonata, symphony, quartet, or other multimovement work; also applied to the final section of an operatic act.

flamenco: Spanish gypsy music, a prominent feature of which is a progression of chords that "slide" up and down a scale, reflecting the fingering technique of the guitar; highly improvisatory and colorful.

flat: A sign (♭) which lowers by a semitone any note before which it is placed.

folkloric music: Music in a style that took shape during the latter part of the nineteenth century, particularly in Eastern European countries; characterized by simple melodic material, vigorous rhythms, and striking and brilliant textures and colors.

free imitation: Imitation in which each entering voice moves freely after presenting the subject, which itself may be varied.

free organum: Organum in which the added voices move in different directions from the cantus firmus, retaining much the same rhythmic pattern.

French overture: The instrumental number which preceded operas and ballets in French baroque theater performances; a slow ceremonious opening section, using dotted rhythms, followed by a quick imitative section, in the manner of a canzona.

frottola: Popular rather than courtly Italian vocal composition of the late fifteenth and early sixteenth centuries; a predecessor of the madrigal.

fugue: Literally, "flight"; hence, a composition in which voices follow or chase each other. Strictly speaking, fugue is a process in which a theme or subject is presented and worked over in contrapuntal imitation by two or more parts. This process lent its name to pieces so composed. Fugal imitation is not as thorough, nor as exact, as canonic imitation.

galant style: The light, popular, elegant style that dominated musical taste in the later eighteenth century. It was characterized by light, simple textures, ingratiating melodies, song and dance idioms, contrasts, and mixing of affective values. It was opposed to the learned style and to the unity of affective value of the Baroque era. It was also called the *free* style as opposed to the *strict.*

gamelan: The Javanese orchestra, consisting principally of struck instruments—gongs, chimes, xylophones, etc.—accompanied by several string and wind instruments.

gavotte: A French dance in moderately quick duple time; a typical feature is its beginning in the middle of a measure, with an upbeat of two quarter notes; well-marked divisions in the phrasing to reflect the steps of the dance itself.

Gesamtkunstwerk: Term used by Wagner to designate the merging of music, language, staging, and pantomime to create a comprehensive work of art.

gigue: A quick dance in six-eight or nine-eight, often treated imitatively. English in origin.

give-and-take: A texture that is basically homophonic, but which shows many aspects of contrapuntal treatment; the melodies are shared between the component voices; incidental imitations enter and disappear; the accompaniment figures have distinct melodic interest. This type of texture is one of the important features of the classic style.

grace note: A short note, ornamenting a principal note which follows it. Grace notes are not counted in the metrical notation of a measure.

ground bass: A melody given to the bass, repeated many times, over which the treble instruments play variations.

half cadence: A harmonic pause upon the dominant, equivalent to a comma or semicolon in language.

harmonic series: When a tone is sounded, the vibrating body (string, reed, pipe, membrane) vibrates, in addition to its full length, in successively smaller fractions. Each of these fractions produces a faint tone auxiliary to the principal or fundamental tone. The combination of all these tones is called the *harmonic series.* For example, C has the following series:

$$\begin{array}{cccccc} C & c & g & c & e & g \\ 1 & \frac{1}{2} & \frac{1}{3} & \frac{1}{4} & \frac{1}{5} & \frac{1}{6} \text{ etc.} \end{array}$$

The tones above the fundamental are called *overtones.* The prominence of certain overtones has much to do with the specific tone color of a voice or instrument.

harmony: The element of music which deals with the relationships tones can form with each other to give a sense of position, stability and instability, and specific sonority value, aside from melodic, rhythmic, or textural considerations.

harpsichord: An important keyboard instrument of the Renaissance and Baroque eras, producing its tone through the plucking of strings by quills. Constructed in many sizes and types.

homophonic: Pertaining to music in which one principal melodic idea is stated at a given time.

hunt: A quick march or dance idiom, using gigue or contredanse patterns, characterized by the use of fanfares.

idée fixe: A term (applied to Berlioz's *Symphonie Fantastique*) which refers to a distinctive melody heard in each movement; this melody represents the "fixation" of the poet-hero upon the idea of his beloved; it interrupts or is part of various episodes in his life. (*See also* leitmotif; thematic transformation.)

imitation: The taking up of the subject or melody by successive voices in turn.

impressionism: A musical style in which subtle textures and colors were used to convey impressions of the physical world, such as the play of light, air, or water; also to suggest exotic, nostalgic, and sentimental subjects.

incidental music: Music intended for performance during the course of a play or other dramatic presentation. Such music may accompany dramatic action, be performed for dances or songs, or it may signal entrances and exits.

intermezzo: An interlude piece; name also given to certain pieces of light or lyric character; also light entertainments given between the acts of serious Renaissance and baroque theatrical performances.

interval: Distance between two tones. Intervals are named according to the staff degrees they encompass. Thus a second covers two degrees; a third, three; etc. Intervals are further qualified according to their exact size. Their dimensions are as follows:

minor second	$\frac{1}{2}$ step
major second	1 step
augmented second	$1\frac{1}{2}$ steps
diminished third	2 half steps
minor third	$1\frac{1}{2}$ steps
major third	2 steps
diminished fourth	1 step, 2 half steps
perfect fourth	$2\frac{1}{2}$ steps
augmented fourth	3 steps
diminished fifth	2 steps, 2 half steps
perfect fifth	$3\frac{1}{2}$ steps
augmented fifth	4 steps
minor sixth	3 steps, 2 half steps
major sixth	$4\frac{1}{2}$ steps
diminished seventh	3 steps, 3 half steps
minor seventh	4 steps, 2 half steps
major seventh	$5\frac{1}{2}$ steps
octave	5 steps, 2 half steps

intonation: In Renaissance music, an instrumental piece used as a prelude to liturgical singing; called intonation because it sets the tone (tonic of the mode) of the song to follow. Generally, tuning of a voice or instrument with regard to accuracy of pitch.

introduction: An opening section preceding the body of a movement, usually in slower tempo than the main part. Often employs the French overture idiom, possibly the aria style, or the Storm and Stress. In classic works, the introduction builds a strong cadential drive to prepare for the advent of the allegro.

inversion: In harmony, placing the root or root *and* third of a chord in the upper voices and thereby causing the third or fifth of a chord to become the lowermost tone. Also, the reversal in direction of the intervals of a melody.

jazz: A style evolved in the early twentieth century, based upon march and dance patterns elaborated by syncopation, melodic nuances, characteristic scoring, and much improvisation upon a basic melody or progression.

jota: A Spanish dance in quick triple time, characterized by shifts between groups of two beats and three beats: *1 2 3   1 2 3* versus *1 2   3 1 2 3.*

key: A tonal center, generally one defined by cadential (leading-tone) action; the system of tones governed by a given tonal center, such as C major, F minor. The key sense in Western music is said to have become fully developed in the late seventeenth century when cadential formulas were first used in great strength and numbers, saturating the harmony.

key area: A section of a composition centering upon one key.

key area form: A form based upon the opposition of key areas; especially applied to the harmonic plan of sonata form, I-V; X-I.

koto: A many-stringed Japanese instrument.

ländler: A German dance in triple meter, similar to the waltz, but with some elements of the minuet.

leading tone: Ordinarily, the seventh degree of the major scale or the seventh degree (raised) of the minor scale. A leading tone, being part of the tension element of a cadential formula, *leads* to its tonic. The term is also applied to any tone which has a leading function in harmony.

learned style: In later eighteenth century, contrapuntal composition; also the strict style, with more rigorous control of dissonance than is found in the galant style.

legato: performed in a smooth manner, without noticeable break in sound. (*See* detaché, staccato.)

leger line: Line added below or above a staff in order to notate tones lying outside the staff.

leitmotif: A significant motive, which may have a distinctive melodic, rhythmic, or harmonic quality and which is assigned to some idea, person, or situation; it is introduced in the musical composition to signal or to develop the idea to which it is attached.

libretto: The text or book of an opera or oratorio.

lied: German for song.

liturgical: Pertaining to Church rites and services.

lute: A plucked string instrument widely used in Renaissance and baroque music.

madrigal: A secular vocal composition of the Renaissance, cultivated first in Italy, then taken up toward the end of the sixteenth century in England.

major scale: A scale in which the order of whole steps and half steps is: 1 1 ½ 1 1 1 ½.

march: A piece in duple time and of steady meter, using incisive (dotted) rhythmic patterns, regular period structure. Tempo varies according to occasion (quick for military, moderate for ceremonial, slow for funeral).

Mass: The most important service of the Catholic Church, commemorating the sacrifice of Christ on the cross.

mastersinger: The fifteenth- and sixteenth-century continuation of the minnesingers. In contrast to their aristocratic forebears, mastersingers were middle-class townsmen and artisans. (German: *Meistersinger.*)

mazurka: Polish dance in quick triple time, with strong accent on beat 2 or 3.

measure: A group of beats marked off on a musical score by a vertical line.

measured organum: Organum in which the upper voice or voices, and sometimes the cantus firmus, move in the measured system of the rhythmic modes, using patterns of long and short tones.

melismatic style: In plainsong, the style of a melody that has melodic elaborations upon one syllable.

melismatic organum: Organum in which the added voice is in melismatic style, while the cantus firmus moves in long notes.

melodic interval: The distance between two tones sounded successively.

melodic motive: A melodic fragment, two notes in length or longer, which gives a distinct impression of manner or style.

melody: A series of tones which moves forward to delineate and complete a meaningful musical shape.

menuet: A dance of French origin, in triple meter, with a moderately quick yet elegant and graceful quality of movement. (Also *minuet.*)

meter: Grouping of beats into small, recurrent units. *Simple duple* meter involves two beats; *simple triple* involves three beats; *compound duple* involves four or six beats subdivided into two subgroups of two or three each; *compound triple* involves triple division, the subgroups containing two or three beats each.

microtones: Intervals smaller than the half step of traditional Western music, used sometimes for ornamentation of a basically diatonic or chromatic harmony, sometimes as constituent elements of the harmony itself.

middle C: The note C at the midpoint of the piano keyboard.

Minnelied: Minnesinger's song.

minnesinger: German counterpart of the troubadour.

minor scale: Scale characterized by the minor third between 1 and 3. The *natural minor scale* has the following order of steps and half steps: 1 $\frac{1}{2}$ 1 1 $\frac{1}{2}$ 1 1. In order to make the minor scale effective cadentially, the seventh degree was made a leading tone with the following order: 1 $\frac{1}{2}$ 1 1 $\frac{1}{2}$ 1$\frac{1}{2}$ $\frac{1}{2}$. This *harmonic minor scale* had to be adjusted to eliminate the awkward melodic interval between 6 and 7. Therefore, in the *melodic minor scale* the order is as follows: 1 $\frac{1}{2}$ 1 1 1 1 $\frac{1}{2}$.

minor triad: A three-note chord, consisting of a perfect fifth and a minor third above the lowermost tone.

modes, medieval and Renaissance: Scales used to codify melodies, according to finals, ranges, and distribution of whole and half steps.

modulation: A formal shift of tonal center, usually confirmed by an authentic cadence in the new key. Also, a change of key.

monody: In the early baroque style, the music for solo singer and chordal accompaniment in recitative style developed around 1600 as a reaction to the highly developed polyphony of the Renaissance. Generally, music for one voice.

motet: A composition based upon measured organum in which one or more of the upper voices has words (*mots*); also an important Ars nova form; a category of Renaissance music.

musette: See bagpipe.

music drama: Term used to distinguish the works of Wagner from other nineteenth-century operas and to emphasize his particular conception of opera.

nationalism: The trend toward the cultivation of national ideas and idioms in the later nineteenth century. Principal among the national schools were the Russian, Bohemian, and Scandinavian. Nationalism was a counter-movement to the international idioms of Germany, France, and Italy.

natural sign: A sign (♮) which cancels the raising or lowering effect of a previous sharp or flat.

neoclassicism: The tendency in the twentieth century to organize music along the lines of eighteenth-century principles of construction, using contrapuntal layouts, well-defined phrase structure, transparent texture, often strongly emphasized cadences and keys.

neoromanticism: The retention, in twentieth-century music, of certain broadly expressive attitudes of romanticism, together with its rich texture and harmony.

New Orleans jazz: The early style of jazz characterized by performance by three or more wind instruments, supported by other instruments which perform a rhythmic function (piano, banjo, percussion, bass); rather free simultaneous improvisation in what is basically a popular kind of march style. *See also* jazz.

obbligato: Literally, "obliged." A part or voice necessary to the full realization of the composition. (*See* ad libitum.) At present, the term has just the opposite meaning, indicating an ornamental part accompanying the principal melody (as a violin or flute supporting a singer).

octave: An interval consisting of five whole steps and two half steps. The most consonant interval in music, since the two notes sound as upper and lower duplicates of each other.

office: In Catholic Church liturgy, the services held at specific hours of the day.

opera: A drama, performed with scenery and action, sung throughout, and accompanied by some instrumental group. Some eighteenth- and nineteenth-century comic operas have occasional spoken dialog.

opera buffa: Comic opera, derived from commedia dell'arte episodes interpolated into serious theater performances in the seventeenth century; great variety of styles and forms, ensemble numbers.

opéra comique: French comic opera of the eighteenth century.

opera seria: Principal operatic type of the later Baroque period; elaborate arias interspersed with recitatives; subject matter drawn from Greco-Roman history or mythology, involving persons of noble birth.

opus: Literally, "work." A composition or group of compositions designated usually with numbers, thus giving the chronological position of the work within the output of a single composer.

oratorio: A dramatic representation of a religious or thoughtful subject, using many of the techniques of opera.

orchestra: A large group of instrumental performers, including string instruments.

organal voice: A voice added to the cantus firmus in organum.

organum: The earliest polyphony, consisting of a plainsong cantus firmus and organal voices.

ornamentation: The art of adding figures to a given musical text, a process which was already in operation during plainsong times and which is still in use today.

ostinato: A ground bass.

overture: The instrumental piece, usually in sonata form, which serves as a prelude to an opera. Also applied to the symphony in eighteenth-century concerts, indicating derivation of the symphony from the operatic overture.

pandiatonism: In twentieth-century music the use of tones from a diatonic scale in chords that do not represent traditional triads and seventh chords.

parallel organum: Organum in which the added voice or voices move parallel to the cantus firmus at the interval of a fourth, fifth, or octave.

parlando: A style of singing in quick, separate, even notes, with a syllable to each note: "patter" singing, featured in opera buffa.

parody: In Renaissance music, the elaboration of a smaller polyphonic composition into a larger one, as, for example, a Mass elaborated from a motet, madrigal, or chanson. In the earlier twentieth century, the use of familiar styles and types of music in a rather grotesquely distorted manner; the waltz is a favorite subject for parody.

passacaglia: See chaconne.

passepied: A French dance in quick triple time.

passion: An oratorio dealing with the sacrifice of Christ.

pedal: A foot-operated mechanism; the pedal keyboard of the organ; *pedal-point* refers to a sustained tone held while other voices move, the passage generally extending for several measures.

pentatonic scale: A scale that has five tones, corresponding to 1 2 3 5 6 of the major scale, or 1 2 4 5 7 of the minor scale; its lack of half tones gives it a special character and a flexibility of use but imposes a very tight limitation on progression in the scale; used as a coloristic device in impressionism.

percussion instruments: Instruments whose tone is produced by striking a membrane, wood block, or bar of metal. Percussion instruments include the kettledrum, snare drum, bass drum, xylophone, chimes, tambourine, and cymbals.

perfect fifth: An interval encompassing five scale degrees, containing three whole steps and one half step. The perfect fifth is one of the strongest embodiments of harmonic stability.

period: A section of music, generally consisting of two or more phrases, ending with a full or conclusive point of arrival and containing a rather fully expressed musical idea.

phase of movement: A musical statement whose progress forward is marked off and controlled by points of departure and arrival. Phases of musical movement are variable in length.

phrase: A fairly short section of music with a well-defined point of arrival, containing clearly formed ideas, yet lacking something in form or sense to be complete.

pictorialism: The linking of distinctive musical ideas to specific pictorial or literary effects; the musical idea suggests by its design the nonmusical concept.

pitch: The level of musical sound, based on the number of vibrations given out by any specified tone.

pizzicato: An indication for string performers to pluck the strings with the fingers.

plagal cadence: A cadence in which the subdominant precedes the tonic. This is a very restful sort of cadence and is heard in the amen phrase at the end of many sacred compositions.

plagal mode: A mode in which the final occurs in the middle of the range or scale.

plainsong: Medieval church song; also referred to as Gregorian chant.

point of arrival: The point at which a phase of movement reaches an end or is marked off from the succeeding phase. This may arrest movement partially or completely.

point of imitation: A section of a piece using imitation.

polka: A Bohemian dance, quick, in duple time, very popular in the nineteenth century.

polonaise: A Polish dance, much favored in the seventeenth and eighteenth centuries; quick triple time.

polychoral: A performance group divided into two or more sections that are opposed to each other in the give-and-take of musical material; applied especially to Venetian music performed in St. Mark's Cathedral during the late Renaissance and the Baroque periods.

polyphonic: Pertaining to music which employs counterpoint.

polytonality: The simultaneous performance of passages in two or more keys; also refers to chords built with tones from more than one key.

prelude: An introductory piece, generally for keyboard; a piece in an improvisatory style.

prima prattica: The polyphonic style of the Renaissance; *see* seconda prattica.

program music: Music written to a story or scenario; the allusions are more specific than in eighteenth-century musical pictorialism and more fully carried out.

psalm tone: A melody, characterized by many repeated tones, used in plainsong to recite the Psalms.

quartet: A group of four performers; a composition for four performers.

quintet: A group of five performers; a composition for five performers.

raga: A melodic pattern in Indian music upon which a composition is elaborated.

ragtime: A form of late nineteenth- and early twentieth-century popular music using syncopated rhythms in a march style with regular phrase structure.

recapitulation: In sonata form, the section following the X, in which the material of the exposition is presented in the home key to resolve the harmonic contrast first established. It acts as a rhyme to the exposition.

recitative: Musical declamation, in no set meter or rhythm; echoes the inflections of speech.

recitative accompagnato: A vocal declamation accompanied by distinctive short figures in the orchestra; employs some of the expressive songlike manner of the aria; no standard key or phrase plan.

recitative secco: Vocal declamation over the sustained or punctuating chords of a keyboard instrument. Less expressive than accompagnato, generally quicker, employing the rhythmic patterns of ordinary speech.

refrain: The principal theme of a rondo. More generally, a section that returns periodically in a song, dance, or larger work.

register: Section of the range of an instrument or voice with a characteristic color. In organ performance, a set of pipes governed by one stop.

remembrance motive: A distinctive motive or passage associated with some situation in an opera and recalled when reference is made again to the situation. Less intensively employed than leitmotif.

repetition: Restatement of any musical effect, melody, rhythm, harmony, texture, phrase, period, etc. Repetition may be literal or varied. In any case, repetition may be taken as counterstatement.

resolution: In counterpoint and harmony, the settling of dissonance or tension by conducting the dissonant tones to tones which are consonant.

retrograde: Reversal of order in the tones of a subject.

rhapsody: An improvisatory piece, along the lines of a fantasia; structurally, often written as a series of episodes.

rhythm: The element which generates, measures, organizes, and controls musical time.

rhythmic modes: Rhythmic patterns used in measured organum; based on poetic meter (long and short syllables).

ricercar: In Renaissance music, the instrumental counterpart or paraphrase of a motet; also, an improvisatory piece much like a toccata or intonation.

ripieno: Literally, "filling up"; the full orchestra in a concerto.

ritardando: Becoming slower in tempo.

ritornello: The orchestral section of an aria, heard at the beginning and end, and sometimes within the body of the aria. Also the tutti section of a concerto.

rococo: An eighteenth-century style, applied to art as well as music, designating a highly ornate type of embellishment.

rondo: A piece built by alternations of refrains and episodes, as in ABACADA.

root position: A chord position in which the lowermost note is the fundamental root or generator. (*See* harmonic series.) In practice this works out so that the root is the lower note of the perfect fifth of the triad. In chords which have no perfect fifth, the root is considered to be the bottom note when the chord is arranged in thirds.

round: A simple type of imitation, in which a number of voices, beginning at different times, sing the same melody over and over again.

1	2	3	4	1	2	3	4
4	**1**	2	3	4	1	2	3
3	4	**1**	2	3	4	1	2
2	3	4	**1**	2	3	4	1

All voices begin with **1.**

rubato: Literally, "robbed." A manner of performance in which time values are stolen from some tones in order to give greater stress or expressive accent to others.

samisen: A three-stringed Japanese instrument.

sarabande: Rather slow dance in triple time, with an accent of length generally upon the second beat of the measure; Spanish in origin.

satire (*and parody*): In the late nineteenth and early twentieth centuries, the distortion and ridiculing of familiar or traditional ideas and musical idioms. This was often done with a strong flavor of bitterness or irony.

scale: A stepwise series of tones, usually denoting a rising line. Scales are qualified according to the arrangement of whole steps and half steps. (*See* major scale, minor scale, mode, whole-tone scale, chromatic scale, diatonic scale.)

scherzo: Italian for "jest." A quick, dancelike movement, which all but supplanted the minuet in the nineteenth-century symphony.

seconda prattica: The new, bold treatment of dissonance for expressive purposes, and generally the heightening of expressive values, in early baroque music.

semitone: A half step; the smallest interval commonly used in Western music.

Sensibility: A style of performance and composition concerned with intimate, capricious, sentimental expression; closely allied to lyric poetry of the later eighteenth century.

sequence: Restatement of a motive or phrase upon several successively higher or lower levels; a way of giving a larger contour to a group of motives or phrases.

serenade: Music for evening, generally light and entertaining in character; especially applied to sets of instrumental pieces often performed outdoors, consisting of marches, dances, variations, and songlike movements, as well as one or more longer movements in sonata or rondo form. Sometimes included virtuoso passages for solo violin or winds. Term used interchangeably with divertimento.

serialism: The organization of musical events through a pattern in which each element has a fixed position in relation to the others; such a pattern is called a series; it governs the order of tones, rhythms, or scoring in a piece.

sextet: A group of six performers; a composition for six performers.

sharp: A sign (♯) which raises by a semitone any note before which it is placed.

signature: The group of sharps or flats and the meter indication of a composition; both are found at the beginning of the piece; the key signature (sharps or flats) is placed at the left of each staff system throughout the piece.

sinfonia: Orchestral introduction to Italian opera; also applied to instrumental episodes in concertato or dramatic works.

singing-allegro: Quick, songlike melodic style with Alberti bass accompaniment or simple rhythmic support, favored in Italian-style compositions of the classic era.

Singspiel: German comic opera of the eighteenth century.

sitar: A lutelike Indian instrument.

solo: A single instrument or voice; a passage performed by a single instrument or voice.

soloistic: Term applied to virtuoso figurations in classic music derived from the baroque concerto.

sonata: From *canzona da sonar.* An important instrumental form of the Baroque period, consisting of three or more movements in alternating slow-fast tempo; performed as a solo or as a piece for a few instruments.

sonata da camera: Sonata performed as chamber music.

sonata da chiesa: Sonata performed as church music.

sonata form: The most important form of the classic era; basically, a long-range harmonic plan (*see* key area form) in which each key area has distinctive thematic material. *See* exposition, development, recapitulation, coda.

soprano: Literally, "above." The highest women's voice; also the highest instrument of a family, such as the soprano saxophone.

sostenuto: Sustained.

Sprechgesang: A type of singing evolved by Wagner to mirror the accents and expressive nuances of his dramatic texts.

Sprechstimme: Vocal performance in which the music is half sung, half spoken; no fixed pitches, only relative rise and fall suggesting the inflection of speech.

staccato: Performed in a markedly detached manner. (*See* detaché, legato.)

staff: The system of five lines upon which music is notated.

stile brisé: Highly ornamented French style, derived from lute music.

stile rappresentativo: See monody, recitative, seconda prattica.

Storm and Stress: Applied to a late eighteenth-century manner concerned with impetuous, agitated, violent expression; influenced by the *Sturm und Drang,* the early stage of German romantic drama and literature.

string instruments: A family of instruments constructed of a sounding box over which strings are stretched. The tone is produced by drawing a bow across the strings or by plucking. The modern orchestral strings are violins, violas, cellos, string basses.

strophic: Characterized by the use of the same music for the stanzas of a poem.

subject: A distinctive melodic statement, generally in a large composition, which will be developed in some fashion after it has been presented.

superius: The soprano, treble, or uppermost voice in a polyphonic setting.

suspension: An effect achieved when one or more voices are held over as one chord moves to another. These voices are *suspended* and create dissonances, which are then directed or resolved into the proper tones of the second chord.

syllabic style: A style in vocal music in which each syllable of the text has a single note. This applies particularly to one style of plainsong.

sympathetic resonance: The vibration caused in a resonating body (string, pipe) when a nearby body of the same length is sounded.

symphonic poem: A one-movement orchestral work with a number of episodes, suitable for epic, heroic, dramatic program music; established by Franz Liszt.

symphony: The most important orchestral form of the late eighteenth and nineteenth centuries. A three- or four-movement work, of which the first movement is always in sonata form.

syncopation: Shift of accent or length from the normal position occupied by a point of arrival; it creates imbalance and intensifies movement.

tactus: The unit of time in Renaissance music.

tarantella: A quick Italian dance in six-eight time, giguelike.

tastar de corde: The technique of the improvisatory ricercar.

temperament: The act of modifying or tempering; applied to the tuning of instruments (especially keyboard) to adjust for minor discrepancies which arise when the ratios of the harmonic series are used.

tempo: Synonym for *pace.* (*See* Chapter 2 for various tempo designations.)

tenor: The voice that sings the cantus firmus in medieval polyphony; the voice which "holds," often in long notes. Generally, a low middle range of voice or instrument, such as a male tenor voice, cello, bassoon, or tenor trombone.

terrace dynamics: The change in strength of sound achieved sharply by alternations of tutti and solo in a concertolike texture.

tessitura: The general working range of a vocal part in a song or aria.

texture: The composite action of the component voices or parts performing at any given time; includes monophonic, unison, single action (isometric), melody and accompaniment, imitative and nonimitative polyphony, and give-and-take.

thematic transformation: The technique of altering the character of a theme without destroying its basic shape or identity; frequently used in romantic music to establish structural unity.

theme: A distinctive melodic statement, usually part of a long movement.

three-part structure Ternary form (ABA), the important feature of which is some sort of contrasting episode setting off two statements of the principal idea, phrase, period, or larger section.

through-composed: Characterized by modification of the music for various stanzas in the musical setting of a poem (*see* strophic) or by little or no repetition of sections.

toccata: Literally, "touched"; applied to a study for keyboard or possibly string instrument in the manner of a fantasia or prelude.

tonal center: A tone which is given prominence in a phrase, period, or larger section acting as a point of reference, arrival, or stability. This prominence can be given by melodic, rhythmic, or, most strongly, harmonic means.

tone row: A distinctive pattern using all twelve tones of the chromatic scale without repetition; this pattern acts as the source material for an entire movement or composition. *See also* serialism.

tonic: The tonal center, the principal note of a key or mode.

total organization: Serialism in which all events in a composition are controlled, including pitch, rhythm, scoring, and dynamics.

treble: A voice or instrument performing in a high range, such as a treble viol. The high range itself, as applied particularly to choral composition.

tremolo: In strings, the rapid repetition of the same note. The term has also been used to designate a rapid alternation between two notes.

triad: A chord of three tones, reducible to a fifth divided by a third.

trill: An ornamental figure consisting of the rapid alternation of a principal note with the note directly above.

trio: A composition for three instruments. Also applied to the second part of a minuet movement, the B of the ABA form. Typically, this second dance featured a group of solo instruments, often three; hence the name, trio.

trio sonata: A texture involving two solo instruments and continuo; a composition using this texture; actually, four performers are required (*see* continuo).

tritone: The augmented fourth, involving three whole steps, as F to B. The term is also applied to inversion of the augmented fourth, i.e., the diminished fifth, since both have a similar function of creating harmonic tension to indicate a tonal center.

troubadours: Poet-musicians of the Middle Ages in southern France.

trouvères: The counterpart of troubadours in northern France.

two-part structure (binary form): A form consisting of two complementary sections. The cadence or the point of arrival of the first part usually gives an impression of being incomplete or of requiring further action; the point of arrival or cadence of the second part acts as a completion of the form.

two-reprise form: A dance-derived form consisting of two sections or periods; the first ends with an open or inconclusive cadence, the second with a conclusive or closed cadence.

tutti: The full ensemble in a baroque instrumental work.

unison: A combination which is created when two or more voices sound the same tone.

upbeat: A note or group of notes preceding an accented tone. The upbeat usually is found immediately preceding the measure line (or bar line).

variation: The alteration or elaboration of one or more features of a subject or theme. Also compositions in which the procedure of variation is the principal means of carrying the structure forward.

verismo: The operatic style that corresponds to literary and artistic realism in the late nineteenth century.

vers mesuré: A type of French sixteenth-century secular vocal music in which the time values of the tones reflect the scansion of the poetic text employed; sung in familiar style.

vibrato: A rapid and very small change of pitch in string-instrument and in vocal performance. Properly handled, in moderation, vibrato can add richness and expressive nuance to give tones.

viola da gamba: The bass of the viol family (six-string instruments), used widely in baroque music to complete the continuo.

whole-tone scale: A scale that uses whole steps exclusively, such as C D E F♯ G♯ B♭; characterized by a vagueness of harmonic focus and a special richness of color.

woodwind instruments: A family of instruments, constructed of a keyed tube of wood (or metal) and producing sound by the vibration of a reed (or double-reed) in the mouthpiece (with the exception of the flute). In addition to flutes, the family includes clarinets, oboes, bassoons, saxophones.

LIST OF
COMPOSERS

Bach, Johann Christian, 1735–1782, b. Leipzig: The youngest son of Johann Sebastian Bach. Composer of orchestral works, chamber music, operas. Very successful in London. He influenced Mozart greatly, particularly with reference to the use of the Italian galant style.

Bach, Johann Sebastian, 1685–1750, b. Eisenach: Greatest master of the late Baroque period. Bach's music represents the final culmination of the baroque style and a synthesis of many different idioms. He wrote in many media and forms, and though he wrote no opera, he employed operatic techniques in his cantatas, passions, and other choral works. Served at Weimar, Cöthen, and Leipzig. Among his important works are the Mass in B minor, the *Well-Tempered Clavier, The Art of the Fugue,* and the six *Brandenburg* Concertos.

Bach, Karl Philipp Emanuel, 1714–1788, b. Weimar: Son of Johann Sebastian Bach. Identified with the *Empfindsamkeit* manner. A brilliant keyboard performer at the court of Frederick the Great. Exerted considerable influence upon Mozart and Haydn. Solo works for keyboard, concertos, orchestral works.

Barber, Samuel, 1910–   , b. West Chester: American composer of orchestral and chamber music. His works, based largely upon traditional forms and harmonic procedures, are frequently performed in America and Europe.

Bartók, Béla, 1881–1945, b. Nagyszentmiklós: Hungarian composer in the forefront of the folkloric trend of the twentieth century. Bartók, moreover, had an extremely eloquent and distinctive personal style which influenced many composers. Important works include six string quartets, Concerto for Orchestra, operas, orchestral works, teaching pieces (*Mikrokosmos*).

Beethoven, Ludwig van, 1770–1827, b. Bonn: German composer whose music represents the culmination of the classic style as well as an important link to nineteenth-century romanticism. He exerted a profound influence upon ideas of musical construction and expression, establishing the concept of the "monumental" symphony, and intensifying expression much beyond the scope of his predecessors. He wrote nine symphonies, of which the Third, the *Eroica,* is a landmark in the history of music. Seventeen string quartets, thirty-two piano sonatas, opera *Fidelio,* five piano concertos, much other chamber music.

Bellini, Vincenzo, 1801–1835, b. Catania, Sicily: Opera composer noted especially for the attractiveness of his melodic style. Chief works are *Norma, I Puritani, La Sonnambula.*

Berg, Alban, 1885–1935, b. Vienna: Together with Von Webern and Schönberg, Berg represents the grand triumvirate of twelve-tone music in the first half of the twentieth century. Pupil of Schönberg. His music tends to be more directly grasped and more openly dramatic than that of his two colleagues. His opera *Wozzeck* is one of the monuments of the modern lyric stage.

Berlioz, Louis Hector, 1803–1869, b. near Grenoble: French composer whose treatment of the orchestra was highly original and imaginative; his textures and phrase structure foreshadowed modern techniques of orchestration and composition. Important works include the *Symphonie Fantastique,* the symphony, *Harold in Italy,* the operas *Benvenuto Cellini* and *The Trojans,* a Requiem Mass, the dramatic symphony *Romeo and Juliet,* and the secular oratorio *The Damnation of Faust.*

Bizet, Georges, 1838–1875, b. Paris: Opera composer whose work *Carmen* is one of the most popular of the entire operatic repertoire. *Carmen* represents the new realistic lyric drama, with emphasis upon sharp dramatic impact, fresh and striking color, and winning melody.

Bloch, Ernest, 1880–1959, b. Geneva: Bloch's music combines various aspects of impressionism, folkloric style, and romanticism, held together by a firm neoclassic command of structure and of polyphonic procedures. Important works include *Schelomo* (rhapsody for violoncello and orchestra), a Violin Concerto, Quintet for Piano and Strings, two concerti grossi, a Sacred Service, chamber music of various types.

Borodin, Aleksandr, 1833–1887, b. St. Petersburg: A member of the group that worked for the establishment of a Russian national school. His music uses many materials based on folk idioms; some compositions are descriptive of Russian or Asiatic scenes, such as the opera *Prince Igor* and the symphonic sketch *On the Steppes of Central Asia.* The Symphony No. 2 in B minor is a well-known concert item.

Boulez, Pierre, 1925–   , b. Montbrison: French composer. Leader in the post-Webern serialist trend, applying total organization to serial techniques. Best known work is *Le Marteau sans Maître,* a suite for contralto and six instruments.

Brahms, Johannes, 1833–1897, b. Hamburg: Principal representative of the classic tradition in nineteenth-century music. Brahms's music, particularly his symphonies, concertos, chamber music, and choral works, has the grand manner and the broad scope associated with great music of the classic era. His songs and small keyboard pieces reflect romantic modes very characteristically. Brahms's style, particularly his rhythms, textures, and broad melodies, was frequently imitated by later composers.

Britten, Benjamin, 1913–   , b. Lowestoft, Suffolk: English composer noted especially for his operas, which include *Peter Grimes, Albert Herring, The Rape of Lucrece, Gloriana, The Turn of the Screw.* Britten has developed a very direct, easily grasped style, drawn from many traditional sources and eminently suited for dramatic purposes.

Bruckner, Anton, 1824-1896, b. Upper Austria: Austrian composer noted especially for his nine symphonies and for sacred music. Bruckner transferred the techniques and the manner of Wagner to orchestral music.

Buxtehude, Dietrich, 1637-1707, b. Hälsingborg: Composer of the North German school, and organist who contributed to the evolution of the suite, the fugue, and German sacred music. Strong influence on Johann Sebastian Bach.

Byrd, William, 1540-1623: Important Tudor composer, versatile in all forms of English Renaissance music. Works include Masses, motets, anthems, madrigals, chamber music, and keyboard music.

Caccini, Giulio, c. 1546-1618, b. Rome: Italian composer who was one of the principal exponents of the new monodic style, in which he wrote madrigals and operas. His *Euridice* is the first opera presented in a public theater. He also wrote a book of madrigals called *Nuove Musiche,* in which new techniques of vocal performance are described.

Carissimi, Giacomo, 1605-1674, b. near Rome: Roman composer noted chiefly for his oratorios. An exponent of the *stile rappresentativo.* His oratorios include *Jephthe, The Judgment of Solomon, Jonah, Balthazar.*

Carter, Elliott, 1908-   , b. New York City: American composer, whose music is stylistically related to that of Stravinsky and Bartók. He has developed a concept of *metric modulation,* which controls changes of pace according to proportional formulas.

Cherubini, Luigi, 1760-1842, b. Florence: Italian composer of operas and instrumental music. Cherubini was admired by Beethoven, upon whom he had considerable influence. He was also an important musical theorist and, as his music shows, a skillful contrapuntalist.

Chopin, Frédéric, 1810-1849, b. near Warsaw: Polish composer; one of the most important figures of the early romantic period. Almost exclusively a composer for piano, Chopin worked out an individual style which explored the sonority resources of his instrument. Works include two concertos for piano, four scherzi, fantasies, ballades, preludes, études, valses, polonaises, mazurkas, etc.

Copland, Aaron, 1900-   , b. Brooklyn: One of the most widely performed American composers. Copland has developed a highly distinctive personal style, based in part upon folk-dance rhythms and American folk melodies. His music turns to subjects of popular interest, such as the orchestral works *El Salón México* and *An Outdoor Overture,* and the ballets *Appalachian Spring* and *Billy the Kid.*

Corelli, Arcangelo, 1653-1713, b. near Imola: Italian composer and violinist. Important in the development of late baroque chamber and orchestral music. Sonatas and concertos comprise his chief works. Teacher of many eighteenth-century violinists.

Couperin, François, 1668-1733, b. Paris: French composer at the court of Louis XIV. Brilliant clavecinist, evolving a distinctive manner of ornamentation. Compositions for organ, clavecin, choral works, chamber music, orchestral works. His keyboard style, explained in his *L'Art de Toucher le Clavecin,* influenced Johann Sebastian Bach.

Cowell, Henry, 1897-1965, b. Menlo Park: American composer notable for experiments in sonority and for works in many forms, including symphonies, chamber music, choral music, stage music. Cowell has been interested also in Oriental musical systems and has introduced Oriental elements into his concert music. He has written books on music and much musical criticism.

Dallapiccola, Luigi, 1904-1975, b. Pisino: Italian composer; works include the opera *Il Prigionero,* chamber music, and orchestral works. Wrote in the twelve-tone system, adapting it to Italianate style.

Debussy, Claude, 1862-1918, b. St. Germain-en-Laye: French composer; the principal figure in musical impressionism. Important works include the opera *Pelléas et Mélisande,* which, in its subtle nuances and calculated understatement, represented a strong reaction against Wagner's emphasis and violence. Debussy wrote many songs, preludes and other works for piano, orchestral works including the nocturnes *La Mer* and *Iberia,* and some chamber music.

Delius, Frederick, 1862-1934, b. Bradford: English composer; one of the foremost exponents of impressionism. Important works include the opera *A Village Romeo and Juliet,* orchestral rhapsody *Brigg Fair,* the orchestral variations with chorus, *Appalachia,* many descriptive works for orchestra, operas, concertos, and choral works.

Des Prés, Josquin, c. 1450-1521, b. Hainaut: Represents the first complete embodiment of Renaissance style, and very likely the finest. His music combines mastery of Netherlands counterpoint (imitation, canon) with a clarity of structure and sureness of harmonic procedure (feeling for cadential action) derived probably from Italian music. He wrote Masses, motets, chansons, some instrumental works.

Donizetti, Gaetano, 1797-1848, b. Bergamo: Italian opera composer. Wrote over sixty operas, including *Don Pasquale, The Daughter of the Regiment, The Elixir of Love, Lucrezia Borgia,* and one of the greatest favorites in the entire operatic repertoire, *Lucia di Lammermoor.* Donizetti's music is distinguished by an extremely elegant, ingratiating melodic style.

Dowland, John, 1562-1626: English composer and lutenist. Works include lute songs, lute solos, and instrumental ensemble pieces.

Dufay, Guillaume, c. 1400-1474: Netherlandish composer, representing the period during which the Renaissance style was evolved. Strong influence upon the generation which followed him. Sacred and secular works which show the tendency toward triadic sonorities.

Dukas, Paul, 1865-1935, b. Paris: French composer of orchestral works, ballets, and an important opera, *Ariane et Barbe-Bleu.* His most noted work, the orchestral scherzo *L'Apprenti-Sorcier* embodies both traditional structural and impressionistic color devices, a combination characteristic of his general style.

Dunstable, John, c. 1370-1453, b. Bedfordshire: English composer; one of the most important figures in the change of style from Ars nova to Renaissance. Spent a number of years in France.

Dvořák, Anton, 1841-1904, b. Muhlhausen: Bohemian composer, whose strong interest in folk subjects is shown in such works as his *From the New World* Symphony, the Slavonic Dances, the American Quartet. Brilliant orchestrator with a vivacious imaginative style of composition. His Symphony in D minor is one of the finest works of its kind after Beethoven.

Elgar, Sir Edward, 1857-1934, b. Broadheath: English composer; Master of the King's Musick. One of the principal representatives of English romanticism, largely influenced by Brahms. Works include oratorios, cantatas, symphonies, chamber music. His *Enigma Variations* for orchestra and the oratorio *The Dream of Gerontius* are among his most celebrated works.

Falla, Manuel de, 1876-1949, b. Cadiz: Spanish composer, particularly important for his use of Spanish idioms and subjects. Works include the ballets *Love, The Magician, The Three-Cornered Hat, Nights in the Gardens of Spain.*

Fauré, Gabriel, 1845-1924, b. Pamiers: French composer, notable for his retention of classic structural and developmental principles, within which he evolved many striking harmonic, melodic, and expressive nuances. He was a teacher and had strong influence upon later generations of French composers. Operas, ballets, orchestral works, chamber music, choral works, of which the Requiem is perhaps best known. Director of the Conservatoire de Musique in Paris.

Franck, César, 1822-1890, b. Liège: Belgian composer and organist. Symbolized reaction against operatic domination of French music; strong influence on later composers, such as D'Indy, Chausson, Ropartz. Works include the famous Symphony in D minor and chamber, organ, and choral music. Franck was constantly trying to reconcile the rich harmonic language of the late nineteenth century with traditional principles of structure.

Frescobaldi, Girolamo, 1583-1643, b. Ferrara: Italian organist and composer who was important in the evolution of a distinctive seventeenth-century keyboard style. Organist of St. Peter's in Rome. Fantasias, ricercare, toccatas, canzone, capriccios, and other types of keyboard music.

Froberger, Johann Jakob, 1616-1667, b. Stuttgart: German composer and organist. Important in the early history of the baroque suite.

Gabrieli, Andrea, c. 1510-1586, b. Venice: Composer and organist, especially important in the evolution of an idiomatic instrumental style in the sixteenth century. Many works in various media.

Gabrieli, Giovanni, 1557-1612, b. Venice: Nephew of Andrea Gabrieli. One of the foremost figures in the evolution of the concertato style, and hence of modern instrumental music. A forerunner of baroque music; teacher of Schütz. Works for divided chorus and for combinations of voices and instruments, including *Sacrae Symphoniae.*

Gershwin, George, 1898-1937, b. Brooklyn: Foremost American representative of the popular style, equally successful in straight song and dance forms or in larger forms which develop and extend jazz material. Works include opera *Porgy and Bess, Rhapsody in Blue,* Concerto in F for piano, *An American in Paris,* and numerous highly successful and long-popular musical comedies, such as *Strike Up the Band, Lady Be Good, Let 'em Eat Cake.*

Gesualdo, Carlo, c. 1560–1613, b. Naples: Composer of madrigals, distinctive for their unusual chromatic style and highly affective manner of expression, marked by strong contrasts.

Glinka, Michail Ivanovitch, 1804–1857, b. Noosspaskoe: Russian composer who pioneered the nationalist movement in his native country. He wrote in a wide range of genres, the most important works being the operas *A Life for the Tsar* and *Russlan and Ludmilla.*

Gluck, Christoph Willibald von, 1714–1787, b. Erasbach: German composer noted especially for his "reform" of opera, in which he substituted a simpler style for the more ornate Italian manner, giving more immediate and direct expression to the dramatic content. His "reform" operas include *Orfeo ed Euridice, Paris and Helen, Iphigenia in Tauris, Iphigenia in Aulis, Armide,* and *Alceste.* Gluck also wrote operas in the Italian style.

Gounod, Charles François, 1818–1893, b. Paris: French composer whose opera *Faust* is one of the most frequently performed works in the operatic repertoire. In addition to other operas, Gounod wrote many sacred works.

Grieg, Edvard, 1843–1907, b. Bergen: Norwegian composer, influential in the establishment of a national school. In his harmonic innovations, his handling of sonority and color, Grieg foreshadows some of the techniques of impressionism. Works include incidental music for Ibsen's drama *Peer Gynt,* Concerto for Piano in A minor, chamber music, and many songs and small works in lyric vein.

Griffes, Charles T., 1884–1920, b. Elmira: American composer, with leanings toward the impressionist style. Works include *Roman Sketches* for piano (including the well-known sketch *The White Peacock*), the symphonic poem *The Pleasure Dome of Kubla Khan,* songs, chamber music. His music shows some Oriental influences.

Handel, Georg Frideric, 1685–1759, b. Halle: German composer who represents, with Johann Sebastian Bach, the culmination of the late Baroque period. Much of his life was spent in England, where he wrote many operas, oratorios (*The Messiah*), concertos, chamber music. His style has unexcelled rhythmic vigor and a bold melodic manner.

Hanson, Howard, 1896–   , b. Wahoo, Nebraska: American composer. Former director of the Eastman School of Music. Principally known for symphonic works and the opera *Merry Mount.*

Harris, Roy, 1898–   , b. Lincoln, Oklahoma: American composer whose works have drawn often from American folk culture and history for subject matter and style. Many orchestral works and compositions in various media.

Haydn, Franz Joseph, 1732–1809, b. Rohrau: Austrian composer; the oldest of the Viennese classic group (*see* Mozart and Beethoven). More than any other, Haydn was responsible for the structural and technical principles underlying the mature classic forms. Wrote 104 symphonies, 88 quartets, oratorios, including *The Seasons* and *The Creation,* keyboard music, choral music, operas. Many years in service with the Esterházy house; later, in London, Haydn composed some of his greatest works.

Hindemith, Paul, 1895–1963, b. near Frankfurt: German composer noted for his classic tendencies, as exemplified in the use of traditional forms, consistent contrapuntal texture, key-controlled structure. Works in many media and forms; his symphony *Mathis der Maler* (from the opera of the same name) is a classic of the modern period. An exponent of "music for practical use," written to accommodate the limitations of amateur performers. Very influential on younger composers.

Honegger, Arthur, 1892–1955, b. Le Havre: Swiss composer, generally linked with the postimpressionist French composers. Wide range of style in his music, from the futuristic sketch *Pacific 231* (impression of a locomotive) to *Pastorale d'Été* (a delicate nature study). Very successful with stage and dramatic music, especially his oratorio *King David* and his music for Claudel's mystery play *Joan of Arc at the Stake.*

Indy, Vincent d', 1851–1931, b. Paris: Noted French composer and music educator. Cofounder of the Schola Cantorum. His music is oriented toward the past, using traditional forms and styles of expression. D'Indy, an important theorist, wrote *Cours de Composition Musicale.*

Isaak, Heinrich, c. 1450–1517: Netherlands composer who held posts in Florence, Vienna, and Rome, thus helping to disseminate the Flemish polyphonic style of composition. Many masses and motets, chorales, and secular works; also instrumental works. *Choralis Constantinus* is a cycle of motets written for the liturgical year for the cathedral of Constance, Switzerland.

Ives, Charles, 1874–1954, b. Danbury: One of the most individual figures of the twentieth century. Within a style basically romantic, Ives experimented with harmonies, textures, sonorities, rhythms, anticipating many of the procedures of modern music. Orchestral works and chamber, keyboard, and theater music.

Jannequin, Clément, c. 1485–?: French composer; the first important representative of sixteenth-century French music; writer of many chansons, some of them extended pictorial representations of scenes or events; also motets and other sacred music.

Kodály, Zoltán, 1882–1967, b. Kecskemét: With Bartók, Kodály represents best the modern Hungarian school. His interest in Hungarian folk music is profound and has influenced his style. His work covers many media; the *Háry János* suite for orchestra, from the opera of the same name, is well known. His style, in addition to folk-music elements, exhibits features of impressionism, romanticism, and contemporary harmonic practices of atonality and polytonality.

Křenek, Ernst, 1900–   , b. Vienna: One of the more noted representatives of twelve-tone music, of the generation following Schönberg. Also interested in jazz as a stylistic resource, as well as other contemporary techniques. His opera *Jonny spielt auf* displays jazz elements; his opera *Karl V* is in the tone-row technique. Křenek has also written small pieces to demonstrate the applicability of tone-row techniques to simple lyric expression.

Landino, Francesco, 1325–1397, b. Florence: The principal representative of Italian Ars nova music. Known for his secular music, madrigals, cacce, ballate. Organist of the Church of Lorenzo. In contrast to the French Ars nova, with its rhythmic complexities, Landino's music displays typical Italian cantilena qualities.

Lassus, Orlandus, c. 1532–1594, b. Hainaut: One of the greatest composers of the late Renaissance, a Netherlandish composer who represents, with Palestrina, the culmination of the Roman sacred style. Lassus also wrote in the style of French chansons, German songs, and Italian madrigals, epitomizing the ideal of the cosmopolitan culture of the Renaissance.

Leoninus (twelfth century): The earlier of the two composers (*see* Perotinus) who represent the Notre Dame school of composition. He was important in establishing the use of rhythmic modes in melismatic organum.

Liszt, Franz, 1811–1886, b. near Ödenburg: Hungarian composer and pianist who was a prototype of the transcendental virtuoso of the romantic period. His brilliant declamatory style of composition and performance, his harmonic innovations, his flamboyant expression had a profound effect upon musical style during his life and afterward. He established a single-movement form with many episodes, called the *symphonic poem,* which suited the many changes of mood and feeling in his music. The most famous of these is *Les Préludes.* Also wrote *Hungarian Rhapsodies,* brilliant piano works, *Faust* Symphony. Influenced Richard Wagner and Richard Strauss.

Lully, Jean Baptiste, 1632–1687, b. Florence: Italian composer who became the virtual dictator of French music at the court of Louis XIV. Established a style of opera, including recitative, and a style of orchestral performance that prevailed in France for almost a century. Lully was responsible also for the establishment of the French overture as an important instrumental form.

MacDowell, Edward, 1861–1908, b. New York City: One of the earliest American composers to receive international recognition. His music includes large-scale compositions modeled after European patterns, such as his concertos for piano. He has also written charming characteristic smaller pieces, such as the *Indian Suite* for orchestra and *Woodland Sketches* for piano.

Machaut, Guillaume de, c. 1300–1377, b. Machaut: The most noted representative of French fourteenth-century music. Composer of secular songs, motets, and the first polyphonic setting of the Mass by a single composer.

Mahler, Gustav, 1860–1911, b. Kalisz: Bohemian composer noted chiefly for his broadly scaled symphonies and for songs with orchestral accompaniment. Conductor of the Metropolitan Opera and New York Philharmonic Society. His style has many facets, a grandiose manner recalling Beethoven and Wagner, a poignant lyricism (perhaps his most convincing vein) in the manner of the Viennese song composers, and a starkness, expressed in clashing dissonances and strange textures, foreshadowing expressionism. Both the lyricism and the expressionist tendencies are manifest in one of his last works, *The Song of the Earth,* a song cycle with orchestra.

Marenzio, Luca, 1553-1599, b. Caccaglio: Italian madrigalist, one of the finest composers in the genre. His works show the tendencies toward chromaticism that foreshadow baroque harmonic and expressive style.

Mason, Daniel Gregory, 1873-1953, b. Brookline: American composer, educator, and writer on music. Works include symphonies and chamber music.

Massenet, Jules, 1842-1912, b. Montaud: French composer of operas, the best known being *Manon* and *Hérodiade.* His music is characterized by an ingratiating melodic style. Professor at the Conservatoire.

Mendelssohn-Bartholdy, Felix, 1809-1847, b. Hamburg: German composer whose elegant style, crystal-clear structural layouts, easy manner, and exquisite melodies have made his music a concert favorite. Well-known works include the *Scotch* and *Italian* Symphonies (Nos. 3 and 4), the violin concerto, music for Shakespeare's *A Midsummer Night's Dream, Hebrides* Overture, *Songs Without Words* for piano. Mendelssohn was largely responsible for the revival of interest in Bach during the nineteenth century.

Menotti, Gian-Carlo, 1911-   , b. Cadigliano: Highly successful composer of operas including *The Medium, The Telephone, The Old Maid and the Thief, Amahl and the Night Visitors, The Consul,* etc.

Meyerbeer, Giacomo, 1791-1864, b. Berlin: Opera composer born in Germany but noted as the founder of French grand opera in Paris in the 1830s. His works include *Robert the Devil, The Huguenots, The Prophet,* and *The African.*

Milhaud, Darius, 1892-1974, b. Aix-en Provence: French composer, a member of the post-Debussy group known as *The Six.* A prolific writer in a wide variety of forms and idioms, from dissonant polytonality to traditional major-minor and modal harmony. His work is characterized by clarity of design and elegance of melodic manner. Works include much chamber music, theater music, operas *David, Medea, Christopher Columbus,* and orchestral music.

Monteverdi, Claudio, 1567-1643, b. Cremona: Italian composer; one of the first and among the greatest composers of the Baroque era. Established opera on a firm footing after the experiments of the Camerata. Pioneer and extremely successful exponent of the new use of dissonance for expressive purposes. Works include operas *Orfeo, The Return of Ulysses, The Coronation of Poppea,* many madrigals, and sacred works.

Moore, Douglas, 1893-1969, b. Cutchogue, N.Y.: American composer of operas, symphonic works, and chamber music. His works include the operas *White Wings, The Devil and Daniel Webster, The Ballad of Baby Doe.* Orchestral music includes *The Pageant of P. T. Barnum, Village Music, A Farm Journal.* Moore's style is clear and straightforward, with strong emphasis upon frank, appealing melody; idioms of traditional American songs and dances appear frequently in his music.

Morley, Thomas 1557-1602: Important Elizabethan composer of madrigals and keyboard music. Organist at St. Paul's Cathedral. Author of the first theoretical treatise on music published in England, *A Plaine and Easie Introduction to Practicall Musicke.*

Moussorgsky, Modest, 1839-1881, b. Pskov: One of the foremost representatives of the Russian nationalist movement. Rejecting Western techniques of building form, he used characteristic folk rhythms and melodies, combining them with a sense of brilliant color and dramatic effect. The opera *Boris Godunov* is his masterpiece. *Pictures at an Exhibition* for piano, later orchestrated by Ravel, is a piquant group of sketches. He had strong influence upon the impressionists.

Mozart, Wolfgang Amadeus, 1756–1791, b. Salzburg: One of the great triumvirate of the Viennese classic era (with Haydn and Beethoven). One of the most astonishing geniuses in the history of music. He represents the full flowering of the eighteenth century in music. He combined dramatic, popular, and learned styles, contributed to the broadening of classic structure, established the modern piano concerto, coordinated buffa and seria styles in opera, expanded the expressive role of harmony in all media. His style is based upon an Italianate, operatic melodic manner strengthened and expanded by a sure sense for counterpoint and harmonic action. Operas *Don Giovanni, The Magic Flute, The Marriage of Figaro, Così fan tutte,* etc., symphonies, concertos, chamber music, choral music, etc.

Offenbach, Jacques, 1819–1880, b. Cologne: Famous French composer of burlesque opera and *opéra comique. Tales of Hoffmann* is his masterpiece; also wrote *Orpheus in the Underworld, La Belle Hélène, The Grand Duchess of Gerolstein,* etc. His music is characterized by vivacious dance rhythms, captivating melodies, and a general effervescence of manner.

Okeghem, Jean d', c. 1430–1495, b. Flanders: Netherlandish composer, spanning the generation between Dufay and Des Prés. Important in establishing imitative counterpoint as a basic technical feature of Renaissance music. Sacred style characterized by long, weaving melodic lines, retaining something of the mystic quality of medieval Gothic music. This is in contrast to the "rational," clearly organized treatment of short motives by Okeghem's pupil Des Prés. Sacred and secular works, some instrumental music. Master of the Chapel Royal in France.

Paganini, Niccolò, 1782–1840, b. Genoa: Supposedly the greatest violin virtuoso in music history. The counterpart of Franz Liszt, with whom he is responsible for establishing the idea of the superhuman performer. His violin compositions, concertos, and studies make fantastic demands upon the technique of the performer.

Palestrina, Giovanni Pierluigi da, 1524–1594, b. Palestrina: The epitome of the Roman sacred school of polyphony. Palestrina's music has served as model for contrapuntal composition for more than three hundred years. Style characterized by smoothness of movement, gently rounded melodic contours, carefully used dissonances, richness and sweetness of sonority. Masses, motets, psalms, hymns, and other sacred music, some madrigals in a quasi-sacred style.

Pergolesi, Giovanni Battista, 1710–1736, b. Jesi: Italian composer chiefly famous for his opera buffa, *La Serva Padrona,* which took Europe by storm in the mid-eighteenth century and which served as a model for succeeding composers in that genre. Also wrote chamber music, serious operas, choral music.

Peri, Jacopo, 1561–1633, b. Florence: A member of the Florentine Camerata and composer of the first opera (*Dafne*) set in the *stile rappresentativo.*

Perotinus (twelfth and thirteenth centuries): The later of the two important composers of the Notre Dame school (*see* Leoninus). Noted for the full realization of modal rhythmic procedure (in all voices) and for some organa in four parts.

Piston, Walter, 1894-   , b. Rockland, Me.: American composer of orchestral and chamber music. Style combines contemporary scoring, rhythmic patterns, and harmonic devices with a classic clarity of structure and purpose. Piston has also written a number of books on music.

Poulenc, Francis, 1899-1963, b. Paris: French composer of the postimpressionist era. His music is attractive and witty.

Prokofiev, Sergei, 1891-1953, b. Sonzovka: Outstanding modern Russian composer, with works in many different media. Operas (*Love of Three Oranges* frequently performed), symphonies, concertos, chamber music, choral music, including *Alexander Nevsky*, a cantata, *Peter and the Wolf*, an immensely successful fairy tale for narrator and orchestra. His style has much melodic appeal; his music addresses itself directly to the audience.

Puccini, Giacomo, 1858-1924, b. Lucca: Principal representative of the Italian verismo school of opera. *La Bohème, Tosca, Madame Butterfly* are standard items in the repertoires of most opera houses. Style distinguished by broad, somewhat sentimental melodies, rich orchestration, with a colorful harmonic support that has many unusual touches. Has influenced much present-day music, including semipopular and theater music.

Purcell, Henry, c. 1659-1695, b. London: The principal representative of English baroque music. His opera *Dido and Aeneas* is one of the masterpieces of dramatic composition. Chamber music, choral music, incidental music for the stage.

Rachmaninov, Sergei, 1873-1943, b. Onega: Russian composer and pianist. Concertos, symphonies, orchestral music, piano works, operas. His music continues the romantic tradition represented earlier by Tchaikovsky.

Rameau, Jean Philippe, 1683-1764, b. Dijon: Important French composer and theorist. Wrote operas in the tradition of Lully, extending harmonic and melodic scope, also orchestration. Author of epoch-making treatises on harmony, the foundation of harmonic theory to the present day.

Ravel, Maurice, 1875-1937, b. Ciboure: French composer. With Debussy, the principal representative of French impressionism. In addition, Ravel displays a neoclassic vein with emphasis upon well-developed melodic lines. Works include the orchestral works *Boléro, La Valse, Rapsodie Espagnole, Daphnis et Chloé, Ma Mère l'Oye* Suite, the opera *L'Heure Espagnole*, and many chamber, keyboard, vocal works.

Rimsky-Korsakov, Nicholas, 1844-1908, b. Tichvin: Russian composer noted for his skill in orchestration and for his brilliant colorful style of composition. Works include the orchestral pieces *Scheherazade, Capriccio Espagnol, Russian Easter* Overture, symphonies, operas, chamber music. He turned frequently to Oriental subjects and idioms for his material. Strong influence on the young Stravinsky. Professor at the St. Petersburg Conservatory.

Rossini, Gioacchino, 1792-1868, b. Pesaro: Italian opera composer, noted especially for *The Barber of Seville*, the last great work in the eighteenth-century opera-buffa tradition. Other operas include the grand opera *William Tell, Semiramide, Cinderella, Tancred,* etc. Overtures to Rossini's operas are popular concert items although most of the operas have rarely been performed recently.

Saint-Saëns, Charles Camille, 1835-1921, b. Paris: Eminent French composer, pianist, and conductor. His opera *Samson and Delilah,* symphonic poems *Danse Macabre, The Spinning Wheel of Omphale,* and his concertos for violin, piano, and cello are frequently heard.

Scarlatti, Alessandro, 1660-1725, b. Palermo: One of the pioneers of the Neapolitan opera; important in the evolution of the da capo aria, the accompanied recitative, and the sinfonia preceding the opera. Composer of much chamber and choral music. Maestro of the royal chapel at Naples.

Scarlatti, Domenico, 1685-1757, b. Naples: Son of Alessandro Scarlatti. Important as a harpsichordist and composer. Wrote hundreds of pieces for his instrument, working out many innovations of figuration, sonority, and harmony, leading to the modern keyboard style. Preferred the galant manner, although he wrote a considerable amount of contrapuntal music.

Schönberg, Arnold, 1874-1951, b. Vienna: Leading figure of the twelve-tone school, which he established in the 1920s. Works show an evolution from Wagnerian and Brahmsian romanticism through expressionism, to a wide range of form and expression in the twelve-tone technique. Began his career in Vienna; in 1936 became professor of music at the University of California at Los Angeles. Works include *Pierrot Lunaire,* a chamber work for voice and instruments, the sextet *Transfigured Night,* four string quartets, opera *Moses and Aaron,* many chamber and keyboard works.

Schubert, Franz, 1797-1828, b. Lichtenthal: Austrian composer; one of the leading figures of early romanticism. His lyric style was embodied in hundreds of exquisite songs and was also evident in his orchestral and chamber music. Regarded as the founder of the German *lied* style. Eight symphonies, of which the great C major ranks among the finest in symphonic literature; considerable chamber music, including *Death and the Maiden* string quartet, *Trout* quintet, choral music.

Schumann, Robert, 1810-1856, b. Zwickau: Important German romantic composer, pianist, and writer on music. Best in smaller forms, songs and short piano pieces such as *Carnaval, Kreisleriana, Scenes from Childhood.* Four symphonies, concertos for piano, violin, cello, chamber music. Schumann's style contains a wealth of harmonic detail and innovation, interesting rhythmic imbalances with regular period structure. Editor and co-founder of *Neue Zeitschrift für Musik.*

Schütz, Heinrich, 1585-1672, b. Köstritz: German composer; the link between the earliest Italian baroque style of Giovanni Gabrieli and the late German baroque. Responsible for much of the systematization of procedures in German sacred music of the seventeenth century. Many sacred and secular works. Music director to the Elector of Saxony.

Scriabin, Alexander, 1872-1915, b. Moscow: Russian composer notable for his efforts to create a new chordal basis for harmony, constructing chords by fourths instead of thirds. This procedure is exemplified in his symphonic poem *Prometheus*. He also tried to coordinate color and sound in performance, prescribing colors to be projected on a screen while music was being performed. In general, his works have a late romantic flavor, his keyboard music showing the influence of Chopin.

Sessions, Roger, 1896-   , b. Brooklyn: Influential American composer, linked stylistically to advanced trends. His manner is serious and introspective. Symphonies, operas, chamber music.

Shostakovitch, Dmitri, 1906-1975, b. St. Petersburg: Russian composer, one of the leading symphonic composers of the mid-century. Uses traditional forms and manners of expression with freshness and imagination. Symphonies, operas, chamber music.

Sibelius, Jean, 1865-1957, b. Tavastehus: Finnish composer; one of the leading symphonic composers of the early modern period. Rather conservative and traditional in his procedures; works are conceived on a grand scale and in serious vein. Principal works are for orchestra, including seven symphonies, many tone poems, and smaller works. Some chamber and vocal music.

Smetana, Friedrich, 1824-1884, b. Leitomischl: Important as a figure in the Bohemian national school. His opera *The Bartered Bride* is his most notable work. He is known also for the set of six orchestral pieces entitled *My Country,* of which *The Moldau* (descriptive of the river Moldau) is familiar to concert audiences everywhere. Smetana's music has a strong flavor of Slavonic song and dance.

Stamitz, Johann, 1717-1757, b. Deutsch-Brod: Bohemian composer who became the leader of the Mannheim orchestra and in this position exerted a profound influence upon the growth of the modern orchestral style.

Strauss, Johann, Jr., 1825-1899, b. Vienna: The Waltz King. Strauss epitomizes the musical spirit of nineteenth-century Vienna with his incomparable waltz melodies, the brilliant scoring of his music, and his rhythmic élan. Among his world-famous waltzes are *The Beautiful Blue Danube, Tales from the Vienna Woods, Roses from the South, The Artist's Life, Wine, Women, and Song,* and many others. His operetta *Die Fledermaus* is a masterpiece of its kind.

Strauss, Richard, 1864-1949, b. Munich: German composer of the late romantic and early modern period, noted first for his tone poems, including *Don Juan, Till Eulenspiegel, Death and Transfiguration;* later for his operas, including *Elektra, Salome, Der Rosenkavalier.* Also wrote many songs, some chamber music. Strauss followed the path laid out by Wagner and Liszt, adding melodic and harmonic elements distinctly Italian in flavor.

Stravinsky, Igor, 1882-1971, b. Oranienbaum: Russian composer; one of the most important figures of the contemporary era. Early works in folkloric style, such as the ballets *Petrouchka, The Firebird, The Rite of Spring,* the cantata *The Wedding;* later works in neoclassic vein, such as the Symphony of Psalms, Octet, opera *The Rake's Progress.* Works in many media. Stravinsky's rhythmic and textural innovations represent a major contribution to twentieth-century musical techniques.

Sullivan, Sir Arthur, 1842-1900, b. London: The musical half of the English team, Gilbert and Sullivan, which produced the comic operas *Trial by Jury, Iolanthe, The Mikado, The Yeomen of the Guard, H.M.S. Pinafore,* etc. Notable for their fine melodies and delightful patter songs.

Tchaikovsky, Pëtr Ilich, 1840-1893, b. Kamsko-Votinsk: Russian composer whose works are among the most popular and frequently performed in all concert literature. Although his works are a little loose in structure, the brilliance of his orchestration, the excellence of his melodies, his sureness of effect, and his vivid imagination have made his music a favorite everywhere. He is unexcelled as a composer for ballet, e.g., *Sleeping Beauty, Swan Lake, Nutcracker.* Of six symphonies, the last three are well known, also his concertos for violin and for piano, the opera *Pique Dame,* the overture-fantasy *Romeo and Juliet.*

Thompson, Randall, 1899- , b. New York: American composer of choral, symphonic, and chamber music. Former professor of music and chairman of the department at Harvard University.

Thomson, Virgil, 1896- , b. Kansas City: American composer and former music critic of the *New York Herald Tribune.* Noted for his opera *Four Saints in Three Acts* (texts by Gertrude Stein). Music for motion pictures (*Plow That Broke the Plains,* etc.). Thomson's style has a strong flavor of traditional American songs and dances.

Varèse, Edgard, 1885-1965, b. Paris: Composer noted for his successful exploration of nontraditional musical techniques, especially in the realm of sonority. His most familiar work is *Ionization* for thirty-five different instruments, mainly percussion.

Vaughan Williams, Ralph, 1872-1958, b. Gloucestershire: One of the most distinguished modern English composers. Symphonies, operas, chamber music, choral music. Strong interest in English folk song, the style of which appears frequently in his music.

Verdi, Giuseppe, 1813-1901, b. Le Roncole: The master of nineteenth-century Italian opera; continued and developed the tradition of eighteen-century opera. The dramatic power, the stageworthiness, the keen psychological insight, the well-delineated melody, and the effective scoring of Verdi's operas mark him as supreme in the genre. His last works, *Otello* and *Falstaff,* show a modification of the set number plan toward a more continuous flow of music and action. *La Traviata, Il Trovatore, Rigoletto,* and *Aida* are probably his most popular works.

Villa-Lobos, Heitor, 1881-1959, b. Rio de Janeiro: Prolific Brazilian composer. Over 1300 works. Strong element of Brazilian folk music in his style.

Vivaldi, Antonio, c. 1675-1741, b. Venice: Important late baroque composer, notable for his brilliant concertos, of which there are hundreds extant. His works served as models for the concertos of Johann Sebastian Bach. (Bach transcribed a number of Vivaldi's concertos.)

Wagner, Richard, 1813-1883, b. Leipzig: Tremendously influential and important German composer; creator of the music drama, an operatic form different in many respects from the other opera types of Wagner's era. Wagner established stylistic trends in harmony, scoring, and expressive content that have had their repercussions to the present day. Works include *Lohengrin, Tannhäuser, The Flying Dutchman, Tristan und Isolde,* the *Ring* Cycle, *Parsifal, The Mastersingers of Nurenberg.* Wrote his own librettos: evolved his own theories of art. Subject of countless books, studies, articles.

Walton, William, 1902-   , b. Oldham: English composer of opera (*Troilus and Cressida*), symphonic works (*Portsmouth Point* Overture), choral works (*Belshazzar's Feast*).

Weber, Karl Maria von, 1786-1826, b. Oldenburg: Early romantic German composer; wrote the first German opera, *Der Freischütz,* distinguished by folk elements such as pastoral locale, German folk music, traditional story. Other works include operas (*Oberon, Euryanthe*), concertos, chamber music, *Invitation to the Dance.* Weber's style is brilliant, facile, with a boldness and dramatic impact suggestive of Beethoven's music.

Webern, Anton von 1883-1945, b. Vienna: The most advanced of the three Viennese tone-row masters (*see* Berg, Schönberg). Webern wrote in a highly condensed, cryptic style, with sparing use of sonority resources. Orchestral, vocal, chamber music. Webern's manner has found many adherents among younger tone-row composers.

Weelkes, Thomas, d. 1623: English madrigal composer, one of the most accomplished in the genre.

Wolf, Hugo, 1860-1903, b. Windischgräz: Austrian composer, noted chiefly for his superb songs, many of which were set to the poems of Edward Mörike.

RECOMMENDED READINGS

Abraham, Gerald, *A Hundred Years of Music,* Gerald Duckworth & Co., London, 1949.
  A survey of romantic and early modern music. Many valuable observations on style and aesthetics.
Apel, Willi, *Harvard Dictionary of Music,* Harvard University Press, Cambridge, Mass., 1944, 1969.
  Compact one-volume dictionary giving information on musical terms and music history. Good bibliographies. No biographical material.
Bekker, Paul, *The Story of the Orchestra,* W. W. Norton & Company, Inc., New York, 1936.
  The history of the modern orchestra from the eighteenth century to the twentieth.
Bukofzer, Manfred, *Music in the Baroque Era,* W. W. Norton & Company, Inc., New York, 1947.
  An excellent history of music from 1600 to 1750. Styles, forms, aesthetics, and sociology are linked together in an informative and interesting manner.
Chase, Gilbert, *America's Music,* McGraw-Hill Book Company, New York, 1955.
  A comprehensive study of American music. A valuable reference.
Einstein, Alfred, *Mozart, His Character, His Work,* W. W. Norton & Company, Inc., New York, 1945.
  Although a biography, the best work in the English language dealing with eighteenth-century classic music. The eighteenth-century scene is set forth in rather full detail.
Einstein, Alfred, *Music in the Romantic Era,* W. W. Norton & Company, Inc., New York, 1947.
  Survey of the principal trends and concepts of nineteenth-century music. Much speculation on style and aesthetics.

Forsyth, Cecil, *Orchestration*, The Macmillan Company, New York, 1936 (rev. ed.).
A comprehensive study of orchestral instruments, both past and present. Valuable reference.

Grout, Donald, *A History of Western Music*, W. W. Norton & Company, Inc., New York, 1960.
A comprehensive history of Western music in one volume. Well documented.

Grove's Dictionary of Music and Musicians, St. Martin's Press, Inc., New York, 1955.
The most comprehensive dictionary of music in the English language. Extended treatment of most topics, both technical and biographical.

Hansen, Peter, *An Introduction to Twentieth Century Music*, Allyn and Bacon, Inc., Boston, 1961.
A compact, well-organized survey of the principal style trends of the modern era.

Lang, Paul Henry, *Music in Western Civilization*, W. W. Norton & Company, Inc., New York, 1941.
A monumental work, encompassing the relation of music to art, philosophy, literature, religion, and politics from Greek times to the end of the nineteenth century. Well written, full of challenging ideas.

Ratner, Leonard G., *Harmony: Structure and Style*, McGraw-Hill Book Company, New York, 1962.
A companion book to *Music: The Listener's Art*, explaining music theory on the basis of the criteria of sound, movement, and arrival; the relation of these criteria to harmonic progression, structure, and style.

Reese, Gustave, *Music in the Middle Ages*, 1940, and *Music in the Renaissance*, 1954, W. W. Norton & Company, Inc., New York.
Two comprehensive studies of music covering the period from Greek music to 1600. A great deal of specific information. Recommended for students engaged in research in these periods.

Slonimsky, Nicolas (ed.), *Baker's Biographical Dictionary of Musicians*, 5th ed. G. Schirmer, Inc., New York, 1958, 1965.
Compact one-volume dictionary providing biographical material. Complement to the Apel dictionary. Good bibliographical references.

Thompson, Oscar (ed.), *International Cyclopedia of Music and Musicians*, 9th ed., ed. Robert Sabin, Dodd, Mead & Company, Inc., New York, 1964.
Good popular reference with a number of extensive articles.

Tovey, Donald Francis, *Essays in Musical Analysis*, Oxford University Press, London, 1935–1939; and musical articles from the *Encyclopaedia Britannica*, Oxford University Press, London, 1944.
Beautifully written articles on specific compositions and musical topics, containing many original and fresh insights on musical style and form. Tovey was one of the soundest musical analysts of our century.

COMPOSERS ON MUSIC

Hindemith, Paul, *A Composer's World*, Harvard University Press, Cambridge, Mass., 1952.

Schönberg, Arnold, *Style and Idea*, Philosophical Library, New York, 1950.

Sessions, Roger, *The Musical Experience of Composer, Performer, and Listener,* Princeton University Press, Princeton, N.J., 1950.

Stravinsky, Igor, *Poetics of Music,* Harvard University Press, Cambridge, Mass., 1947.

BIOGRAPHIES (arranged chronologically by composer)

Schrade, Leo, *Monteverdi, Creator of Modern Music,* W. W. Norton & Company, Inc., New York, 1950.

Westrup, J. A., *Purcell,* J. M. Dent & Sons, Ltd., London, 1938.

David, H. T., and A. J. Mendel, *The Bach Reader,* W. W. Norton & Company, Inc., New York, 1945.

Spitta, P., *Johann Sebastian Bach,* Novello, London, 1899 (the monumental work on Bach).

Flower, Newman, *George Frideric Handel,* Charles Scribner's Sons, New York, 1948.

Kirkpatrick, Ralph. *Domenico Scarlatti,* Princeton University Press, Princeton, N.J., 1953.

Einstein, Alfred, *Gluck,* E. P. Dutton & Co., Inc., New York, 1936.

Geiringer, Karl, *Haydn, a Creative Life in Music,* W. W. Norton & Company, Inc., New York, 1946.

Einstein, Alfred, *Mozart, His Character, His Work,* W. W. Norton & Company, Inc., New York, 1945.

Thayer, Alexander, *Beethoven,* The Beethoven Association, New York, 1921 (a monumental work on Beethoven's life).

Burk, John, *The Life and Work of Beethoven,* Random House, Inc., New York, 1943.

Tovey, Donald F., *Beethoven,* Oxford University Press, London, 1945.

Brown, Maurice J. E., *Schubert: A Critical Biography,* St. Martin's Press, Inc., New York, 1958.

Barzun, Jacques, *Berlioz and the Romantic Century,* Little, Brown & Company, Boston, 1950.

Weinstock, Herbert, *Chopin, the Man and His Music,* Alfred A. Knopf, Inc., New York, 1949.

Chissell, Joan, *Schumann,* J. M. Dent & Sons, Ltd., London, 1948.

Newman, Ernest, *The Man Liszt,* Charles Scribner's Sons, New York, 1935.

Newman, Ernest, *Wagner as a Man and Artist,* Alfred A. Knopf, Inc., New York, 1924.

Toye, F., *Giuseppe Verdi: His Life and Works,* William Heinemann, Ltd., London, 1931.

Geiringer, Karl, *Brahms, His Life and Work,* Houghton Mifflin Company, Boston, 1936.

Calvocoressi, M. D., *Musorgsky,* J. M. Dent & Sons, Ltd., London, 1946.

Vallas, L., *Claude Debussy: His Life and Works,* Oxford University Press, London, 1933.

Demuth, N., *Ravel,* J. M. Dent & Sons, Ltd., London, 1947.

Stevens, H., *The Life and Music of Béla Bartók,* Oxford University Press, New York, 1953.

Vlad, Roman, *Stravinsky,* Oxford University Press, London, 1960.

	MEDIEVAL	RENAISSANCE	BAROQUE
QUALITIES OF SOUND	thin, light sound; medium register; variety of vocal and instrumental color	richer, fuller sound; medium registers with greater importance of bass level; moderate strength	wide variety of instrumental and vocal sonorities; contrasts between full and thin; greater range in registers; often great strength and amount of sound
TEXTURE	1 to 4 parts, relatively equal; polyphonic action	3 to 6 or more parts; some chordal texture; principal texture remains polyphonic; fuller sound tends to disguise polyphony	polarity between soprano and bass; middle voices add fullness; some chordal texture; principally polyphonic action
CONSONANCE	4ths, 5ths, 8ves, unisons; consonance represents stability and arrival; open intervals	3rds, 6ths, 5ths, 8ves, unisons; 4th treated as dissonance at times; high concentration of consonance; triad sounds	3rds, 6ths, 5ths, 8ves, unisons; 4th partial dissonance; consonance equals stability
DISSONANCE	2nds, 7ths used ornamentally, with frequent clashes between lines; in earliest polyphony, 3rds, 6ths treated as dissonant	preparation and resolution of dissonances; elimination of clashes	increase in amount and intensity of dissonance; many "tritone" dissonances
HARMONIC ACTION	incidental cadences; few leading tones; light definition of tonal center; little sense of harmonic progression	appearance of strong cadences at phrase endings; more leading tones; beginning of key sense; increase in feeling of harmonic drive	much stronger and more pervasive cadential action; full emergence of key sense; active, compact harmonic flow with strong feeling of drive
MOVEMENT	steady, moderate, gentle pace; some variation in manner of movement; mild accentuation by length	steady, moderate pace; considerable difference in manner in different styles; growing vigor of movement in secular and instrumental music; gentle accentuation	in early baroque, sharp contrasts of pace, often with uncertain flow; in late baroque, vigorous, steady, "motoric" pace throughout a piece; wide range of pace and manner present; growing vigor of accent
ARRIVAL	gentle, clear points of arrival; some leading-tone action in polyphony; open and closed cadences in dances	gentle points of arrival; stronger cadences occasionally and at end of piece; well-defined caesuras and cadences in dance music	relatively few but strong cadential points
PHRASE STRUCTURE	relatively short phrases; symmetry in dance music	relatively short phrases in dance music; in polyphonic music, continuous flow, covering cadences, extending phases of movement; symmetry in dance music	in dance music, symmetrical phrase structure; relatively short phases of movement; in other music, continuous expansion, building broad phases

CLASSIC	ROMANTIC	MODERN	
wide variety of instrumental and vocal sonorities; brilliant sound, transparent; much contrast between light and full; wide dynamic range; exploration of higher registers	increase in fullness, richness, and denseness of sound; concern with special color effects; striking contrasts; widened range of pitch and dynamics	extremes of transparency and density; experiments in new sonority effects; sharp contrasts of color; tendency to reduce the "sweetness" of sound	QUALITIES OF SOUND
2, 3 to many parts; emphasis on principal melody, with some polyphony, some give-and-take	tendency toward amplification of lines by doublings; active part-writing, often with rich ornamentation; 3, 4 to many parts	1, 2 to many parts; prominent polyphonic action, also give-and-take; also use of baroque, classic, romantic textural layouts	TEXTURE
same consonance values as preceding eras	same consonance values as before; lesser proportion of consonance than previously	consonance no longer a synonym for stability, although traditional ideas of consonance and dissonance still have considerable force	CONSONANCE
dissonance used for harmonic tension, for dramatic emphasis, often without preparation; many "tritone" dissonances	greater saturation of dissonance, often without intervening consonance; dissonances make rich sounds, and represent instability; tritone, 7ths, 9ths, altered intervals	as a rule, considerable saturation of dissonance, with dissonances frequently at points of arrival; functional distinction between consonance and dissonance disappears frequently	DISSONANCE
saturation of cadential action; long-range definition, long-range contrast of key; very strong harmonic drive	retention of classic cadence feeling with tendency toward deceptive and elided resolutions; rapid elusive shifts of tonal center; harmonic color an objective; weakened harmonic drives	partial abandonment of older chord types; substitutes for older cadences; rapid shifts of tonal areas; modal, atonal, polytonal, tone-row, microtonal systems; little harmonic drive	HARMONIC ACTION
wide range of pace and manner; strongly influenced by typical song and dance manners; steady, active pace, with strong accentuation	wide range of pace and manner; appearance of imbalanced, unsteady qualities of movement; preference for slower pace, less vigorous accent	emphasis on active, percussively accented pace, with cross-rhythms and imbalances, often in rapidly paced music; wide range of pace and manner; uncertain, shifting pace often found	MOVEMENT
clear, frequent, strong points of arrival; momentum often carries beyond, aiming for emphatic cadential points	obscured cadences, disguised points of arrival more frequent	in neo-classic and folkloric music well-defined points of arrival; in expressionistic music, uncertain sense of arrival	ARRIVAL
well-defined period structure in all forms and types; extension of periods	in small pieces, clear periodization in symmetrical structure; in larger works, tendency toward asymmetrical phrase structure	as a rule, asymmetrical phrase structure; some use of baroque continuous expansion and classic periodization	PHRASE STRUCTURE

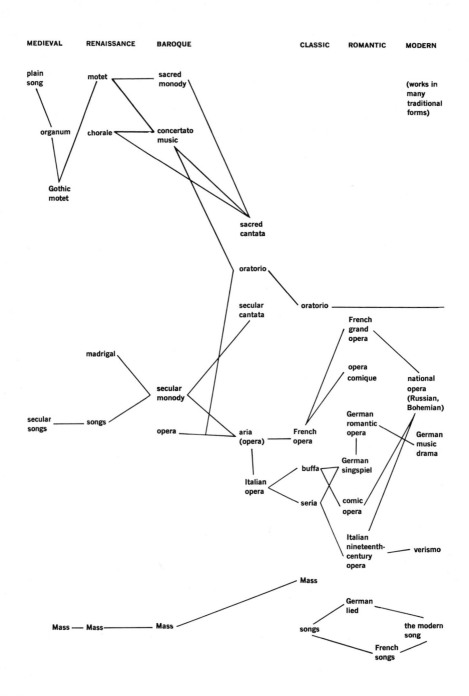

MEDIEVAL	RENAISSANCE	BAROQUE	CLASSIC	ROMANTIC	MODERN

plain song

motet

sacred monody

(works in many traditional forms)

organum

chorale

concertato music

Gothic motet

sacred cantata

oratorio

secular cantata

oratorio

French grand opera

opera comique

national opera (Russian, Bohemian)

madrigal

secular monody

German romantic opera

German music drama

secular songs

songs

opera

aria (opera)

French opera

German singspiel

buffa

Italian opera

seria

comic opera

Italian nineteenth-century opera

verismo

Mass

German lied

the modern song

Mass — Mass — Mass

Mass

songs

French songs

EVOLUTION OF INSTRUMENTAL MUSIC

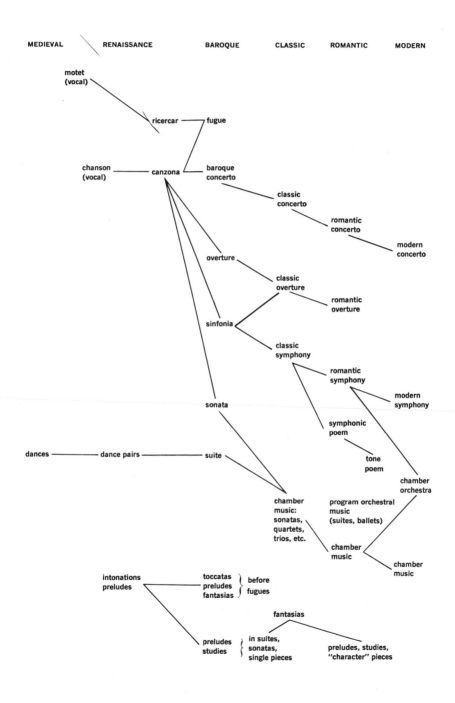

MEDIEVAL   RENAISSANCE   BAROQUE   CLASSIC   ROMANTIC   MODERN

motet (vocal)

ricercar — fugue

chanson (vocal) — canzona — baroque concerto

classic concerto

romantic concerto

modern concerto

overture

classic overture

romantic overture

sinfonia

classic symphony

romantic symphony

modern symphony

sonata

symphonic poem

dances — dance pairs — suite

tone poem

chamber orchestra

chamber music: sonatas, quartets, trios, etc.

program orchestral music (suites, ballets)

chamber music

chamber music

intonations preludes

toccatas preludes fantasias } before fugues

fantasias

preludes studies { in suites, sonatas, single pieces

preludes, studies, "character" pieces

INDEX